Mediterranean Instant Pot for Beginners

600 Effortless Mediterranean Instant Pot Recipes to Lose Weight & Boost Your Health

Gaffney Horon

© Copyright 2020 Gaffney Horon - All Rights Reserved.

In no way is it legal to reproduce, duplicate, or transmit any part of this document by either electronic means or in printed format. Recording of this publication is strictly prohibited, and any storage of this material is not allowed unless with written permission from the publisher. All rights reserved.

The information provided herein is stated to be truthful and consistent, in that any liability, regarding inattention or otherwise, by any usage or abuse of any policies, processes, or directions contained within is the solitary and complete responsibility of the recipient reader. Under no circumstances will any legal liability or blame be held against the publisher for any reparation, damages, or monetary loss due to the information herein, either directly or indirectly.

Respective authors own all copyrights not held by the publisher.

Legal Notice:

This book is copyright protected. This is only for personal use. You cannot amend, distribute, sell, use, quote or paraphrase any part of the content within this book without the consent of the author or copyright owner. Legal action will be pursued if this is breached.

Disclaimer Notice:

Please note the information contained within this document is for educational and entertainment purposes only. Every attempt has been made to provide accurate, up-to-date and reliable, complete information. No warranties of any kind are expressed or implied. Readers acknowledge that the author is not engaging in the rendering of legal, financial, medical or professional advice.

By reading this document, the reader agrees that under no circumstances are we responsible for any losses, direct or indirect, which are incurred as a result of the use of information contained within this document, including, but not limited to, errors, omissions, or inaccuracies.

Table of contents

Introduction	13
Chapter 1: Why the Mediterranean Diet?	14
What is the Mediterranean diet?	14
The history of the Mediterranean diet?	14
The Science Behind Mediterranean diet	14
Benefits of the Mediterranean diet	15
Chapter 2: Instant Pot Basics	16
Instant pot benefits	16
The main functions	17
Cleaning tips	18
Chapter 3: Breakfast & Brunch	19
Vegetable Quinoa	19
Quinoa Breakfast Bowls	19
Delicious Breakfast Potato Mix	19
Perfect Breakfast Oatmeal	20
Mix Berry Oatmeal	20
Warm Pumpkin Oats	20
Blueberry Breakfast Oatmeal	21
Pear Oatmeal	21
Sprout Potato Salad	21
Peach Blueberry Oatmeal	22
Breakfast Jalapeno Egg Cups	22
Almond Peach Oatmeal	22
Breakfast Cobbler	23
Breakfast Cauliflower Rice Bowl	23
Healthy Zucchini Kale Tomato Salad	23
Walnut Banana Oatmeal	24
Breakfast Rice Bowls	24
Healthy Dry Fruit Porridge	25
Rosemary Broccoli Cauliflower Mash	25
Zucchini Pudding	25
Mushroom Tomato Egg Cups	26
Feta Spinach Egg Cups	26
Breakfast Carrot Oatmeal	26
Potato Breakfast Hash	27
Cranberry Oatmeal	27
Healthy Buckwheat Porridge	27
Apricot Oats	28
Simple Breakfast Quinoa	28
Irish Oatmeal	28
Slow Cook Apple Oatmeal	29
Chocolate Quinoa Bowl	29
Coconut Strawberry Oatmeal	29
Egg Cauliflower Salad	29
Quick & Healthy Apple Squash Porridge	30
Healthy Cauliflower Mushroom Salad	30
Olive Squash Salad	31
Almond Blueberry Quinoa	31

Quinoa Pudding	31
Breakfast Potato Salad	32
Pepper Chickpea Salad	32
Healthy Vegetable Breakfast	32
Pumpkin Oatmeal	33
Pumpkin Steel Cut Oatmeal	33
Nut & Sweet Potato Breakfast	34
Healthy Quinoa Rice Bowls	34
Buckwheat Breakfast Bowls	34
Breakfast Potato Salad	35
Breakfast Rice Bowls	35
Carrot Rice Pudding	35
Chia Carrot Oatmeal	36
Millet Oats	36
Pear Breakfast Rice	36
Almond Peach Oatmeal	37
Garlic Potatoes	37
Spinach Egg Breakfast	37
Potato Cheese Frittata	38
Spinach Frittata	38
Date Apple Oats	39
Mushroom Cheese Breakfast	39
Simple Lemon Quinoa	39
Chapter 4: Soups & Stews	**41**
Nutritious Kidney Bean Soup	41
Healthy Vegetable Soup	41
Hearty Pork Stew	41
Mixed Lentil Stew	42
Spinach Chicken Stew	42
Delicious Okra Chicken Stew	43
Lamb Stew	43
Easy & Delicious Beef Stew	44
Tomato Chickpeas Stew	44
Chicken Lentil Stew	44
Garlic Squash Broccoli Soup	45
Chicken Rice Soup	45
Mussels Soup	45
Simple Black Bean Soup	46
Creamy Chicken Soup	46
Cheesy Chicken Soup	46
Italian Salsa Chicken Soup	47
Italian Chicken Stew	47
Creamy Carrot Tomato Soup	48
Healthy Lentil Soup	48
Creamy Cauliflower Soup	48
Spinach Lentil Soup	49
Easy Lemon Chicken Soup	49
Basil Zucchini Soup	49
Tomato Pepper Soup	50
Sausage Potato Soup	50

Roasted Tomatoes Soup 51
Healthy Cabbage Soup 51
Basil Broccoli Soup 51
Mushroom Carrot Soup 52
Spinach Cauliflower Soup 52
Delicious Chicken Wild Rice Soup 52
Kidney Bean Soup 53
Pepper Chicken Soup 53
Chili Chicken Soup 54
Creamy Potato Soup 54
Healthy Carrot Soup 54
Creamy Squash Cauliflower Soup 55
Creamy Lentil Soup 55
Lentil Veggie Soup 55
Lentil Tomato Soup 56
Onion Soup 56
Chicken Noodle Soup 56
Easy Cauliflower Soup 57
Cheese Kale Soup 57
Chicken Kale Soup 57
Cabbage Soup 58
Celery Soup 58
Pepper Pumpkin Soup 58
Curried Zucchini Soup 59

Chapter 5: Pasta, Grains & Beans 60
Delicious Chicken Pasta 60
Flavors Taco Rice Bowl 60
Flavorful Mac & Cheese 60
Cucumber Olive Rice 61
Flavors Herb Risotto 61
Delicious Pasta Primavera 62
Roasted Pepper Pasta 62
Cheese Basil Tomato Rice 62
Mac & Cheese 63
Tuna Pasta 63
Vegan Olive Pasta 64
Italian Mac & Cheese 64
Italian Chicken Pasta 64
Delicious Greek Chicken Pasta 65
Pesto Chicken Pasta 65
Spinach Pesto Pasta 65
Fiber Packed Chicken Rice 66
Tasty Greek Rice 66
Bulgur Salad 67
Perfect Herb Rice 67
Herb Polenta 67
Vegetable Herb Rice 68
Cheesy Polenta 68
Healthy Red Lentils 68
Quick & Easy Couscous 69

Healthy Green Bean Rice 69
Cheese Herb Rice 69
Garlic Zucchini Rice 70
Leek Rice Pilaf 70
Healthy Spinach Rice 71
Italian Pesto Pasta 71
Salsa Chicken Rice 71
Salsa Avocado Rice 72
Nutritious Rice 72
Rosemary Black Beans 72
Creamy Italian Pasta 73
Tasty Tomato Risotto 73
Cheesy Zucchini Pasta 73
Kidney Bean Salad 74
Lentil Rice 74
Chicken Risotto 74
Rosemary Beans & Lentils 75
Tasty Saucy Beans 75
Garlic Onion Pinto Beans 76
Classic Greek Lentils & Rice 76
Creamy & Tasty Risotto 76
Curried Beans 77
Tasty Salsa Beans 77
Brown Rice Pilaf 77
Corn Risotto 78

Chapter 6: Vegetables 79
Potato Salad 79
Greek Green Beans 79
Healthy Vegetable Medley 79
Spicy Zucchini 80
Healthy Garlic Eggplant 80
Carrot Potato Medley 80
Lemon Herb Potatoes 81
Flavors Basil Lemon Ratatouille 81
Garlic Basil Zucchini 82
Feta Green Beans 82
Garlic Parmesan Artichokes 82
Delicious Pepper Zucchini 83
Celery Carrot Brown Lentils 83
Lemon Artichokes 84
Easy Chili Pepper Zucchinis 84
Delicious Okra 84
Tomato Dill Cauliflower 85
Parsnips with Eggplant 85
Easy Garlic Beans 85
Eggplant with Olives 85
Vegan Carrots & Broccoli 86
Zucchini Tomato Potato Ratatouille 86
Easy Curried Spinach Chickpeas 87
Vegan Sweet Potato Hummus 87

Quinoa Veggie Ratatouille 87
Vegetable Chili 88
Vegan Basil Artichoke Olive 88
Lemon Basil Eggplants 89
Delicious Cauliflower Rice 89
Spicy Mushrooms 89
Delicious Baby Carrots 90
Easy Bell Pepper Gumbo 90
Healthy Chickpea & Broccoli 90
Nutritious Potato Lentils 91
Rosemary Potatoes 91
Delicious Italian Bell Pepper 91
Pesto Zucchini 92
Pesto Cauliflower 92
Italian Tomato Mushrooms 93
Chickpea & Potato 93
Zesty Green Beans 93
Rosemary Garlic Zucchini 94
Healthy Baby Carrots 94
Greek Cauliflower Rice 94
Tomato & Cheese Mix 95
Beans & Mushrooms 95
Radish & Asparagus 96
Spicy Cauliflower 96
Creamy Lemon Bell Peppers 96
Creamy Dill Potatoes 97

Chapter 7: Appetizers 98
Spicy Pepper Eggplant Spread 98
Pinto Bean Dip 98
Spicy Jalapeno Spinach Artichoke Dip 98
Perfect Black Bean Dip 99
Flavorful Italian Peppers 99
Cheese Stuff Artichokes 99
Sausage Queso Dip 100
Chocolate Hummus 100
Tasty Spinach Artichoke Dip 101
Rosemary Hummus 101
Homemade Salsa 101
Cheesy Corn Dip 102
Light & Creamy Garlic Hummus 102
Perfect Queso 103
Creamy Potato Spread 103
Cucumber Tomato Okra Salsa 103
Parmesan Potatoes 104
Creamy Artichoke Dip 104
Homemade Salsa 104
Delicious Eggplant Caponata 105
Flavorful Roasted Baby Potatoes 105
Perfect Italian Potatoes 105
Garlic Pinto Bean Dip 106

Creamy Eggplant Dip	106
Jalapeno Chickpea Hummus	106
Tasty Black Bean Dip	107
Healthy Kidney Bean Dip	107
Creamy Pepper Spread	108
Healthy Spinach Dip	108
Kidney Bean Spread	108
Tomato Cucumber Salsa	109
Spicy Berry Dip	109
Rosemary Cauliflower Dip	109
Tomato Olive Salsa	110
Easy Tomato Dip	110
Balsamic Bell Pepper Salsa	111
Spicy Chicken Dip	111
Slow Cooked Cheesy Artichoke Dip	111
Olive Eggplant Spread	112
Pepper Tomato Eggplant Spread	112

Chapter 8: Poultry 113

Flavorful Mediterranean Chicken	113
Artichoke Olive Chicken	113
Easy Chicken Piccata	113
Garlic Thyme Chicken Drumsticks	114
Tender Chicken & Mushrooms	114
Delicious Chicken Casserole	115
Perfect Chicken & Rice	115
Moroccan Chicken	116
Flavorful Cafe Rio Chicken	116
Zesty Veggie Chicken	116
Creamy Chicken Breasts	117
Cheese Garlic Chicken & Potatoes	117
Easy Chicken Scampi	118
Protein Packed Chicken Bean Rice	118
Pesto Vegetable Chicken	118
Greek Chicken Rice	119
Flavorful Chicken Tacos	119
Quinoa Chicken Bowls	120
Quick Chicken with Mushrooms	120
Herb Garlic Chicken	121
Delicious Chicken Cacciatore	121
Pesto Chicken	121
One Pot Chicken & Potatoes	122
Lemon Olive Chicken	122
Shredded Greek Chicken	123
Creamy Greek Chicken	123
Delicious Gyro Chicken	124
Moroccan Spiced Chicken	124
Moist & Tender Turkey Breast	125
Tasty Turkey Chili	125

Chapter 9: Beef 126

Moist Shredded Beef	126

- Hearty Beef Ragu 126
- Dill Beef Brisket 126
- Tasty Beef Stew 127
- Meatloaf 127
- Flavorful Beef Bourguignon 127
- Delicious Beef Chili 128
- Rosemary Creamy Beef 128
- Spicy Beef Chili Verde 129
- Carrot Mushroom Beef Roast 129
- Italian Beef Roast 129
- Thyme Beef Round Roast 130
- Jalapeno Beef Chili 130
- Beef with Tomatoes 131
- Tasty Beef Goulash 131
- Beef & Beans 131
- Delicious Ground Beef 132
- Bean Beef Chili 132
- Garlic Caper Beef Roast 133
- Cauliflower Tomato Beef 133
- Artichoke Beef Roast 133
- Italian Beef 134
- Greek Chuck Roast 134
- Beanless Beef Chili 135
- Sage Tomato Beef 135
- Rosemary Beef Eggplant 135
- Lemon Basil Beef 136
- Thyme Ginger Garlic Beef 136
- Beef Shawarma 136
- Beef Curry 137

Chapter 10: Pork 138
- Pork with Vegetables 138
- Garlic Parsley Pork Chops 138
- Creamy Leek Pork Chops 138
- Walnut Pork Chops 139
- Balsamic Pork Chops 139
- Pork & Mushrooms 140
- Pork Rice 140
- Delicious Pork Roast 140
- Meatloaf 141
- Pork Roast with Potatoes 141
- Herb Pork 141
- Basil Pork Broccoli 142
- Spinach Pork 142
- Pork Chops with Sprouts 142
- Pork with Beans 143
- Bell Pepper Pork Chops 143
- Capers Pork Chops 144
- Balsamic Pork with Kale 144
- Simple Paprika Pork Chops 144
- Delicious Pork Carnitas 145

Creamy Pork Chops	145
Pulled Pork Butt	145
Salsa Pork	146
Lime Salsa Pork Chops	146
Pork with Carrots Potatoes	146
Simple Shredded Pork	147
Cheese Pork Chops	147
Tasty Pork Carnitas	147
Pork Rice	148
Simple Lemon Pepper Pork Chops	148
Chapter 11: Lamb	**149**
Lamb Stew	149
Carrot Bean Lamb Stew	149
Delicious Salsa Lamb	149
Tomato Lamb Chops	150
Healthy Quinoa Lamb	150
Sweet Potato lamb	150
Lamb & Kale	151
Tomato Pea Lamb Chops	151
Delicious Lamb Curry	151
Flavors Lamb Ribs	152
Meatballs in Sauce	152
Lamb Basil Salad	153
Lamb Shanks	153
Vegetable Lamb Chops	153
Italian Lamb Tomatoes	154
Lamb with Sprouts	154
Garlic Mushrooms Lamb Chops	154
Eggplant & Lamb	155
Lemon Garlic Lamb Riblets	155
Mediterranean Lamb	155
Tasty Lamb Leg	156
Kale Sprouts & Lamb	156
Herb Veggie Lamb	157
Italian Lamb Stew	157
Curried Lamb Stew	157
Artichoke Lamb Curry	158
Lamb with Beans	158
Garlic Coriander Lamb Chops	158
Healthy Lamb & Couscous	159
Tomato Oregano Lamb Stew	159
Chapter 12: Seafood & Fish	**160**
Delicious Lemon Butter Cod	160
Italian White Fish Fillets	160
Rosemary Salmon	160
Shrimp Salad	161
Chili Lime Salmon	161
Steamed Salmon	161
Rosemary Mussels	162
Basil Fish Curry	162

Italian Fish Stew	163
Thyme Mussels	163
Mediterranean Fish Fillets	163
Flavors Cioppino	164
Delicious Shrimp Alfredo	164
Tomato Olive Fish Fillets	164
Shrimp Scampi	165
Easy Salmon Stew	165
Italian Tuna Pasta	165
Garlicky Clams	166
Delicious Fish Tacos	166
Pesto Fish Fillet	167
Tuna Risotto	167
Salsa Fish Fillets	167
Coconut Clam Chowder	168
Feta Tomato Sea Bass	168
Stewed Mussels & Scallops	168
Healthy Halibut Soup	169
Creamy Fish Stew	169
Nutritious Broccoli Salmon	170
Shrimp Zoodles	170
Healthy Carrot & Shrimp	170
Salmon with Potatoes	171
Honey Garlic Shrimp	171
Simple Lemon Clams	171
Crab Stew	172
Honey Balsamic Salmon	172
Spicy Tomato Crab Mix	172
Dijon Fish Fillets	173
Lemoney Prawns	173
Lemon Cod Peas	173
Quick & Easy Shrimp	174
Chapter 13: Desserts	**175**
Chocolate Nut Spread	175
Fruit Nut Bowl	175
Applesauce	175
Sweet Coconut Raspberries	176
Creamy Fruit Bowls	176
Delicious Berry Crunch	176
Cinnamon Apple	177
Sweet Vanilla Pears	177
Tapioca Pudding	177
Apple Orange Stew	177
Lime Pears	178
Cauliflower Rice Pudding	178
Lime Orange Jam	178
Sweet Pear Stew	179
Vanilla Apple Compote	179
Apple Dates Mix	179
Choco Rice Pudding	180

Grapes Stew 180
Chocolate Rice 180
Raisins Cinnamon Peaches 180
Lemon Pear Compote 181
Strawberry Stew 181
Walnut Apple Pear Mix 181
Cinnamon Pear Jam 182
Delicious Apple Pear Cobbler 182
Coconut Rice Pudding 182
Pear Sauce 183
Sweet Peach Jam 183
Warm Peach Compote 183
Spiced Pear Sauce 183
Honey Fruit Compote 184
Creamy Brown Rice Pudding 184
Lemon Cranberry Sauce 184
Blackberry Jam 185
Chunky Apple Sauce 185
Maple Syrup Cranberry Sauce 185
Raisin Pecan Baked Apples 186
Healthy Zucchini Pudding 186
Cinnamon Apple Rice Pudding 186
Coconut Risotto Pudding 186
Chapter 14: 30-Day Meal Plan 188
Conclusion 192

Introduction

The Mediterranean diet is one of the most studied diets worldwide. It is the oldest diet plan that comes from Mediterranean regions situated on the coast of the Mediterranean Sea. It is one of the healthy food eating habits that allow you to eat natural and fresh ingredients. If your goal is weight loss and you want to switch yourself towards a healthy lifestyle then you are at the right place.

In this book, you have found all about the Mediterranean diet from its history to the health benefits of the Mediterranean diet and science behind the diet. Mediterranean diet helps you various medical conditions such as it helps you to lose your weight, it is also effective on type-2 diabetes, it maintains your blood sugar level, keeps you stress-free and reduces the risk of heart-related disease. Using this book, you have to adopt a healthy diet with a healthy cooking method popularly known as instant pot cooking. This book guides you all about instant pot cooking from the basics of instant pot, benefits of using an instant pot, functions of the instant pot and instant pot cleaning tips. This book is the combination of a healthy Mediterranean diet with a healthy instant pot cooking method.

My goal here is that you should understand all about the Mediterranean diet, its health benefits, and science behind the Mediterranean diet. The books also introduce you with a healthy cooking appliance known as an instant pot with its benefits. There are different types of 450 Mediterranean recipes found in this book. All the recipes in this book are selected from globally inspired dishes. The recipes given in this book are written with their exact cooking and preparation time. There are various books are available in the market on this topic thanks for choosing my book. I hope the information given in this book helps you with your Mediterranean journey.

Chapter 1: Why the Mediterranean Diet?

Mediterranean diet is not just a diet plan it is one of the healthy eating lifestyles. Most of the scientific study and research conducted over the Mediterranean diet proves that the Mediterranean diet helps to reduce your excess weight, cancer cell reduction and also reduces the risk of cardiovascular diseases.

Most of the scientific study also proves that the food consumption during the Mediterranean diet like vegetables, whole grain, nuts, fish and seasonable fruits improves blood vessels functions and reduce the risk of metabolic syndrome.

What is the Mediterranean diet?

Mediterranean diet is one of the traditional diets comes from different Mediterranean countries and regions. Mediterranean diet is basically a plant-based diet that allows you high consumption of vegetables, fruits, nuts, beans, grains, fish and olive oil. Mediterranean diet is a rich fat diet, it allows near about 40 percent of calories from fat. It also allows for consuming a moderate amount of protein and low consumption of meat and dairy products.

Mediterranean diet linked with good health and a healthier heart, it helps to reduce your health issues like diabetes and heart-related disease.

The history of the Mediterranean diet?

Mediterranean diet is one of the oldest diets plans popular in worldwide. It is near about more than three thousand years old diet plan. Mediterranean is the name of the sea situated between Asia, Europe and Africa. Mediterranean diet is an eating habit of people's lives around the coast of the Mediterranean Sea like Italy, France, Spain, Greece and Morocco. There are near about 22 countries situated near the Mediterranean Sea. The large amounts of seasonable fruits are available during four seasons because of mild climate.

There are large numbers of olive trees found in Mediterranean regions. Near about 90 percent of the world, olive trees are grown in Mediterranean regions. Due to large sea coast fishing is the main occupation by most of the people in this region and fish is part of the Mediterranean diet. Most of the scientific study conducted over Mediterranean diet proves that the diet helps to reduce the all-cause mortality. It also reduces the risk of heart-related disease and early death.

The Science Behind Mediterranean diet

Mediterranean diet is one of the high-fat diets that allow near about 40 percent of calories from fat. It is the most studied and healthiest diet worldwide.

The scientific research and study show that the peoples who follow the Mediterranean diet have lower the risk of cardiac mortality and heart disease. The study shows that the Mediterranean diet is a high-fat diet; during the diet, our body consumes a high intake of unsaturated fat and low intake of saturated fat. Unsaturated fats help to increase the HDL (Good Cholesterol) level into your body. Olive oil is one of the main fats used during the Mediterranean diet. Olive oils are full of monounsaturated fats that help to control your diabetes. It improves your insulin sensitivity and controls your diabetes. If you don't have diabetes then it helps to reduce the risk of developing diabetes.

Another study shows that the Mediterranean diet reduces the risk of stomach cancer and also reducing the risk of breast cancer in women.

Benefits of the Mediterranean diet

Mediterranean diet is one of the oldest diets in the world comes with various types of health benefits. Some of the important benefits are as follows.

- Improves heart health

During the Mediterranean diet, olive oil is used as a primary fat. This olive oil contains healthy fat known as monounsaturated fat helps to increase the HDL (Good Cholesterol) level and reduce the LDL (Bad Cholesterol) level. Fish is also part of the Mediterranean lifestyle, fish contains Omega-3 fatty acid which helps to improve the heart health and reduce the risk of heart failure, strokes, and sudden cardiac death.

- Help to maintain blood sugar level

According to the American Heart Association, the Mediterranean diet is low in sugar. It is very effective in type-2 diabetes patients and helps to maintain the blood sugar level. Mediterranean diet is rich in monounsaturated fats which help to reduce the cholesterol level and maintain your blood sugar level.

- Increase your lifespan

Mediterranean region's climate is clear and pollution-free climate. Due to this, you have to find fresh vegetables, seasonable fruits, beans, olives and fish in this region. All of the natural and fresh foods are full of antioxidants, which helps to reduce the inflammation in your body and slow down your aging process. It also reduces the risk of heart-related disease, inflammation, Alzheimer's and depression. The peoples live in Mediterranean regions have a longer lifespan.

- Protects from cancer

Mediterranean diet is one of the simple plant-based food diet. It allows high fat moderate protein and low consumption of red meat. Most of the scientific study and research show that reduction of red meat from your diet and increase the consumption of olive oil and fish into your daily diet will help to reduce the risk of several common cancers. Fish contains omega-3 fatty acids which reduce the risk of cancer.

- Fight against depression

The foods associated with the Mediterranean diet have anti-inflammatory properties which help to reduce the depression and help to improve your mood. One of the scientific research studies shows that the peoples who follow the Mediterranean diet have 98.6 percent of lower the risk of depression.

Chapter 2: Instant Pot Basics

The instant pot is one of the modern kitchen cooking appliances that run over microprocessor technology. It is a small electric pressure-cooking appliance that comes with various smart functions. The instant pot is acts as a multi-cooker appliance which not only used for pressure cooking but also performs the task of 7 different kitchen appliances. Instant pot multi cooker is used as a pressure cooker, slow cooker, steamer, rice cooker and more. The instant pot is the perfect choice for those people who want delicious food with less time. It not only save your kitchen countertop space but also saves your cooing time.

Instant pot cooks your food under high pressure without compromising the nutritional values in the food. It comes with a digital display panel and different function buttons over instant pot panel. Some of the function buttons are pre-programmed you never need to select the time and temperature setting for the functions. You can also operate it manually by setting time and temperature. The functions are varied, depending upon the type of instant pot model you used.

Instant pot benefits

The instant pot is an electric pressure cooker appliance comes with various benefits described as follows:

1. Save your cooking time and energy

Instant pot cooks your food under high pressure. It cooks your food very little time due to this instant pot save your cooking time. Compare to other traditional cooking appliances instant pot requires very less energy to cook your food. The inner pot of instant pot comes with fully insulated, due to this reason it takes very less energy to heat up. Compare to any other traditional cooking appliance your instant pot saves near about 70 percent of energy.

2. Preserves essential vitamins and nutrients

Most of the essential vitamins and nutrients are lost during the cooking process because most of them are water-soluble. Your instant pot requires very less water while pressure-cooks your food. The pot filled with full of steam is sufficient to cook your veggies without losing vitamin and nutrient values. While cooking food into instant pot heat, steam and pressure are equally distributed into the inner pot this will gives you even cooking. It not only just preserves vitamins and nutrients but also maintains the color and flavor of your food.

3. Safe to use

Instant pot is one of the advanced cooking appliances that run over microprocessor technology. It comes with inner temperature and pressure sensing technology which helps to regulate the inner temperature and pressure automatically. Your instant pot comes with 10-built in safety mechanism. This technology makes your instant pot super safe and reliable cooking appliance.

4. Kills harmful micro-organisms

Instant pot cooks your food under high pressure. The inner temperature goes 212 °F which is higher than the boiling pot of water. Due to this, all harmful microorganisms like bacteria, fungi and viruses are killed under high pressure.

Aflatoxins are one kind of fungal poison carried by wheat, beans, and rice. Just heating food with a boiling point is not sufficient to destroy Aflatoxins. Pressure cooking is one of the ways to destroy these types of fungal poison.

5. Multi-cooker appliance

Instant pot is a small electric pressure cooker work as a multi-cooker. It performs the task of a 7-different cooking appliance. It not only used for pressure cooking but also work as a steamer, rice cooker, slow cooker, Sauté food like frying pan, soup maker, baking cakes and cookies. The functions of instant pot are depending upon the model you choose.

The main functions

The instant pot comes with various types of function buttons which are described as follows:

1. Soup

This function is used to make soup, broth, and stock. While using this function instant pot automatically adjusts the inner pressure and temperature to avoid boiling inner liquid heavily.

2. Meat / Stew

This function is used to cook your favorite meat and stew recipes into the instant pot. You can also adjust the setting manually depending on the color and texture of the food you want. The default cooking time under this setting is 35 minutes under high pressure.

3. Manual

This function is used to adjust the time and temperature manually by pressing the + / - settings.

4. Steam

This function is used to steam your seafood and veggies. When you are using this function make sure steam rack are inserted properly otherwise there are chances to burn and stick your food. This function is also used to reheat your food.

5. Slow cook

This function is used for slow cooking purpose it converts your instant pot into the slow cooker. While using this function always remember that the pressure valve set at the venting position. This function has 4 hours of default cooking time. You can also adjust the time by pressing manual function + / -

6. Sauté

This function is used to sauté food like frying pan. When you are using this function pressure cooker lid must be open.

7. Keep Warm / Cancel

This function is used to cancel your current running function. After pressing this function your instant pot goes keep warm mode where certain temperature (145°F to 172°F) is maintained to keep your food warm.

8. Rice

This is one of the fully automatic functions that comes with the instant pot. It converts your instant pot into the rice cooker. Cooking time and cooking temperature depending on the quantity of rice and water in the inner pot.

9. Beans

This function is used to cook all types of your favorite beans. This function runs on default 30 minutes of time under high pressure. You can also adjust the time and temperature manually by pressing + / - buttons.

Cleaning tips

After finishing your cooking cleaning is one of the necessary processes. Here are some important cleaning tips are given as follows:

- Before starting the cleaning process always remember to unplug instant pot main unit.
- Instant pot housing is made up of electric components so never immersed it in water. Just wipe the interior and exterior carefully.
- While cleaning heating elements use a brush to remove dried food particles.
- Wash instant pot lid with soapy water and clean it with dry cloth from both sides.
- Always remember to check and clean the steam valve.
- Pull silicon ring for cleaning purpose and clean it properly. You can clean it in dishwasher. After cleaning check, the ring for damage. If any damage found then change the ring with a new one.
- Clean your inner pot and steam rack into the dishwasher because they are dishwasher safe.
- After cleaning finally reassemble all the parts of instant pot. Make sure the sealing ring is placed its position correctly.

Chapter 3: Breakfast & Brunch

Vegetable Quinoa

Preparation Time: 10 minutes; Cooking Time: 1 minute; Serve: 6
Ingredients:
- 1 cup quinoa, rinsed and drained
- 1 1/2 cups water
- 4 cups spinach, chopped
- 1 bell pepper, chopped
- 2 carrots, chopped
- 1 celery stalk, chopped
- 1/3 cup feta cheese, crumbled
- 1/2 cup olives, sliced
- 1/3 cup pesto
- 2 tomatoes, chopped
- Pepper
- Salt

Directions:
1. Add quinoa, spinach, bell pepper, carrots, celery, water, pepper, and salt into the instant pot and stir well.
2. Seal pot with lid and cook on high for 1 minute.
3. Once done, allow to release pressure naturally for 10 minutes then release remaining using quick release. Remove lid.
4. Add remaining ingredients and stir everything well.
5. Serve and enjoy.

Nutritional Value (Amount per Serving):
Calories 226; Fat 10.7 g; Carbohydrates 26 g; Sugar 4.4 g; Protein 7.9 g; Cholesterol 11 mg

Quinoa Breakfast Bowls

Preparation Time: 10 minutes; Cooking Time: 4 minutes; Serve: 4
Ingredients:
- 1 cup quinoa, rinsed and drained
- 1 cucumber, chopped
- 1 red bell pepper, chopped
- 1/2 cup olives, pitted and sliced
- 1 tbsp fresh basil, chopped
- 2 tbsp fresh lemon juice
- 1 tsp lemon zest, grated
- 1 1/2 cups water
- Pepper
- Salt

Directions:
1. Add quinoa, lemon zest, lemon juice, water, pepper, and salt into the instant pot and stir well.
2. Seal pot with lid and cook on high for 4 minutes.
3. Once done, allow to release pressure naturally for 10 minutes then release remaining using quick release. Remove lid.
4. Add remaining ingredients and stir well.
5. Serve immediately and enjoy it.

Nutritional Value (Amount per Serving):
Calories 199; Fat 4.6 g; Carbohydrates 33.6 g; Sugar 3 g; Protein 7 g; Cholesterol 0 mg

Delicious Breakfast Potato Mix

Preparation Time: 10 minutes; Cooking Time: 15 minutes; Serve: 6
Ingredients:
- 5 potatoes, peeled and cut into wedges
- 3/4 cup mozzarella cheese, shredded
- 1 1/2 tbsp fresh basil, chopped
- 1/2 cup sour cream
- 2 tbsp olive oil
- 1/2 cup onion, chopped
- 1/4 cup vegetable stock
- Pepper
- Salt

Directions:

1. Add oil into the inner pot of instant pot and set the pot on sauté mode.
2. Add onion and sauté for 2-3 minutes.
3. Add potatoes, vegetable stock, pepper, and salt and stir well.
4. Seal pot with lid and cook on high for 12 minutes.
5. Once done, allow to release pressure naturally for 10 minutes then release remaining using quick release. Remove lid.
6. Add remaining ingredients and stir well.
7. Serve and enjoy.

Nutritional Value (Amount per Serving):
Calories 218; Fat 9.5 g; Carbohydrates 29.8 g; Sugar 2.5 g; Protein 4.7 g; Cholesterol 10 mg

Perfect Breakfast Oatmeal

Preparation Time: 10 minutes; Cooking Time: 4 minutes; Serve: 4
Ingredients:
- 1 cup steel-cut oats
- 3/4 cup unsweetened shredded coconut
- 1/4 tsp ground ginger
- 1/4 tsp ground nutmeg
- 1/2 tsp ground cinnamon
- 1/4 cup raisins
- 1 apple, chopped
- 1 1/2 cup carrots, shredded
- 1 cup unsweetened almond milk
- 3 cups of water

Directions:
1. Add all ingredients except raisins and shredded coconut into the instant pot and stir well.
2. Seal pot with lid and cook on high for 4 minutes.
3. Once done, allow to release pressure naturally. Remove lid.
4. Stir well and top with raisins and shredded coconut and serve.

Nutritional Value (Amount per Serving):
Calories 297; Fat 14.4 g; Carbohydrates 38.2 g; Sugar 14.9 g; Protein 5.2 g; Cholesterol 0 mg

Mix Berry Oatmeal

Preparation Time: 10 minutes; Cooking Time: 4 minutes; Serve: 4
Ingredients:
- 1 cup steel-cut oats
- 1/4 tsp ground cinnamon
- 1/2 tsp vanilla extract
- 2 tbsp maple syrup
- 3.5 fresh mixed berries
- 14.5 oz coconut milk

Directions:
1. Spray instant pot from inside with cooking spray.
2. Add all ingredients into the inner pot of instant pot and stir well.
3. Seal pot with lid and cook on high for 4 minutes.
4. Once done, allow to release pressure naturally for 10 minutes then release remaining using quick release. Remove lid.
5. Stir well and serve.

Nutritional Value (Amount per Serving):
Calories 412; Fat 26.3 g; Carbohydrates 41.3 g; Sugar 18.4 g; Protein 5.9 g; Cholesterol 0 mg

Warm Pumpkin Oats

Preparation Time: 10 minutes; Cooking Time: 10 minutes; Serve: 4
Ingredients:
- 1 cup steel-cut oats
- 1/4 tsp ground cinnamon
- 2 1/2 tbsp maple syrup
- 1 tsp vanilla
- 2 cups unsweetened almond milk
- 1/4 cup pumpkin puree

- 1 cup pumpkin coffee creamer
- Pinch of salt

Directions:
1. Spray instant pot from inside with cooking spray.
2. Add oats, almond milk, coffee creamer, vanilla, and salt into the instant pot and stir well.
3. Seal pot with a lid and select manual and set timer for 10 minutes.
4. Once done, allow to release pressure naturally for 10 minutes then release remaining using quick release. Remove lid.
5. Add remaining ingredients and stir well.
6. Serve and enjoy.

Nutritional Value (Amount per Serving):
Calories 139; Fat 3.5 g; Carbohydrates 26 g; Sugar 9.5 g; Protein 3.4 g; Cholesterol 0 mg

Blueberry Breakfast Oatmeal

Preparation Time: 10 minutes; Cooking Time: 3 minutes; Serve: 4

Ingredients:
- 1 cup steel-cut oats
- 1 tbsp maple syrup
- 3 cups of water
- 3/4 cup fresh blueberries
- Pinch of salt

Directions:
1. Spray instant pot from inside with cooking spray.
2. Add all ingredients into the inner pot of instant pot and stir well.
3. Seal pot with lid and cook on high for 3 minutes.
4. Once done, allow to release pressure naturally. Remove lid.
5. Stir well and serve.

Nutritional Value (Amount per Serving):
Calories 106; Fat 1.4 g; Carbohydrates 21.1 g; Sugar 5.9 g; Protein 2.9 g; Cholesterol 0 mg

Pear Oatmeal

Preparation Time: 10 minutes; Cooking Time: 13 minutes; Serve: 4

Ingredients:
- 1 cup steel-cut oatmeal
- 2 cups of water
- 1/4 tsp vanilla
- 2 tbsp maple syrup
- 1 1/4 tsp pumpkin pie spice
- 2 pears, peeled and diced
- Pinch of salt

Directions:
1. Spray instant pot from inside with cooking spray.
2. Add pears, pumpkin pie spice, and maple syrup into the instant pot and stir well and cook on sauté mode for 2 minutes.
3. Add remaining ingredients and stir well.
4. Seal pot with a lid and select manual and set timer for 10 minutes.
5. Once done, allow to release pressure naturally for 10 minutes then release remaining using quick release. Remove lid.
6. Stir well and serve.

Nutritional Value (Amount per Serving):
Calories 89; Fat 1 g; Carbohydrates 29.8 g; Sugar 16.2 g; Protein 1.7 g; Cholesterol 0 mg

Sprout Potato Salad

Preparation Time: 10 minutes; Cooking Time: 12 minutes; Serve: 4

Ingredients:
- 1 1/2 lbs Brussels sprouts, shredded
- 1 tbsp paprika

- 3 tbsp tomato puree
- 1/4 cup vegetable stock
- 1 carrot, chopped
- 1 tsp garlic, minced
- 1 onion, chopped
- 3 potatoes, peeled and cut into wedges
- Pepper
- Salt

Directions:
1. Add all ingredients into the instant pot.
2. Seal pot with a lid and select manual and set timer for 12 minutes.
3. Once done, allow to release pressure naturally for 10 minutes then release remaining using quick release. Remove lid.
4. Stir well and serve.

Nutritional Value (Amount per Serving):
Calories 213; Fat 1 g; Carbohydrates 47 g; Sugar 8.2 g; Protein 9.4 g; Cholesterol 0 mg

Peach Blueberry Oatmeal

Preparation Time: 10 minutes; Cooking Time: 4 hours; Serve: 4
Ingredients:
- 1 cup steel-cut oats
- 1/2 cup blueberries
- 3 1/2 cups unsweetened almond milk
- 7 oz can peach
- Pinch of salt

Directions:
1. Spray instant pot from inside with cooking spray.
2. Add all ingredients into the instant pot and stir well.
3. Seal the pot with a lid and select slow cook mode and cook on low for 4 hours.
4. Stir well and serve.

Nutritional Value (Amount per Serving):
Calories 150; Fat 4.5 g; Carbohydrates 25.4 g; Sugar 8.6 g; Protein 3.9 g; Cholesterol 0 mg

Breakfast Jalapeno Egg Cups

Preparation Time: 10 minutes; Cooking Time: 8 minutes; Serve: 6
Ingredients:
- 12 eggs, lightly beaten
- 1/4 tsp garlic powder
- 1/2 tsp lemon pepper seasoning
- 3 jalapeno peppers, chopped
- 1 cup cheddar cheese, shredded
- Pepper
- Salt

Directions:
1. Pour 1 1/2 cups of water into the instant pot then place steamer rack in the pot.
2. In a bowl, whisk eggs with lemon pepper seasoning, garlic powder, pepper, and salt.
3. Stir in jalapenos and cheese.
4. Pour mixture between six jars and seal jar with a lid.
5. Place jars on top of the rack in the instant pot.
6. Seal pot with a lid and select manual and set timer for 8 minutes.
7. Once done, allow to release pressure naturally for 10 minutes then release remaining using quick release. Remove lid.
8. Serve and enjoy.

Nutritional Value (Amount per Serving):
Calories 212; Fat 15.2 g; Carbohydrates 3.2 g; Sugar 2.1 g; Protein 16.1 g; Cholesterol 347 mg

Almond Peach Oatmeal

Preparation Time: 10 minutes; Cooking Time: 10 minutes; Serve: 2
Ingredients:

- 1 cup unsweetened almond milk
- 2 cups of water
- 1 cup oats
- 2 peaches, diced
- Pinch of salt

Directions:
1. Spray instant pot from inside with cooking spray.
2. Add all ingredients into the instant pot and stir well.
3. Seal pot with a lid and select manual and set timer for 10 minutes.
4. Once done, allow to release pressure naturally for 10 minutes then release remaining using quick release. Remove lid.
5. Stir and serve.

Nutritional Value (Amount per Serving):
Calories 234; Fat 4.8 g; Carbohydrates 42.7 g; Sugar 6.9 g; Protein 7.3 g; Cholesterol 0 mg

Breakfast Cobbler

Preparation Time: 10 minutes; Cooking Time: 12 minutes; Serve: 4

Ingredients:
- 2 lbs apples, cut into chunks
- 1 1/2 cups water
- 1/4 tsp nutmeg
- 1 1/2 tsp cinnamon
- 1/2 cup dry buckwheat
- 1/2 cup dates, chopped
- Pinch of ground ginger

Directions:
1. Spray instant pot from inside with cooking spray.
2. Add all ingredients into the instant pot and stir well.
3. Seal pot with a lid and select manual and set timer for 12 minutes.
4. Once done, release pressure using quick release. Remove lid.
5. Stir and serve.

Nutritional Value (Amount per Serving):
Calories 195; Fat 0.9 g; Carbohydrates 48.3 g; Sugar 25.8 g; Protein 3.3 g; Cholesterol 0 mg

Breakfast Cauliflower Rice Bowl

Preparation Time: 10 minutes; Cooking Time: 12 minutes; Serve: 6

Ingredients:
- 1 cup cauliflower rice
- 1/2 tsp red pepper flakes
- 1 1/2 tsp curry powder
- 1/2 tbsp ginger, grated
- 1 cup vegetable stock
- 4 tomatoes, chopped
- 3 cups broccoli, chopped
- Pepper
- Salt

Directions:
1. Spray instant pot from inside with cooking spray.
2. Add all ingredients into the instant pot and stir well.
3. Seal pot with lid and cook on high for 12 minutes.
4. Once done, allow to release pressure naturally for 10 minutes then release remaining using quick release. Remove lid.
5. Stir and serve.

Nutritional Value (Amount per Serving):
Calories 44; Fat 0.8 g; Carbohydrates 8.2 g; Sugar 3.8 g; Protein 2.8 g; Cholesterol 0 mg

Healthy Zucchini Kale Tomato Salad

Preparation Time: 10 minutes; Cooking Time: 20 minutes; Serve: 4

Ingredients:

- 1 lb kale, chopped
- 2 tbsp fresh parsley, chopped
- 1 tbsp vinegar
- 1/2 cup can tomato, crushed
- 1 tsp paprika
- 1 cup zucchini, cut into cubes
- 1 cup grape tomatoes, halved
- 2 tbsp olive oil
- 1 onion, chopped
- 1 leek, sliced
- Pepper
- Salt

Directions:
1. Add oil into the inner pot of instant pot and set the pot on sauté mode.
2. Add leek and onion and sauté for 5 minutes.
3. Add kale and remaining ingredients and stir well.
4. Seal pot with lid and cook on high for 15 minutes.
5. Once done, allow to release pressure naturally for 10 minutes then release remaining using quick release. Remove lid.
6. Stir and serve.

Nutritional Value (Amount per Serving):
Calories 162; Fat 7.3 g; Carbohydrates 22.2 g; Sugar 4.8 g; Protein 5.2 g; Cholesterol 0 mg

Walnut Banana Oatmeal

Preparation Time: 10 minutes; Cooking Time: 3 minutes; Serve: 2
Ingredients:
- 1/2 cup steel-cut oats
- 1 cup of water
- 1 cup unsweetened almond milk
- 1 tsp honey
- 2 tbsp walnuts, chopped
- 1/2 banana, chopped

Directions:
1. Spray instant pot from inside with cooking spray.
2. Add oats, water, and almond milk into the instant pot and stir well.
3. Seal pot with lid and cook on high for 3 minutes.
4. Once done, release pressure using quick release. Remove lid.
5. Stir in honey, walnut, and banana and serve.

Nutritional Value (Amount per Serving):
Calories 183; Fat 7.8 g; Carbohydrates 25.2 g; Sugar 6.8 g; Protein 5.4 g; Cholesterol 0 mg

Breakfast Rice Bowls

Preparation Time: 10 minutes; Cooking Time: 8 minutes; Serve: 4
Ingredients:
- 1 cup of brown rice
- 1 tsp ground cinnamon
- 1/4 cup almonds, sliced
- 2 tbsp sunflower seeds
- 1/4 cup pecans, chopped
- 1/4 cup walnuts, chopped
- 2 cup unsweetened almond milk
- Pinch of salt

Directions:
1. Spray instant pot from inside with cooking spray.
2. Add all ingredients into the instant pot and stir well.
3. Seal pot with lid and cook on high for 8 minutes.
4. Once done, allow to release pressure naturally for 5 minutes then release remaining using quick release. Remove lid.
5. Stir well and serve.

Nutritional Value (Amount per Serving):
Calories 291; Fat 12 g; Carbohydrates 40.1 g; Sugar 0.4 g; Protein 7.6 g; Cholesterol 0 mg

Healthy Dry Fruit Porridge

Preparation Time: 10 minutes; Cooking Time: 8 hours; Serve: 6
Ingredients:
- 2 cups steel-cut oats
- 1/8 tsp ground nutmeg
- 1 tsp vanilla
- 1 1/2 tsp cinnamon
- 1/2 cup dry apricots, chopped
- 1/2 cup dry cranberries, chopped
- 1/2 cup dates, chopped
- 1/2 cup raisins
- 8 cups of water
- Pinch of salt

Directions:
1. Spray instant pot from inside with cooking spray.
2. Add all ingredients into the instant pot and stir well.
3. Seal the pot with a lid and select slow cook mode and cook on low for 8 hours.
4. Stir well and serve.

Nutritional Value (Amount per Serving):
Calories 196; Fat 2 g; Carbohydrates 42 g; Sugar 18.4 g; Protein 4.5 g; Cholesterol 0 mg

Rosemary Broccoli Cauliflower Mash

Preparation Time: 10 minutes; Cooking Time: 12 minutes; Serve: 3
Ingredients:
- 2 cups broccoli, chopped
- 1 lb cauliflower, cut into florets
- 1 tsp dried rosemary
- 1/4 cup olive oil
- 1 tsp garlic, minced
- Salt

Directions:
1. Add broccoli and cauliflower into the instant pot. Pour enough water into the pot to cover broccoli and cauliflower.
2. Seal pot with lid and cook on high for 12 minutes.
3. Once done, allow to release pressure naturally. Remove lid.
4. Drain broccoli and cauliflower well and clean the instant pot.
5. Add oil into the pot and set the pot on sauté mode.
6. Add broccoli, cauliflower, rosemary, garlic, and salt and cook for 10 minutes.
7. Mash the broccoli and cauliflower mixture using a potato masher until smooth.
8. Serve and enjoy.

Nutritional Value (Amount per Serving):
Calories 205; Fat 17.2 g; Carbohydrates 12.6 g; Sugar 4.7 g; Protein 4.8 g; Cholesterol 0 mg

Zucchini Pudding

Preparation Time: 10 minutes; Cooking Time: 10 minutes; Serve: 4
Ingredients:
- 2 cups zucchini, grated
- 1/2 tsp ground cardamom
- 1/4 cup swerve
- 5 oz half and half
- 5 oz unsweetened almond milk
- Pinch of salt

Directions:
1. Spray instant pot from inside with cooking spray.
2. Add all ingredients into the instant pot and stir well.
3. Seal pot with lid and cook on high for 10 minutes.
4. Once done, allow to release pressure naturally for 10 minutes then release remaining using quick release. Remove lid.
5. Stir well and serve.

Nutritional Value (Amount per Serving):
Calories 62; Fat 4.7 g; Carbohydrates 18.9 g; Sugar 16 g; Protein 1.9 g; Cholesterol 13 mg

Mushroom Tomato Egg Cups

Preparation Time: 10 minutes; Cooking Time: 5 minutes; Serve: 4
Ingredients:
- 4 eggs
- 1/2 cup tomatoes, chopped
- 1/2 cup mushrooms, chopped
- 2 tbsp fresh parsley, chopped
- 1/4 cup half and half
- 1/2 cup cheddar cheese, shredded
- Pepper
- Salt

Directions:
1. In a bowl, whisk the egg with half and half, pepper, and salt.
2. Add tomato, mushrooms, parsley, and cheese and stir well.
3. Pour egg mixture into the four small jars and seal jars with lid.
4. Pour 1 1/2 cups of water into the instant pot then place steamer rack in the pot.
5. Place jars on top of the steamer rack.
6. Seal pot with lid and cook on high for 5 minutes.
7. Once done, release pressure using quick release. Remove lid.
8. Serve and enjoy.

Nutritional Value (Amount per Serving):
Calories 146; Fat 10.9 g; Carbohydrates 2.5 g; Sugar 1.2 g; Protein 10 g; Cholesterol 184 mg

Feta Spinach Egg Cups

Preparation Time: 10 minutes; Cooking Time: 8 minutes; Serve: 4
Ingredients:
- 6 eggs
- 1/4 tsp garlic powder
- 1 tomato, chopped
- 1/4 cup feta cheese, crumbled
- 1 cup spinach, chopped
- 1/2 cup mozzarella cheese, shredded
- Pepper
- salt

Directions:
1. Pour 1 1/2 cups of water into the instant pot then place steamer rack in the pot.
2. In a bowl, whisk eggs with garlic powder, pepper, and salt.
3. Add remaining ingredients and stir well.
4. Spray four ramekins with cooking spray.
5. Pour egg mixture into the ramekins and place ramekins on top of the rack.
6. Seal pot with lid and cook on high for 8 minutes.
7. Once done, release pressure using quick release. Remove lid.
8. Serve and enjoy.

Nutritional Value (Amount per Serving):
Calories 134; Fat 9.3 g; Carbohydrates 2 g; Sugar 1.4 g; Protein 11 g; Cholesterol 256 mg

Breakfast Carrot Oatmeal

Preparation Time: 10 minutes; Cooking Time: 10 minutes; Serve: 2
Ingredients:
- 1 cup steel-cut oats
- 1/2 cup raisins
- 1/2 tsp ground nutmeg
- 1/2 tsp ground cinnamon
- 2 carrots, grated
- 2 cups of water
- 2 cups unsweetened almond milk
- 1 tbsp honey

Directions:
1. Spray instant pot from inside with cooking spray.
2. Add all ingredients into the instant pot and stir well.
3. Seal pot with lid and cook on high for 10 minutes.
4. Once done, release pressure using quick release. Remove lid.

5. Stir and serve.

Nutritional Value (Amount per Serving):
Calories 365; Fat 6.6 g; Carbohydrates 73.8 g; Sugar 33.7 g; Protein 8.1 g; Cholesterol 0 mg

Potato Breakfast Hash

Preparation Time: 10 minutes; Cooking Time: 10 minutes; Serve: 2

Ingredients:
- 1 sweet potato, diced
- 1 cup bell pepper, chopped
- 1 tsp cumin
- 1 tbsp olive oil
- 1 potato, diced
- 1/2 tsp pepper
- 1 tsp paprika
- 1/2 tsp garlic, minced
- 1/4 cup vegetable stock
- 1/2 tsp salt

Directions:
1. Add all ingredients into the instant pot and stir well.
2. Seal pot with lid and cook on high for 10 minutes.
3. Once done, release pressure using quick release. Remove lid.
4. Stir and serve.

Nutritional Value (Amount per Serving):
Calories 206; Fat 7.7 g; Carbohydrates 32.9 g; Sugar 7.6 g; Protein 4 g; Cholesterol 0 mg

Cranberry Oatmeal

Preparation Time: 10 minutes; Cooking Time: 6 minutes; Serve: 2

Ingredients:
- 1/2 cup steel-cut oats
- 1 cup unsweetened almond milk
- 1 1/2 tbsp maple syrup
- 1/4 tsp cinnamon
- 1/4 tsp vanilla
- 1/4 cup dried cranberries
- 1 cup of water
- 1 tsp lemon zest, grated
- 1/4 cup orange juice

Directions:
1. Add all ingredients into the heat-safe dish and stir well.
2. Pour 1 cup of water into the instant pot then place the trivet in the pot.
3. Place dish on top of the trivet.
4. Seal pot with lid and cook on high for 6 minutes.
5. Once done, allow to release pressure naturally for 10 minutes then release remaining using quick release. Remove lid.
6. Serve and enjoy.

Nutritional Value (Amount per Serving):
Calories 161; Fat 3.2 g; Carbohydrates 29.9 g; Sugar 12.4 g; Protein 3.4 g; Cholesterol 0 mg

Healthy Buckwheat Porridge

Preparation Time: 10 minutes; Cooking Time: 6 minutes; Serve: 2

Ingredients:
- 1 cup buckwheat groats, rinsed
- 1 tsp ground cinnamon
- 1 banana, sliced
- 3 cups unsweetened almond milk
- Pinch of salt

Directions:
1. Spray instant pot from inside with cooking spray.
2. Add all ingredients into the instant pot and stir well.
3. Seal pot with lid and cook on high for 6 minutes.
4. Once done, release pressure using quick release. Remove lid.

5. Stir and serve.

Nutritional Value (Amount per Serving):
Calories 316; Fat 7.3 g; Carbohydrates 59.8 g; Sugar 8.8 g; Protein 9.8 g; Cholesterol 0 mg

Apricot Oats

Preparation Time: 10 minutes; Cooking Time: 3 minutes; Serve: 2
Ingredients:
- 1 cup steel-cut oats
- 1 cup dried apricots, chopped
- 1 1/2 cups water
- 1 1/2 cups unsweetened almond milk

Directions:
1. Spray instant pot from inside with cooking spray.
2. Add all ingredients into the instant pot and stir well.
3. Seal pot with lid and cook on high for 3 minutes.
4. Once done, release pressure using quick release. Remove lid.
5. Stir and serve.

Nutritional Value (Amount per Serving):
Calories 222; Fat 5.8 g; Carbohydrates 37.7 g; Sugar 7.4 g; Protein 7.1 g; Cholesterol 0 mg

Simple Breakfast Quinoa

Preparation Time: 10 minutes; Cooking Time: 1 minute; Serve: 6
Ingredients:
- 1 1/2 cups quinoa, rinsed and drained
- 2 1/2 cups water
- 1/2 tsp vanilla
- 2 tbsp maple syrup
- 1/4 tsp ground cinnamon
- Pinch of salt

Directions:
1. Spray instant pot from inside with cooking spray.
2. Add all ingredients into the instant pot and stir well.
3. Seal pot with lid and cook on high for 1 minute.
4. Once done, allow to release pressure naturally for 10 minutes then release remaining using quick release. Remove lid.
5. Fluff quinoa using fork and serve.

Nutritional Value (Amount per Serving):
Calories 175; Fat 2.6 g; Carbohydrates 31.9 g; Sugar 4 g; Protein 6 g; Cholesterol 0 mg

Irish Oatmeal

Preparation Time: 10 minutes; Cooking Time: 5 minutes; Serve: 2
Ingredients:
- 1 cup steel-cut oats
- 1 tbsp maple syrup
- 1/4 tsp cinnamon
- 1 tbsp raisins
- 1 tbsp dried apricots, chopped
- 1 tbsp dried cranberries
- 1 cup apple juice
- 3 cups of water
- Pinch of salt

Directions:
1. Spray instant pot from inside with cooking spray.
2. Add all ingredients into the instant pot and stir well.
3. Seal pot with lid and cook on high for 5 minutes.
4. Once done, allow to release pressure naturally for 10 minutes then release remaining using quick release. Remove lid.
5. Stir well and serve.

Nutritional Value (Amount per Serving):

Calories 256; Fat 2.9 g; Carbohydrates 53.1 g; Sugar 21.6 g; Protein 5.7 g; Cholesterol 0 mg

Slow Cook Apple Oatmeal

Preparation Time: 10 minutes; Cooking Time: 3 hours; Serve: 4
Ingredients:
- 1 1/2 cups rolled oats
- 1 tbsp honey
- 2 apples, diced
- 1 cup unsweetened almond milk
- 2 1/2 cups water
- Pinch of salt

Directions:
1. Spray instant pot from inside with cooking spray.
2. Add all ingredients into the instant pot and stir well.
3. Seal the pot with a lid and select slow cook mode and cook on low for 3 hours.
4. Stir well and serve.

Nutritional Value (Amount per Serving):
Calories 200; Fat 3.1 g; Carbohydrates 41 g; Sugar 16.2 g; Protein 4.6 g; Cholesterol 0 mg

Chocolate Quinoa Bowl

Preparation Time: 10 minutes; Cooking Time: 1 minute; Serve: 2
Ingredients:
- 1 1/2 cups quinoa, rinsed and drained
- 1/4 tsp cinnamon
- 1/2 tsp vanilla
- 1/2 tbsp unsweetened cocoa powder
- 2 tbsp maple syrup
- 1 cup unsweetened almond milk
- 1 1/2 cups water
- Pinch of salt

Directions:
1. Spray instant pot from inside with cooking spray.
2. Add all ingredients into the instant pot and stir well.
3. Seal pot with lid and cook on high for 1 minute.
4. Once done, allow to release pressure naturally for 10 minutes then release remaining using quick release. Remove lid.
5. Fluff quinoa using fork and serve.

Nutritional Value (Amount per Serving):
Calories 549; Fat 9.7 g; Carbohydrates 97.3 g; Sugar 12.1 g; Protein 18.8 g; Cholesterol 0 mg

Coconut Strawberry Oatmeal

Preparation Time: 10 minutes; Cooking Time: 10 minutes; Serve: 6
Ingredients:
- 1 cup fresh strawberries, halved
- 1 cup coconut flakes
- 1 tsp ground cinnamon
- 1/2 cup coconut cream
- 2 cups unsweetened almond milk

Directions:
1. Spray instant pot from inside with cooking spray.
2. Add all ingredients into the instant pot and stir well.
3. Seal pot with lid and cook on high for 10 minutes.
4. Once done, release pressure using quick release. Remove lid.
5. Stir and serve.

Nutritional Value (Amount per Serving):
Calories 115; Fat 10.5 g; Carbohydrates 6 g; Sugar 2.7 g; Protein 1.4 g; Cholesterol 0 mg

Egg Cauliflower Salad

Preparation Time: 10 minutes; Cooking Time: 14 minutes; Serve: 4

Ingredients:
- 4 eggs, hard-boiled, peeled and cubed
- 2 tbsp fresh parsley, chopped
- 1 tbsp vinegar
- 2 tbsp green onion, chopped
- 2 tbsp mayonnaise
- 1/2 cup heavy cream
- 1 1/2 cup vegetable stock
- 2 cups cauliflower florets
- 1/4 cup grape tomatoes, halved
- Pepper
- Salt

Directions:
1. Pour 1 1/2 cups of stock into the instant pot the place steamer basket in the pot.
2. Add cauliflower florets into the steamer basket.
3. Seal pot with lid and cook on high for 14 minutes.
4. Once done, allow to release pressure naturally for 10 minutes then release remaining using quick release. Remove lid.
5. Transfer cauliflower florets into the large mixing bowl. Add remaining ingredients into the bowl and mix well.
6. Serve and enjoy.

Nutritional Value (Amount per Serving):
Calories 163; Fat 12.5 g; Carbohydrates 6.3 g; Sugar 2.7 g; Protein 7.3 g; Cholesterol 186 mg

Quick & Healthy Apple Squash Porridge

Preparation Time: 10 minutes; Cooking Time: 8 minutes; Serve: 2

Ingredients:
- 2 apples, cored and sliced
- 1/2 cup water
- 1 tbsp maple syrup
- 1/4 tsp ground cinnamon
- 1/4 tsp ground ginger
- 1/2 squash, peeled and sliced
- Pinch of salt

Directions:
1. Spray instant pot from inside with cooking spray.
2. Add all ingredients except maple syrup into the instant pot and stir well.
3. Seal pot with lid and cook on high for 8 minutes.
4. Once done, release pressure using quick release. Remove lid.
5. Add maple syrup and stir well and using immersion blender blend apple mixture until smooth.
6. Serve and enjoy.

Nutritional Value (Amount per Serving):
Calories 151; Fat 0.5 g; Carbohydrates 39.5 g; Sugar 30 g; Protein 1.2 g; Cholesterol 0 mg

Healthy Cauliflower Mushroom Salad

Preparation Time: 10 minutes; Cooking Time: 20 minutes; Serve: 4

Ingredients:
- 1 cup cauliflower rice
- 1 tbsp chives, chopped
- 1 cup vegetable stock
- 1 tbsp garlic, minced
- 2 tbsp fresh lemon juice
- 2 cups mushrooms, sliced
- 2 tbsp olive oil
- 1 small onion, chopped
- 1/4 cup grape tomatoes, halved
- Pepper
- Salt

Directions:
1. Add oil into the inner pot of instant pot and set the pot on sauté mode.
2. Add garlic, onion, and mushrooms and sauté for 5 minutes.
3. Add remaining ingredients and stir well.

4. Seal pot with lid and cook on high for 15 minutes.
5. Once done, allow to release pressure naturally for 10 minutes then release remaining using quick release. Remove lid.
6. Stir well and serve.

Nutritional Value (Amount per Serving):
Calories 97; Fat 7.7 g; Carbohydrates 6 g; Sugar 3 g; Protein 2.7 g; Cholesterol 0 mg

Olive Squash Salad

Preparation Time: 10 minutes; Cooking Time: 14 minutes; Serve: 4
Ingredients:
- 1 lb squash, peeled and cut into cubes
- 1/2 cup olives, pitted and halved
- 2 tomatoes, cut into chunks
- 1/4 cup vegetable stock
- 1 tbsp sunflower seeds
- 1 tbsp olive oil
- 2 tbsp green onion, chopped
- Pepper
- Salt

Directions:
1. Add oil into the inner pot of instant pot and set the pot on sauté mode.
2. Add sunflower seeds and green onion and sauté for 1 minute.
3. Add remaining ingredients and stir well.
4. Seal pot with lid and cook on high for 13 minutes.
5. Once done, allow to release pressure naturally for 10 minutes then release remaining using quick release. Remove lid.
6. Stir well and serve.

Nutritional Value (Amount per Serving):
Calories 84; Fat 6 g; Carbohydrates 7.7 g; Sugar 3.7 g; Protein 2.3 g; Cholesterol 0 mg

Almond Blueberry Quinoa

Preparation Time: 10 minutes; Cooking Time: 1 minute; Serve: 2
Ingredients:
- 1/2 cup quinoa, rinsed and drained
- 1/4 tsp ground cinnamon
- 1/2 cup blueberries
- 2 tbsp almonds, sliced
- 1 1/2 cups unsweetened almond milk

Directions:
1. Spray instant pot from inside with cooking spray.
2. Add quinoa, cinnamon, and milk and stir well.
3. Seal pot with lid and cook on high for 1 minute.
4. Once done, allow to release pressure naturally. Remove lid.
5. Add blueberries and almonds and stir well.
6. Serve and enjoy.

Nutritional Value (Amount per Serving):
Calories 242; Fat 8.3 g; Carbohydrates 35.5 g; Sugar 3.9 g; Protein 8.3 g; Cholesterol 0 mg

Quinoa Pudding

Preparation Time: 10 minutes; Cooking Time: 5 minutes; Serve: 4
Ingredients:
- 1 1/2 cups quinoa, rinsed and drained
- 2 tbsp walnuts, chopped
- 1 1/2 cups coconut cream
- 1 1/2 cups almond milk
- 1 1/2 tsp cinnamon

Directions:
1. Spray instant pot from inside with cooking spray.

2. Add all ingredients except walnuts into the instant pot and stir well.
3. Seal pot with lid and cook on high for 5 minutes.
4. Once done, allow to release pressure naturally for 10 minutes then release remaining using quick release. Remove lid.
5. Top with walnuts and serve.

Nutritional Value (Amount per Serving):
Calories 522; Fat 29.9 g; Carbohydrates 54.2 g; Sugar 8.5 g; Protein 12.9 g; Cholesterol 0 mg

Breakfast Potato Salad

Preparation Time: 10 minutes; Cooking Time: 12 minutes; Serve: 4

Ingredients:
- 2 lbs potatoes, peeled and cut into wedges
- 1 1/2 cups water
- 1/4 cup balsamic vinegar
- 1/4 cup olive oil
- 1 tsp thyme, chopped
- 1 small onion, chopped
- Pepper
- Salt

Directions:
1. Pour water into the instant pot then place steamer basket in the pot.
2. Add potato wedges into the basket.
3. Seal pot with lid and cook on high for 12 minutes.
4. Once done, allow to release pressure naturally for 10 minutes then release remaining using quick release. Remove lid.
5. Transfer potato wedges into the large mixing bowl. Add remaining ingredients to the bowl and mix well.
6. Serve and enjoy.

Nutritional Value (Amount per Serving):
Calories 275; Fat 12.9 g; Carbohydrates 37.6 g; Sugar 3.4 g; Protein 4 g; Cholesterol 0 mg

Pepper Chickpea Salad

Preparation Time: 10 minutes; Cooking Time: 15 minutes; Serve: 4

Ingredients:
- 2 cups chickpeas, soaked overnight & drained
- 3 tbsp olive oil
- 1/4 cup balsamic vinegar
- 1 tbsp chives, chopped
- 1 onion, chopped
- 2 celery stalks, chopped
- 1 carrot, chopped
- 1/2 tsp chili powder
- 1 tsp paprika
- 1 1/2 cups bell pepper, chopped
- 1/2 tsp garlic, minced
- 3 cups vegetable stock
- Pepper
- Salt

Directions:
1. Add all ingredients into the inner pot of instant pot and stir well.
2. Seal pot with lid and cook on high for 15 minutes.
3. Once done, allow to release pressure naturally for 10 minutes then release remaining using quick release. Remove lid.
4. Stir well and serve.

Nutritional Value (Amount per Serving):
Calories 498; Fat 16.9 g; Carbohydrates 69.8 g; Sugar 15.7 g; Protein 20.7 g; Cholesterol 0 mg

Healthy Vegetable Breakfast

Preparation Time: 10 minutes; Cooking Time: 10 minutes; Serve: 4

Ingredients:
- 1 cup grape tomatoes, halved
- 1 cup mushrooms, sliced
- 2 cups okra, sliced
- 3 tbsp olive oil
- 1 1/2 cups onion, chopped
- 1/2 cup balsamic vinegar
- 1 tbsp thyme, chopped
- 2 tbsp fresh basil, chopped
- 2 cups bell pepper, chopped
- 2 cups zucchini, chopped
- 1 cup of water
- Pepper
- Salt

Directions:
1. Add all ingredients into the inner pot of instant pot and stir well.
2. Seal pot with lid and cook on high for 10 minutes.
3. Once done, release pressure using quick release. Remove lid.
4. Stir well and serve.

Nutritional Value (Amount per Serving):
Calories 176; Fat 11.1 g; Carbohydrates 17.3 g; Sugar 8.2 g; Protein 3.8 g; Cholesterol 0 mg

Pumpkin Oatmeal

Preparation Time: 10 minutes; Cooking Time: 12 minutes; Serve: 4

Ingredients:
- 1 cup steel-cut oats
- 1 cup butternut squash, shredded
- 1/2 tsp vanilla
- 1/4 cup walnuts, chopped
- 1/4 tsp ground nutmeg
- 1/2 tsp lemon zest, grated
- 1/4 tsp ground ginger
- 1/3 cup maple syrup
- 1/4 cup raisins
- 3 1/2 cups almond milk
- Pinch of salt

Directions:
1. Spray instant pot from inside with cooking spray.
2. Add all ingredients except walnuts and vanilla into the instant pot and stir well.
3. Seal pot with lid and cook on high for 12 minutes.
4. Once done, allow to release pressure naturally for 10 minutes then release remaining using quick release. Remove lid.
5. Add vanilla and walnuts and stir well.
6. Serve and enjoy.

Nutritional Value (Amount per Serving):
Calories 723; Fat 56.2 g; Carbohydrates 55.4 g; Sugar 29.2 g; Protein 10 g; Cholesterol 0 mg

Pumpkin Steel Cut Oatmeal

Preparation Time: 10 minutes; Cooking Time: 10 minutes; Serve: 4

Ingredients:
- 2 cups steel-cut oats
- 1/2 cup pumpkin seeds, toasted
- 2 1/2 tbsp maple syrup
- 1 cup pumpkin puree
- 3 cups of water
- 1/4 tsp ground cinnamon
- Pinch of salt

Directions:
1. Spray instant pot from inside with cooking spray.
2. Add all ingredients except maple syrup and pumpkin seeds into the instant pot and stir well.
3. Seal pot with lid and cook on high for 10 minutes.
4. Once done, release pressure using quick release. Remove lid.
5. Add maple syrup and stir well.

6. Top with pumpkin seeds and serve.

Nutritional Value (Amount per Serving):
Calories 302; Fat 10.8 g; Carbohydrates 44.2 g; Sugar 10 g; Protein 10.3 g; Cholesterol 0 mg

Nut & Sweet Potato Breakfast

Preparation Time: 10 minutes; Cooking Time: 15 minutes; Serve: 4

Ingredients:
- 4 sweet potatoes, peeled and cut into cubes
- 1 tbsp pecans, chopped
- 1 tbsp walnut, chopped
- 1 tbsp almond, chopped
- 1/4 tsp ground nutmeg
- 1 cup heavy cream
- 1 tbsp maple syrup

Directions:
1. Spray instant pot from inside with cooking spray.
2. Add all ingredients except maple syrup into the instant pot and stir well.
3. Seal pot with lid and cook on high for 15 minutes.
4. Once done, allow to release pressure naturally for 10 minutes then release remaining using quick release. Remove lid.
5. Stir in maple syrup and serve.

Nutritional Value (Amount per Serving):
Calories 295; Fat 15.7 g; Carbohydrates 36.6 g; Sugar 3.8 g; Protein 3.5 g; Cholesterol 41 mg

Healthy Quinoa Rice Bowls

Preparation Time: 10 minutes; Cooking Time: 12 minutes; Serve: 4

Ingredients:
- 1/2 cup brown rice
- 1 cup quinoa
- 1/2 tsp ground cinnamon
- 1 tsp vanilla
- 1/2 tsp ground nutmeg
- 1/4 cup almonds, chopped
- 1/4 cup pecans, chopped
- 1/4 cup walnuts, chopped
- 4 cups unsweetened almond milk

Directions:
1. Spray instant pot from inside with cooking spray.
2. Add all ingredients into the instant pot and stir well.
3. Seal pot with lid and cook on high for 12 minutes.
4. Once done, allow to release pressure naturally for 5 minutes then release remaining using quick release. Remove lid.
5. Stir and serve.

Nutritional Value (Amount per Serving):
Calories 376; Fat 15 g; Carbohydrates 50 g; Sugar 0.6 g; Protein 12 g; Cholesterol 0 mg

Buckwheat Breakfast Bowls

Preparation Time: 10 minutes; Cooking Time: 15 minutes; Serve: 4

Ingredients:
- 1 cup buckwheat
- 1 tsp ground cinnamon
- 1 tbsp almonds, chopped
- 1 tbsp walnuts, chopped
- 1 cup heavy cream
- 2 cups almond milk

Directions:
1. Spray instant pot from inside with cooking spray.
2. Add all ingredients into the instant pot and stir well.
3. Seal pot with lid and cook on high for 15 minutes.

4. Once done, allow to release pressure naturally for 10 minutes then release remaining using quick release. Remove lid.
5. Stir and serve.

Nutritional Value (Amount per Serving):
Calories 547; Fat 43.1 g; Carbohydrates 38.9 g; Sugar 4.1 g; Protein 9.8 g; Cholesterol 41 mg

Breakfast Potato Salad

Preparation Time: 10 minutes; Cooking Time: 15 minutes; Serve: 4

Ingredients:
- 1 lb baby potatoes, peeled and cut in half
- 1 cup vegetable stock
- 2 tbsp balsamic vinegar
- 2 tbsp olive oil
- 1 tbsp rosemary, chopped
- 4 eggs, hard-boiled, peeled and cut into wedges
- 2 tbsp green onion, chopped
- Pepper
- Salt

Directions:
1. Pour the stock into the instant pot then place steamer basket in the pot.
2. Add potato into the basket.
3. Seal pot with lid and cook on high for 15 minutes.
4. Once done, allow to release pressure naturally for 10 minutes then release remaining using quick release. Remove lid.
5. Transfer potato into the large mixing bowl. Add remaining ingredients to the bowl and mix well.
6. Serve and enjoy.

Nutritional Value (Amount per Serving):
Calories 196; Fat 11.7 g; Carbohydrates 15.5 g; Sugar 0.6 g; Protein 8.6 g; Cholesterol 164 mg

Breakfast Rice Bowls

Preparation Time: 10 minutes; Cooking Time: 20 minutes; Serve: 4

Ingredients:
- 1 cup of brown rice
- 1 tbsp fresh basil, chopped
- 1/4 cup salsa
- 3/4 cup olives, pitted and sliced
- 1 tbsp olive oil
- 1 onion, chopped
- 2 cups vegetable stock
- Pepper
- Salt

Directions:
1. Add oil into the inner pot of instant pot and set the pot on sauté mode.
2. Add onion and sauté for 2 minutes.
3. Add rice and cook for 3 minutes.
4. Add remaining ingredients and stir well.
5. Seal pot with lid and cook on high for 15 minutes.
6. Once done, allow to release pressure naturally for 10 minutes then release remaining using quick release. Remove lid.
7. Stir well and serve.

Nutritional Value (Amount per Serving):
Calories 250; Fat 7.6 g; Carbohydrates 41.8 g; Sugar 2 g; Protein 4.5 g; Cholesterol 0 mg

Carrot Rice Pudding

Preparation Time: 10 minutes; Cooking Time: 15 minutes; Serve: 4

Ingredients:

- 1 cup of rice
- 1 cup carrot, grated
- 1/4 tsp ground nutmeg
- 1 tsp vanilla
- 3 cups unsweetened almond milk
- Pinch of salt

Directions:
1. Spray instant pot from inside with cooking spray.
2. Add all ingredients into the instant pot and stir well.
3. Seal pot with lid and cook on high for 15 minutes.
4. Once done, allow to release pressure naturally for 10 minutes then release remaining using quick release. Remove lid.
5. Stir and serve.

Nutritional Value (Amount per Serving):
Calories 214; Fat 3 g; Carbohydrates 41.4 g; Sugar 1.6 g; Protein 4.3 g; Cholesterol 0 mg

Chia Carrot Oatmeal

Preparation Time: 10 minutes; Cooking Time: 10 minutes; Serve: 6
Ingredients:
- 1 cup steel-cut oats
- 1/4 cup chia seeds
- 1 cup carrot, grated
- 1 1/2 tsp ground cinnamon
- 4 cups almond milk

Directions:
1. Spray instant pot from inside with cooking spray.
2. Add all ingredients except chia seeds into the instant pot and stir well.
3. Seal pot with lid and cook on high for 10 minutes.
4. Once done, allow to release pressure naturally for 10 minutes then release remaining using quick release. Remove lid.
5. Stir in chia seeds and serve.

Nutritional Value (Amount per Serving):
Calories 434; Fat 39.4 g; Carbohydrates 20.9 g; Sugar 6.4 g; Protein 5.8 g; Cholesterol 0 mg

Millet Oats

Preparation Time: 10 minutes; Cooking Time: 10 minutes; Serve: 4
Ingredients:
- 2 apples, cored and chopped
- 3 cups almond milk
- 1/2 cup steel-cut oats
- 3/4 cup millet

Directions:
1. Spray instant pot from inside with cooking spray.
2. Add all ingredients into the instant pot and stir well.
3. Seal pot with lid and cook on high for 10 minutes.
4. Once done, allow to release pressure naturally for 10 minutes then release remaining using quick release. Remove lid.
5. Stir and serve.

Nutritional Value (Amount per Serving):
Calories 653; Fat 45.4 g; Carbohydrates 59.6 g; Sugar 17.7 g; Protein 9.9 g; Cholesterol 0 mg

Pear Breakfast Rice

Preparation Time: 10 minutes; Cooking Time: 15 minutes; Serve: 4
Ingredients:
- 1 1/2 cups rice
- 3 cups almond milk
- 2 pears, cored and sliced
- 2 tbsp maple syrup
- 1 tsp ground cinnamon

Directions:
1. Spray instant pot from inside with cooking spray.
2. Set instant pot on sauté mode. Add rice and sauté for 5 minutes.
3. Add remaining ingredients except for maple syrup and stir well.
4. Seal pot with lid and cook on high for 10 minutes.
5. Once done, allow to release pressure naturally for 10 minutes then release remaining using quick release. Remove lid.
6. Stir in maple syrup and serve.

Nutritional Value (Amount per Serving):
Calories 755; Fat 43.6 g; Carbohydrates 88.5 g; Sugar 22.2 g; Protein 9.5 g; Cholesterol 0 mg

Almond Peach Oatmeal

Preparation Time: 10 minutes; Cooking Time: 4 minutes; Serve: 4

Ingredients:
- 2 cups rolled oats
- 2 tbsp flax meal
- 1/2 cup almonds, sliced
- 1 tsp vanilla
- 1 peach, chopped
- 4 cups of water
- Pinch of salt

Directions:
1. Spray instant pot from inside with cooking spray.
2. Add all ingredients except flax meal and almonds into the instant pot and stir well.
3. Seal pot with lid and cook on high for 3 minutes.
4. Once done, allow to release pressure naturally for 10 minutes then release remaining using quick release. Remove lid.
5. Stir in flax meal and almonds and serve.

Nutritional Value (Amount per Serving):
Calories 257; Fat 10 g; Carbohydrates 34.9 g; Sugar 4.5 g; Protein 9 g; Cholesterol 0 mg

Garlic Potatoes

Preparation Time: 10 minutes; Cooking Time: 5 minutes; Serve: 2

Ingredients:
- 1 lb potatoes, cut into chunks
- 2 tbsp fresh parsley, chopped
- 1/4 cup vegetable stock
- 1 tsp garlic, minced
- 1 tbsp olive oil
- Pepper
- Salt

Directions:
1. Add oil in instant pot and set the pot on sauté mode.
2. Add garlic, potatoes, and salt and sauté for 5 minutes. Add stock and stir well.
3. Seal pot with lid and cook on high for 5 minutes.
4. Once done, release pressure using quick release. Remove lid.
5. Garnish with parsley and serve.

Nutritional Value (Amount per Serving):
Calories 221; Fat 7.3 g; Carbohydrates 36.5 g; Sugar 2.7 g; Protein 4.1 g; Cholesterol 0 mg

Spinach Egg Breakfast

Preparation Time: 10 minutes; Cooking Time: 8 minutes; Serve: 2

Ingredients:
- 6 eggs
- 1 tomato, chopped
- 1/2 cup mozzarella cheese, shredded
- 1 cup spinach, chopped
- 1/4 cup feta cheese, crumbled
- Pepper

- Salt

Directions:
1. Pour 1 cup of water into the instant pot then place the steamer rack in the pot.
2. In a bowl, whisk eggs with pepper and salt. Add remaining ingredients and stir well.
3. Spray heat-safe dish with cooking spray. Pour egg mixture into the prepared dish and place dish on top of the steamer rack.
4. Seal pot with lid and cook on high for 8 minutes.
5. Once done, release pressure using quick release. Remove lid.
6. Serve and enjoy.

Nutritional Value (Amount per Serving):
Calories 267; Fat 18.5 g; Carbohydrates 3.8 g; Sugar 2.7 g; Protein 22 g; Cholesterol 511 mg

Potato Cheese Frittata

Preparation Time: 10 minutes; Cooking Time: 10 minutes; Serve: 2

Ingredients:
- 6 eggs
- 1/2 cup cheddar cheese, shredded
- 1/4 cup almond milk
- 1/2 small onion, chopped
- 1/2 bell pepper, chopped
- 1 small potato, peeled and chopped
- Pepper
- Salt

Directions:
1. Pour 1 cup of water into the instant pot then place the steamer rack in the pot.
2. In a bowl, whisk eggs with pepper and salt. Add remaining ingredients and stir well.
3. Spray heat-safe dish with cooking spray.
4. Pour egg mixture into the prepared dish and place dish on top of the steamer rack.
5. Seal pot with lid and cook on high for 10 minutes.
6. Once done, release pressure using quick release. Remove lid.
7. Serve and enjoy.

Nutritional Value (Amount per Serving):
Calories 454; Fat 29.8 g; Carbohydrates 21.8 g; Sugar 5.1 g; Protein 26.6 g; Cholesterol 521 mg

Spinach Frittata

Preparation Time: 10 minutes; Cooking Time: 15 minutes; Serve: 4

Ingredients:
- 6 eggs
- 1/2 cup tomato, chopped
- 1 cup fresh spinach
- 1 tsp Italian seasoning
- 1 tbsp heavy cream
- Pepper
- Salt

Directions:
1. In a bowl, whisk eggs with remaining ingredients.
2. Spray a 7-inch baking dish with cooking spray.
3. Pour egg mixture into the prepared baking dish. Cover dish with foil.
4. Pour 1 1/2 cups of water into the instant pot then place steamer rack in the pot.
5. Place baking dish on top of the steamer rack.
6. Seal pot with lid and cook on high for 15 minutes.
7. Once done, release pressure using quick release. Remove lid.
8. Serve and enjoy.

Nutritional Value (Amount per Serving):
Calories 117; Fat 8.4 g; Carbohydrates 1.9 g; Sugar 1.2 g; Protein 8.8 g; Cholesterol 251 mg

Date Apple Oats

Preparation Time: 10 minutes; Cooking Time: 4 minutes; Serve: 2
Ingredients:
- 1/4 cup oats
- 1/4 tsp vanilla
- 14 tsp cinnamon
- 2 dates, chopped
- 1 apple, chopped
- 1/2 cup water

Directions:
1. Spray instant pot from inside with cooking spray.
2. Add all ingredients to the instant pot and stir well.
3. Seal pot with lid and cook on high for 4 minutes.
4. Once done, allow to release pressure naturally for 10 minutes then release remaining using quick release. Remove lid.
5. Stir well and serve.

Nutritional Value (Amount per Serving):
Calories 161; Fat 1.1 g; Carbohydrates 41.6 g; Sugar 17.4 g; Protein 2.5 g; Cholesterol 0 mg

Mushroom Cheese Breakfast

Preparation Time: 10 minutes; Cooking Time: 12 minutes; Serve: 4
Ingredients:
- 5 eggs
- 2 tbsp olive oil
- 1 onion, chopped
- 2 tbsp chives, minced
- 1 1/2 cups mushrooms, sliced
- 1/2 cup almond milk
- 1/2 tbsp cheddar cheese
- 1 bell pepper, chopped
- Pepper
- Salt

Directions:
1. Add oil into the instant pot and set the pot on sauté mode.
2. Add mushrooms and sauté for 2 minutes. Transfer mushrooms on a plate and clean the instant pot.
3. In a bowl, whisk eggs with pepper and salt. Add mushrooms, onion, chives, almond milk, cheese, and bell pepper into the egg mixture and whisk well.
4. Spray baking dish with cooking spray.
5. Pour 1 1/2 cups of water into the instant pot then place steamer rack in the pot.
6. Pour egg mixture into the prepared baking dish. Cover dish with foil.
7. Place baking dish on top of the steamer rack.
8. Seal pot with lid and cook on high for 10 minutes.
9. Once done, release pressure using quick release. Remove lid.
10. Serve and enjoy.

Nutritional Value (Amount per Serving):
Calories 238; Fat 20.1 g; Carbohydrates 7.9 g; Sugar 4.6 g; Protein 9.3 g; Cholesterol 206 mg

Simple Lemon Quinoa

Preparation Time: 10 minutes; Cooking Time: 1 minute; Serve: 4
Ingredients:
- 2 cups quinoa, rinsed and drained
- 1 fresh lemon juice
- 2 tbsp fresh parsley, chopped
- 3 cups of water
- 1/4 tsp salt

Directions:
1. Spray instant pot from inside with cooking spray.
2. Add all ingredients except lemon juice and parsley into the pot. Stir well.
3. Seal pot with lid and cook on high for 1 minute.

4. Once done, allow to release pressure naturally for 10 minutes then release remaining using quick release. Remove lid.
5. Add parsley and lemon juice.
6. Stir and serve.

Nutritional Value (Amount per Serving):
Calories 317; Fat 5.3 g; Carbohydrates 54.9 g; Sugar 0.3 g; Protein 12.2 g; Cholesterol 0 mg

Chapter 4: Soups & Stews

Nutritious Kidney Bean Soup

Preparation Time: 10 minutes; Cooking Time: 1 hour 40 minutes; Serve: 8
Ingredients:
- 3 cups red kidney beans, soaked overnight & drain
- 1/4 cup fresh parsley, chopped
- 6 cups of water
- 1/4 cup olive oil
- 1 1/2 tbsp tomato paste
- 2 bell peppers, chopped
- 2 carrots, chopped
- 1 tbsp garlic, minced
- 1 onion, chopped
- 1 tsp salt

Directions:
1. Add oil into the inner pot of instant pot and set the pot on sauté mode.
2. Add garlic and onion and sauté until onion is softened.
3. Add carrots and bell peppers and sauté for 3-5 minutes.
4. Add beans, parsley, tomato paste, water, and salt and stir everything well.
5. Seal pot with lid and cook on high for 1 hour 40 minutes.
6. Once done, release pressure using quick release. Remove lid.
7. Stir well and serve.

Nutritional Value (Amount per Serving):
Calories 312; Fat 7.2 g; Carbohydrates 48.4 g; Sugar 4.7 g; Protein 16.4 g; Cholesterol 0 mg

Healthy Vegetable Soup

Preparation Time: 10 minutes; Cooking Time: 15 minutes; Serve: 4
Ingredients:
- 1 cup can tomatoes, chopped
- 1 small zucchini, diced
- 3 oz kale, sliced
- 1 tbsp garlic, chopped
- 5 button mushrooms, sliced
- 2 carrots, peeled and sliced
- 2 celery sticks, sliced
- 1/2 red chili, sliced
- 1 onion, diced
- 1 tbsp olive oil
- 1 bay leaf
- 4 cups vegetable stock
- 1/4 tsp salt

Directions:
1. Add oil into the inner pot of instant pot and set the pot on sauté mode.
2. Add carrots, celery, onion, and salt and cook for 2-3 minutes.
3. Add mushrooms and chili and cook for 2 minutes.
4. Add remaining ingredients and stir everything well.
5. Seal pot with lid and cook on high for 10 minutes.
6. Once done, allow to release pressure naturally for 10 minutes then release remaining using quick release. Remove lid.
7. Stir well and serve.

Nutritional Value (Amount per Serving):
Calories 100; Fat 3.8 g; Carbohydrates 15.1 g; Sugar 6.6 g; Protein 3.5 g; Cholesterol 0 mg

Hearty Pork Stew

Preparation Time: 10 minutes; Cooking Time: 15 minutes; Serve: 4
Ingredients:
- 1/2 lb ground pork
- 1 tbsp fresh lemon juice
- 1/4 cup fresh parsley, chopped
- 1 cup of water
- 14 oz can tomatoes, chopped

- 2 cups can navy beans, rinsed and drained
- 3 medium potatoes, peeled and diced
- 1 tbsp garlic, chopped
- 1/2 tsp red pepper flakes
- 1 tsp dried thyme
- 1 carrot, peeled and diced
- 2 celery sticks, diced
- 1 onion, diced
- 2 tbsp olive oil
- 2 tsp salt

Directions:
1. Add oil into the inner pot of instant pot and set the pot on sauté mode.
2. Add carrot, celery, onion, and 1 tsp salt and sauté for 5 minutes.
3. Add meat and cook for 2-4 minutes.
4. Add remaining ingredients except for lemon juice and parsley and stir everything well.
5. Seal pot with lid and cook on high for 6 minutes.
6. Once done, allow to release pressure naturally for 10 minutes then release remaining using quick release. Remove lid.
7. Add lemon juice and stir well.
8. Garnish with parsley and serve.

Nutritional Value (Amount per Serving):
Calories 446; Fat 9.9 g; Carbohydrates 62.6 g; Sugar 7.8 g; Protein 29.1 g; Cholesterol 41 mg

Mixed Lentil Stew

Preparation Time: 10 minutes; Cooking Time: 30 minutes; Serve: 4
Ingredients:
- 1 1/2 cups mixed lentils, rinsed
- 1/4 cup fresh cilantro, chopped
- 12 oz can chickpeas, drained and rinsed
- 1 tsp dried oregano
- 1 tsp ground sumac
- 1 tsp ground ginger
- 1 tsp garlic powder
- 1 tbsp ground cumin
- 1 tbsp paprika
- 28 oz can tomatoes, diced
- 2 zucchini, chopped
- 1 bell pepper, chopped
- 3 carrots, chopped
- 1 sweet potato, chopped
- 1 onion, chopped
- 4 1/2 cups vegetable broth
- Pepper
- Salt

Directions:
1. Add all ingredients except chickpeas and cilantro into the inner pot of instant pot and stir well.
2. Seal pot with lid and cook on high for minutes.
3. Once done, release pressure using quick release. Remove lid.
4. Add cilantro and chickpeas and stir well.
5. Serve and enjoy.

Nutritional Value (Amount per Serving):
Calories 523; Fat 4.2 g; Carbohydrates 102.6 g; Sugar 16.4 g; Protein 22.5 g; Cholesterol 0 mg

Spinach Chicken Stew

Preparation Time: 10 minutes; Cooking Time: 25 minutes; Serve: 4
Ingredients:
- 2 cups spinach, chopped
- 1 lb chicken breasts, skinless, boneless, and cut into chunks
- 1/2 cup can tomato, crushed
- 1 cup chicken stock
- 1 onion, chopped
- 1 tbsp olive oil
- Pepper
- Salt

Directions:
1. Add oil into the inner pot of instant pot and set the pot on sauté mode.
2. Add chicken and onion and sauté for 5 minutes.
3. Add remaining ingredients and stir well.
4. Seal pot with lid and cook on low for 20 minutes.
5. Once done, allow to release pressure naturally for 10 minutes then release remaining using quick release. Remove lid.
6. Stir well and serve.

Nutritional Value (Amount per Serving):
Calories 266; Fat 12.2 g; Carbohydrates 4.2 g; Sugar 1.4 g; Protein 33.9 g; Cholesterol 101 mg

Delicious Okra Chicken Stew

Preparation Time: 10 minutes; Cooking Time: 20 minutes; Serve: 4

Ingredients:
- 1 lb chicken breasts, skinless, boneless, and cubed
- 1 lemon juice
- 1/4 cup fresh parsley, chopped
- 1 tbsp olive oil
- 12 oz can tomatoes, crushed
- 1 tsp allspice
- 14 oz okra, chopped
- 2 cups chicken stock
- 1 tsp garlic, minced
- 1 onion, chopped
- Pepper
- Salt

Directions:
1. Add oil into the inner pot of instant pot and set the pot on sauté mode.
2. Add chicken and onion and sauté until chicken is lightly brown about 5 minutes.
3. Add remaining ingredients except for the parsley and stir well.
4. Seal pot with lid and cook on high pressure 15 for minutes.
5. Once done, allow to release pressure naturally for 10 minutes then release remaining using quick release. Remove lid.
6. Stir well and serve.

Nutritional Value (Amount per Serving):
Calories 326; Fat 12.6 g; Carbohydrates 15.8 g; Sugar 6.2 g; Protein 36.4 g; Cholesterol 101 mg

Lamb Stew

Preparation Time: 10 minutes; Cooking Time: 25 minutes; Serve: 4

Ingredients:
- 1 3/4 lbs lamb shoulder, cut into chunks
- 1/4 cup fresh parsley, chopped
- 1 tsp dried basil
- 3/4 tsp dried oregano
- 1 tbsp olive oil
- 1/2 cup onion, chopped
- 14 oz can tomatoes, chopped
- 1 tbsp garlic, minced
- 1/4 cup chicken broth
- Pepper
- Salt

Directions:
1. Add oil into the inner pot of instant pot and set the pot on sauté mode.
2. Add meat, garlic, and onion and sauté for 5 minutes.
3. Add remaining ingredients except for the parsley and stir well.
4. Seal pot with lid and cook on high pressure 20 for minutes.
5. Once done, release pressure using quick release. Remove lid.
6. Garnish with parsley and serve.

Nutritional Value (Amount per Serving):
Calories 434; Fat 18.2 g; Carbohydrates 7.6 g; Sugar 4.1 g; Protein 57.4 g; Cholesterol 179 mg

Easy & Delicious Beef Stew

Preparation Time: 10 minutes; Cooking Time: 30 minutes; Serve: 4
Ingredients:
- 1 1/2 lbs beef stew meat, cut into cubed
- 1/2 cup sweet corn
- 1 cup can tomato, crushed
- 1 cup chicken stock
- 4 carrots, chopped
- 1 onion, chopped
- 1 tbsp olive oil
- Pepper
- Salt

Directions:
1. Add oil into the inner pot of instant pot and set the pot on sauté mode.
2. Add onion and meat and sauté for 5 minutes.
3. Add remaining ingredients and stir well.
4. Seal pot with lid and cook on high pressure 25 for minutes.
5. Once done, allow to release pressure naturally for 10 minutes then release remaining using quick release. Remove lid.
6. Stir and serve.

Nutritional Value (Amount per Serving):
Calories 410; Fat 14.4 g; Carbohydrates 14 g; Sugar 4.8 g; Protein 54.4 g; Cholesterol 152 mg

Tomato Chickpeas Stew

Preparation Time: 10 minutes; Cooking Time: 25 minutes; Serve: 4
Ingredients:
- 1 lb can chickpeas, rinsed and drained
- 18 oz can tomatoes, chopped
- 1/2 tsp red pepper flakes
- 2 tbsp olive oil
- 1 tsp dried oregano
- 1 tsp garlic, minced
- 1 onion, chopped
- Pepper
- Salt

Directions:
1. Add oil into the inner pot of instant pot and set the pot on sauté mode.
2. Add onion and garlic and sauté for 5 minutes.
3. Add remaining ingredients and stir well.
4. Seal pot with lid and cook on high pressure 20 for minutes.
5. Once done, allow to release pressure naturally for 10 minutes then release remaining using quick release. Remove lid.
6. Serve and enjoy.

Nutritional Value (Amount per Serving):
Calories 236; Fat 8.4 g; Carbohydrates 35.3 g; Sugar 5.6 g; Protein 7.2 g; Cholesterol 0 mg

Chicken Lentil Stew

Preparation Time: 10 minutes; Cooking Time: 25 minutes; Serve: 6
Ingredients:
- 2 lbs chicken thighs, boneless & skinless
- 1 tbsp olive oil
- 1 cup onion, chopped
- 4 cups chicken stock
- 8 oz green lentils, soak for 1 hour
- 28 oz can tomato, diced
- Pepper
- Salt

Directions:
1. Add oil into the inner pot of instant pot and set the pot on sauté mode.
2. Add onion and sauté for 5 minutes.
3. Add the rest of the ingredients and stir well.

4. Seal pot with lid and cook on high for minutes.
5. Once done, release pressure using quick release. Remove lid.
6. Shred chicken using a fork.
7. Stir well and serve.

Nutritional Value (Amount per Serving):
Calories 479; Fat 14.3 g; Carbohydrates 29.8 g; Sugar 5 g; Protein 55.1 g; Cholesterol 135 mg

Garlic Squash Broccoli Soup

Preparation Time: 10 minutes; Cooking Time: 15 minutes; Serve: 4

Ingredients:
- 1 lb butternut squash, peeled and diced
- 1 lb broccoli florets
- 1 tsp dried basil
- 1 tsp paprika
- 2 1/2 cups vegetable stock
- 1 tsp garlic, minced
- 1 tbsp olive oil
- 1 onion, chopped
- Salt

Directions:
1. Add oil into the inner pot of instant pot and set the pot on sauté mode.
2. Add onion and garlic and sauté for 3 minutes.
3. Add remaining ingredients and stir well.
4. Seal pot with lid and cook on high pressure 12 for minutes.
5. Once done, allow to release pressure naturally for 10 minutes then release remaining using quick release. Remove lid.
6. Blend soup using an immersion blender until smooth.
7. Serve and enjoy.

Nutritional Value (Amount per Serving):
Calories 137; Fat 4.1 g; Carbohydrates 24.5 g; Sugar 6.1 g; Protein 5 g; Cholesterol 0 mg

Chicken Rice Soup

Preparation Time: 10 minutes; Cooking Time: 9 minutes; Serve: 4

Ingredients:
- 1 lb chicken breast, boneless
- 2 thyme sprigs
- 1 tsp garlic, chopped
- 1/4 tsp turmeric
- 1 tbsp olive oil
- 2 tbsp fresh parsley, chopped
- 2 tbsp fresh lemon juice
- 1/4 cup rice
- 1/2 cup celery, diced
- 1/2 cup onion, chopped
- 2 carrots, chopped
- 5 cups vegetable stock
- Pepper
- Salt

Directions:
1. Add oil into the inner pot of instant pot and set the pot on sauté mode.
2. Add garlic, onion, carrots, and celery and sauté for 3 minutes.
3. Add the rest of the ingredients and stir well.
4. Seal pot with lid and cook on high for 6 minutes.
5. Once done, release pressure using quick release. Remove lid.
6. Shred chicken using a fork.
7. Serve and enjoy.

Nutritional Value (Amount per Serving):
Calories 237; Fat 6.8 g; Carbohydrates 16.6 g; Sugar 3.4 g; Protein 26.2 g; Cholesterol 73 mg

Mussels Soup

Preparation Time: 10 minutes; Cooking Time: 3 minutes; Serve: 2

Ingredients:
- 6 oz mussels, cleaned
- 2 tsp Italian seasoning
- 2 tbsp olive oil
- 1 cup grape tomatoes, chopped
- 4 cups chicken stock
- 1/4 cup fish sauce

Directions:
1. Add all ingredients into the inner pot of instant pot and stir well.
2. Seal pot with lid and cook on high for 3 minutes.
3. Once done, release pressure using quick release. Remove lid.
4. Stir well and serve.

Nutritional Value (Amount per Serving):
Calories 256; Fat 18.6 g; Carbohydrates 9.9 g; Sugar 5.5 g; Protein 14.1 g; Cholesterol 27 mg

Simple Black Bean Soup

Preparation Time: 10 minutes; Cooking Time: 40 minutes; Serve: 8

Ingredients:
- 1 lb black beans, soaked overnight
- 1 tbsp olive oil
- 1 tbsp fresh parsley, chopped
- 1 onion, chopped
- 7 cups vegetable stock
- 2 tbsp vinegar
- Pepper
- Salt

Directions:
1. Add all ingredients except parsley and vinegar into the instant pot and stir well.
2. Seal pot with lid and cook on high pressure 40 for minutes.
3. Once done, allow to release pressure naturally for 10 minutes then release remaining using quick release. Remove lid.
4. Stir in parsley and vinegar and serve.

Nutritional Value (Amount per Serving):
Calories 220; Fat 2.7 g; Carbohydrates 37.5 g; Sugar 2.4 g; Protein 12.8 g; Cholesterol 0 mg

Creamy Chicken Soup

Preparation Time: 10 minutes; Cooking Time: 10 minutes; Serve: 6

Ingredients:
- 2 lbs chicken breast, boneless and cut into chunks
- 8 oz cream cheese
- 2 tbsp taco seasoning
- 1 cup of salsa
- 2 cups chicken stock
- 28 oz can tomatoes, diced
- Salt

Directions:
1. Add all ingredients except cream cheese into the instant pot.
2. Seal pot with lid and cook on high pressure 10 for minutes.
3. Once done, allow to release pressure naturally. Remove lid.
4. Remove chicken from pot and shred using a fork. Return shredded chicken to the pot.
5. Add cream cheese and stir well.
6. Serve and enjoy.

Nutritional Value (Amount per Serving):
Calories 471; Fat 24.1 g; Carbohydrates 19.6 g; Sugar 6.2 g; Protein 43.9 g; Cholesterol 157 mg

Cheesy Chicken Soup

Preparation Time: 10 minutes; Cooking Time: 15 minutes; Serve: 4

Ingredients:
- 12 oz chicken thighs, boneless
- 1 cup heavy cream
- 2 cups cheddar cheese, shredded
- 3 cups chicken stock

- 2 tbsp olive oil
- 1/2 cup celery, chopped
- 1/4 cup hot sauce
- 1 tsp garlic, minced
- 1/4 cup onion, chopped

Directions:
1. Add all ingredients except cream and cheese into the instant pot and stir well.
2. Seal pot with lid and cook on high pressure 15 for minutes.
3. Once done, allow to release pressure naturally. Remove lid.
4. Shred the chicken using a fork.
5. Add cream and cheese and stir until cheese is melted.
6. Serve and enjoy.

Nutritional Value (Amount per Serving):
Calories 568; Fat 43.6 g; Carbohydrates 3.6 g; Sugar 1.5 g; Protein 40.1 g; Cholesterol 176 mg

Italian Salsa Chicken Soup

Preparation Time: 10 minutes; Cooking Time: 25 minutes; Serve: 6
Ingredients:
- 1 lb chicken breasts, boneless and cut into chunks
- 3 cups chicken stock
- 8 oz cream cheese
- 1 1/2 cups salsa
- 1 tsp Italian seasoning
- 2 tbsp fresh parsley, chopped
- Pepper
- Salt

Directions:
1. Add all ingredients except cream cheese and parsley into the instant pot and stir well.
2. Seal pot with lid and cook on high for 25 minutes.
3. Once done, release pressure using quick release. Remove lid.
4. Remove chicken from pot and shred using a fork. Return shredded chicken to the pot.
5. Add cream cheese and stir well and cook on sauté mode until cheese is melted.
6. Serve and enjoy.

Nutritional Value (Amount per Serving):
Calories 301; Fat 19.4 g; Carbohydrates 5.6 g; Sugar 2.5 g; Protein 26.1 g; Cholesterol 109 mg

Italian Chicken Stew

Preparation Time: 10 minutes; Cooking Time: 12 minutes; Serve: 6
Ingredients:
- 1 lb chicken breasts, boneless
- 2 potatoes, peeled and diced
- 3 carrots, cut into chunks
- 2 celery stalks, cut into chunks
- 1 onion, diced
- 1 tsp garlic, minced
- 1 tsp ground sage
- 1/2 tsp thyme
- 1/2 tsp dried basil
- 3 cups chicken stock
- Pepper
- Salt

Directions:
1. Add all ingredients into the inner pot of instant pot and stir well.
2. Seal pot with lid and cook on high for 12 minutes.
3. Once done, allow to release pressure naturally for 10 minutes then release remaining using quick release. Remove lid.
4. Remove chicken from pot and shred using a fork. Return shredded chicken to the pot.
5. Stir well and serve.

Nutritional Value (Amount per Serving):
Calories 220; Fat 6 g; Carbohydrates 16.7 g; Sugar 3.5 g; Protein 23.9 g; Cholesterol 67 mg

Creamy Carrot Tomato Soup

Preparation Time: 10 minutes; Cooking Time: 10 minutes; Serve: 6
Ingredients:
- 4 oz can tomatoes, diced
- 1/2 cup heavy cream
- 1 cup vegetable broth
- 1 tbsp dried basil
- 1 onion, chopped
- 4 large carrots, peeled and chopped
- 1/4 cup olive oil
- Pepper
- Salt

Directions:
1. Add oil into the inner pot of instant pot and set the pot on sauté mode.
2. Add onion and carrots and sauté for 5 minutes.
3. Add the rest of ingredients except heavy cream and stir well.
4. Seal pot with lid and cook on high pressure 5 for minutes.
5. Once done, allow to release pressure naturally. Remove lid.
6. Stir in heavy cream and blend soup using an immersion blender until smooth.
7. Serve and enjoy.

Nutritional Value (Amount per Serving):
Calories 144; Fat 12.4 g; Carbohydrates 7.8 g; Sugar 3.9 g; Protein 1.8 g; Cholesterol 14 mg

Healthy Lentil Soup

Preparation Time: 10 minutes; Cooking Time: 30 minutes; Serve: 8
Ingredients:
- 1 cup red lentils
- 1 tsp fresh lemon juice
- 8 cups vegetable broth
- 1 tsp ground cumin
- 1 tbsp garlic, chopped
- 2 carrots, chopped
- 1 onion, chopped
- 1 split pea
- Pepper
- Salt

Directions:
1. Add all ingredients except lemon juice into the instant pot and stir well.
2. Seal pot with lid and cook on high pressure 30 for minutes.
3. Once done, allow to release pressure naturally. Remove lid.
4. Stir in Lemont juice and serve.

Nutritional Value (Amount per Serving):
Calories 121; Fat 0.4 g; Carbohydrates 21.8 g; Sugar 4 g; Protein 7.1 g; Cholesterol 0 mg

Creamy Cauliflower Soup

Preparation Time: 10 minutes; Cooking Time: 23 minutes; Serve: 4
Ingredients:
- 1 lb cauliflower florets, chopped
- 2 tbsp fresh chives, chopped
- 1 tsp curry powder
- 2 cups vegetable stock
- 14 oz coconut cream
- 1 onion, chopped
- 1 tbsp garlic, minced
- 1 tbsp olive oil
- Pepper
- Salt

Directions:
1. Add oil into the inner pot of instant pot and set the pot on sauté mode.
2. Add onion and garlic and sauté for 3 minutes.
3. Add the rest of the ingredients and stir well.
4. Seal pot with lid and cook on high for 20 minutes.
5. Once done, allow to release pressure naturally for 10 minutes then release remaining using quick release. Remove lid.

6. Blend soup using an immersion blender until smooth.
7. Serve and enjoy.

Nutritional Value (Amount per Serving):
Calories 306; Fat 27.4 g; Carbohydrates 15.6 g; Sugar 7.6 g; Protein 5.3 g; Cholesterol 0 mg

Spinach Lentil Soup

Preparation Time: 10 minutes; Cooking Time: 30 minutes; Serve: 4

Ingredients:
- 4 cups spinach
- 2 cups green lentils
- 4 cups vegetable stock
- 1 tsp Italian seasoning
- 14 oz can tomatoes, chopped
- 2 tsp thyme, chopped
- 1 tsp garlic, minced
- 1 carrot, chopped
- 1 onion, chopped
- 2 celery stalks, chopped
- Pepper
- Salt

Directions:
1. Add all ingredients except spinach into the inner pot of instant pot and stir well.
2. Seal pot with lid and cook on high for 25 minutes.
3. Once done, allow to release pressure naturally for 10 minutes then release remaining using quick release. Remove lid.
4. Add spinach and stir well and cook on sauté mode for 5 minutes.
5. Stir well and serve.

Nutritional Value (Amount per Serving):
Calories 398; Fat 1.7 g; Carbohydrates 69.8 g; Sugar 8.3 g; Protein 27.5 g; Cholesterol 1 mg

Easy Lemon Chicken Soup

Preparation Time: 10 minutes; Cooking Time: 10 minutes; Serve: 2

Ingredients:
- 1 1/2 lbs chicken breasts, boneless
- 3 cups chicken stock
- 1 tbsp fresh lemon juice
- 1/2 tsp garlic powder
- 1/2 onion, chopped
- Pepper
- Salt

Directions:
1. Add all ingredients except lemon juice into the inner pot of instant pot and stir well.
2. Seal pot with lid and cook on high for 10 minutes.
3. Once done, allow to release pressure naturally. Remove lid.
4. Remove chicken from pot and shred using a fork. Return shredded chicken to the pot.
5. Stir in lemon juice and serve.

Nutritional Value (Amount per Serving):
Calories 676; Fat 26.2 g; Carbohydrates 4.4 g; Sugar 2.6 g; Protein 99.9 g; Cholesterol 303 mg

Basil Zucchini Soup

Preparation Time: 10 minutes; Cooking Time: 15 minutes; Serve: 4

Ingredients:
- 2 zucchini, chopped
- 2 tbsp fresh basil, chopped
- 30 oz vegetable stock
- 1 tbsp garlic, minced
- 2 cups tomatoes, chopped
- 1 1/2 cup corn
- 1 onion, chopped
- 1 celery stalk, chopped
- 1 tbsp olive oil
- Pepper
- Salt

Directions:

1. Add oil into the inner pot of instant pot and set the pot on sauté mode.
2. Add onion and garlic and sauté for 5 minutes.
3. Add remaining ingredients except for basil and stir well.
4. Seal pot with lid and cook on high for 10 minutes.
5. Once done, allow to release pressure naturally for 10 minutes then release remaining using quick release. Remove lid.
6. Stir in basil and serve.

Nutritional Value (Amount per Serving):
Calories 139; Fat 4.8 g; Carbohydrates 23 g; Sugar 8.7 g; Protein 5.2 g; Cholesterol 0 mg

Tomato Pepper Soup

Preparation Time: 10 minutes; Cooking Time: 20 minutes; Serve: 4

Ingredients:
- 1 lb tomatoes, chopped
- 2 red bell peppers, chopped
- 1/2 tsp red pepper flakes
- 1/2 tbsp dried basil
- 1 tsp garlic powder
- 6 cups vegetable stock
- 2 celery stalk, chopped
- 3 tbsp tomato paste
- 1 onion, chopped
- 2 tbsp olive oil
- Pepper
- Salt

Directions:
1. Add oil into the inner pot of instant pot and set the pot on sauté mode.
2. Add onion, red pepper flakes, basil, and garlic powder and sauté for 5 minutes.
3. Add remaining ingredients and stir well.
4. Seal pot with lid and cook on high for 15 minutes.
5. Once done, allow to release pressure naturally for 10 minutes then release remaining using quick release. Remove lid.
6. Blend soup using an immersion blender until smooth.
7. Serve and enjoy.

Nutritional Value (Amount per Serving):
Calories 134; Fat 7.7 g; Carbohydrates 16 g; Sugar 10 g; Protein 3.2 g; Cholesterol 0 mg

Sausage Potato Soup

Preparation Time: 10 minutes; Cooking Time: 20 minutes; Serve: 6

Ingredients:
- 1 lb Italian sausage, crumbled
- 1 cup half and half
- 1 cup kale, chopped
- 6 cups chicken stock
- 1/2 tsp dried oregano
- 3 potatoes, peeled and diced
- 1 tsp garlic, minced
- 1 onion, chopped
- 1 tbsp olive oil
- Pepper
- Salt

Directions:
1. Add oil into the inner pot of instant pot and set the pot on sauté mode.
2. Add sausage, garlic, and onion and sauté for 5 minutes.
3. Add the rest of the ingredients and stir well.
4. Seal pot with lid and cook on high for 15 minutes.
5. Once done, allow to release pressure naturally for 10 minutes then release remaining using quick release. Remove lid.
6. Stir and serve.

Nutritional Value (Amount per Serving):
Calories 426; Fat 29.1 g; Carbohydrates 22.3 g; Sugar 2.8 g; Protein 18.9 g; Cholesterol 78 mg

Roasted Tomatoes Soup

Preparation Time: 10 minutes; Cooking Time: 5 minutes; Serve: 2
Ingredients:
- 14 oz can fire-roasted tomatoes
- 1 1/2 cups vegetable stock
- 1/4 cup zucchini, grated
- 1/2 tsp dried oregano
- 1/2 tsp dried basil
- 1/2 cup heavy cream
- 1/2 cup parmesan cheese, grated
- 1 cup cheddar cheese, grated
- Pepper
- Salt

Directions:
1. Add tomatoes, stock, zucchini, oregano, basil, pepper, and salt into the instant pot and stir well.
2. Seal pot with lid and cook on high for 5 minutes.
3. Once done, release pressure using quick release. Remove lid.
4. Set pot on sauté mode. Add heavy cream, parmesan cheese, and cheddar cheese and stir well and cook until cheese is melted.
5. Serve and enjoy.

Nutritional Value (Amount per Serving):
Calories 460; Fat 34.8 g; Carbohydrates 13.5 g; Sugar 6 g; Protein 24.1 g; Cholesterol 117 mg

Healthy Cabbage Soup

Preparation Time: 10 minutes; Cooking Time: 15 minutes; Serve: 4
Ingredients:
- 1 cabbage head, shredded
- 4 cups vegetable stock
- 1/4 cup fresh parsley, chopped
- 1 tbsp garlic, minced
- 2 tbsp olive oil
- 1 onion, chopped
- 1/2 lb carrots, sliced
- Pepper
- Salt

Directions:
1. Add oil into the inner pot of instant pot and set the pot on sauté mode.
2. Add onion and garlic and sauté for 5 minutes.
3. Add the rest of the ingredients and stir well.
4. Seal pot with lid and cook on high for 10 minutes.
5. Once done, allow to release pressure naturally for 10 minutes then release remaining using quick release. Remove lid.
6. Stir and serve.

Nutritional Value (Amount per Serving):
Calories 149; Fat 7.4 g; Carbohydrates 20.4 g; Sugar 10.4 g; Protein 3.7 g; Cholesterol 0 mg

Basil Broccoli Soup

Preparation Time: 10 minutes; Cooking Time: 15 minutes; Serve: 6
Ingredients:
- 1 lb broccoli florets
- 1 tbsp olive oil
- 1 tsp chili powder
- 1 tsp dried basil
- 6 cups vegetable stock
- 1 onion, chopped
- 2 leeks, chopped
- Pepper
- Salt

Directions:
1. Add oil into the inner pot of instant pot and set the pot on sauté mode.
2. Add onion and leek and sauté for 5 minutes.
3. Add the rest of the ingredients and stir well.

4. Seal pot with lid and cook on high for 10 minutes.
5. Once done, allow to release pressure naturally for 10 minutes then release remaining using quick release. Remove lid.
6. Blend soup using an immersion blender until smooth.
7. Serve and enjoy.

Nutritional Value (Amount per Serving):
Calories 79; Fat 2.9 g; Carbohydrates 12.1 g; Sugar 4 g; Protein 3.2 g; Cholesterol 0 mg

Mushroom Carrot Soup

Preparation Time: 10 minutes; Cooking Time: 20 minutes; Serve: 4

Ingredients:
- 16 oz mushrooms, sliced
- 1 carrot, chopped
- 4 cups vegetable stock
- 1 tsp dried thyme
- 1 tbsp garlic, minced
- 1 onion, chopped
- 1 celery stalk, chopped
- 1 tbsp olive oil
- Pepper
- Salt

Directions:
1. Add oil into the inner pot of instant pot and set the pot on sauté mode.
2. Add onion, garlic, celery, and carrot and sauté for 5 minutes.
3. Add mushrooms and sauté for 5 minutes.
4. Add the rest of the ingredients and stir well.
5. Seal pot with lid and cook on high for 10 minutes.
6. Once done, allow to release pressure naturally for 10 minutes then release remaining using quick release. Remove lid.
7. Blend soup using an immersion blender until smooth.
8. Serve and enjoy.

Nutritional Value (Amount per Serving):
Calories 82; Fat 4 g; Carbohydrates 9.7 g; Sugar 4.6 g; Protein 4.6 g; Cholesterol 0 mg

Spinach Cauliflower Soup

Preparation Time: 10 minutes; Cooking Time: 10 minutes; Serve: 2

Ingredients:
- 1 cup cauliflower, chopped
- 3 cups spinach, chopped
- 1 tsp garlic powder
- 2 tbsp olive oil
- 3 cups vegetable broth
- 1/2 cup heavy cream
- Pepper
- Salt

Directions:
1. Add all ingredients except cream into the inner pot of instant pot and stir well.
2. Seal pot with lid and cook on high for 10 minutes.
3. Once done, release pressure using quick release. Remove lid.
4. Stir in cream and blend soup using an immersion blender until smooth.
5. Serve and enjoy.

Nutritional Value (Amount per Serving):
Calories 309; Fat 27.4 g; Carbohydrates 7.5 g; Sugar 2.8 g; Protein 10.4 g; Cholesterol 41 mg

Delicious Chicken Wild Rice Soup

Preparation Time: 10 minutes; Cooking Time: 17 minutes; Serve: 4

Ingredients:
- 2 chicken breasts, boneless and cubed
- 1 tbsp fresh parsley, chopped
- 5 oz wild rice
- 28 oz chicken stock

- 1 cup carrot, chopped
- 2 tbsp olive oil
- 1 onion, chopped
- Pepper
- Salt

Directions:
1. Add oil into the inner pot of instant pot and set the pot on sauté mode.
2. Add carrot, onion, and chicken and sauté for 5 minutes.
3. Add remaining ingredients and stir well.
4. Seal pot with lid and cook on high for 12 minutes.
5. Once done, allow to release pressure naturally for 10 minutes then release remaining using quick release. Remove lid.
6. Stir well and serve.

Nutritional Value (Amount per Serving):
Calories 356; Fat 13.3 g; Carbohydrates 32.5 g; Sugar 4 g; Protein 27.5 g; Cholesterol 65 mg

Kidney Bean Soup

Preparation Time: 10 minutes; Cooking Time: 15 minutes; Serve: 6

Ingredients:
- 1 lb kidney beans, soaked overnight and drained
- 1 tsp paprika
- 7 cups chicken stock
- 1 tomato, chopped
- 1 tbsp garlic, chopped
- 1 onion, chopped
- 1 tbsp olive oil
- Pepper
- Salt

Directions:
1. Add oil into the inner pot of instant pot and set the pot on sauté mode.
2. Add garlic and onion and sauté for 3 minutes.
3. Add remaining ingredients and stir well.
4. Seal pot with lid and cook on high for 12 minutes.
5. Once done, allow to release pressure naturally for 10 minutes then release remaining using quick release. Remove lid.
6. Stir and serve.

Nutritional Value (Amount per Serving):
Calories 299; Fat 3.9 g; Carbohydrates 50 g; Sugar 3.5 g; Protein 18.3 g; Cholesterol 0 mg

Pepper Chicken Soup

Preparation Time: 10 minutes; Cooking Time: 20 minutes; Serve: 4

Ingredients:
- 2 lbs chicken breasts, boneless and cut into chunks
- 1 tbsp parsley, chopped
- 1 cup coconut cream
- 6 cups chicken stock
- 3 bell peppers, chopped
- 1 tsp garlic, minced
- 1 small onion, chopped
- 2 tbsp olive oil
- Pepper
- Salt

Directions:
1. Add oil into the inner pot of instant pot and set the pot on sauté mode.
2. Add bell peppers, onion, and garlic and sauté for 5 minutes.
3. Add chicken and sauté for 5 minutes.
4. Add remaining ingredients and stir well.
5. Seal pot with lid and cook on high for 10 minutes.
6. Once done, allow to release pressure naturally for 10 minutes then release remaining using quick release. Remove lid.

7. Stir and serve.

Nutritional Value (Amount per Serving):
Calories 681; Fat 39.2 g; Carbohydrates 13.1 g; Sugar 8.3 g; Protein 69.2 g; Cholesterol 202 mg

Chili Chicken Soup

Preparation Time: 10 minutes; Cooking Time: 10 minutes; Serve: 2

Ingredients:
- 1/2 lb cook chicken, shredded
- 7 oz can tomatoes, chopped
- 1/4 tsp cayenne
- 1/4 tsp chili powder
- 1/2 cup mozzarella cheese, shredded
- 2 tbsp hot sauce
- 1 tbsp olive oil
- 1 1/2 cups chicken stock
- Pepper
- Salt

Directions:
1. Add all ingredients into the inner pot of instant pot and stir well.
2. Seal pot with lid and cook on high for 10 minutes.
3. Once done, allow to release pressure naturally. Remove lid.
4. Stir well and serve.

Nutritional Value (Amount per Serving):
Calories 294; Fat 13.9 g; Carbohydrates 26.7 g; Sugar 24.4 g; Protein 17.7 g; Cholesterol 75 mg

Creamy Potato Soup

Preparation Time: 10 minutes; Cooking Time: 10 minutes; Serve: 4

Ingredients:
- 3/4 lb potato, peeled and diced
- 2 leeks, sliced
- 4 cups vegetable stock
- 1 tsp garlic, minced
- 1 onion, chopped
- 1 tbsp olive oil
- Pepper
- Salt

Directions:
1. Add oil into the inner pot of instant pot and set the pot on sauté mode.
2. Add onion and sauté for 2 minutes.
3. Add garlic and leek and sauté for 2 minutes.
4. Add remaining ingredients and stir well.
5. Seal pot with lid and cook on high for 6 minutes.
6. Once done, allow to release pressure naturally for 10 minutes then release remaining using quick release. Remove lid.
7. Blend soup using an immersion blender until smooth.
8. Serve and enjoy.

Nutritional Value (Amount per Serving):
Calories 141; Fat 3.8 g; Carbohydrates 24.9 g; Sugar 4.3 g; Protein 3.1 g; Cholesterol 0 mg

Healthy Carrot Soup

Preparation Time: 10 minutes; Cooking Time: 10 minutes; Serve: 4

Ingredients:
- 1 3/4 lbs carrots, chopped
- 1 tsp coriander powder
- 1 onion, chopped
- 1 tbsp olive oil
- 4 cups vegetable stock
- 1/4 cup fresh coriander, chopped
- Pepper
- Salt

Directions:
1. Add oil into the inner pot of instant pot and set the pot on sauté mode.
2. Add onion and sauté until onion is softened.

3. Add remaining ingredients and stir well.
4. Seal pot with lid and cook on high for 5 minutes.
5. Once done, allow to release pressure naturally for 10 minutes then release remaining using quick release. Remove lid.
6. Blend soup using an immersion blender until smooth.
7. Serve and enjoy.

Nutritional Value (Amount per Serving):
Calories 129; Fat 3.6 g; Carbohydrates 23 g; Sugar 11.6 g; Protein 2.3 g; Cholesterol 0 mg

Creamy Squash Cauliflower Soup

Preparation Time: 10 minutes; Cooking Time: 8 minutes; Serve: 6

Ingredients:
- 1 cauliflower head, cut into florets
- 1 bell pepper, diced
- 1 small butternut squash, peeled and chopped
- 1/2 tsp dried parsley
- 1/2 tsp dried mix herbs
- 1 cup vegetable stock
- 1/4 cup yogurt
- 1 onion, chopped
- Pepper
- Salt

Directions:
1. Add all ingredients except yogurt into the instant pot.
2. Seal pot with lid and cook on high for 8 minutes.
3. Once done, release pressure using quick release. Remove lid.
4. Stir in yogurt and blend soup using an immersion blender until smooth.
5. Serve and enjoy.

Nutritional Value (Amount per Serving):
Calories 54; Fat 0.3 g; Carbohydrates 11.3 g; Sugar 4.4 g; Protein 2.5 g; Cholesterol 1 mg

Creamy Lentil Soup

Preparation Time: 10 minutes; Cooking Time: 12 minutes; Serve: 4

Ingredients:
- 2 cups split red lentils, soak for 30 minutes
- 1 cup potatoes, peeled and diced
- 1 onion, chopped
- 4 cups vegetable stock
- Pepper
- Salt

Directions:
1. Add all ingredients into the instant pot.
2. Seal pot with lid and cook on high for 12 minutes.
3. Once done, allow to release pressure naturally for 10 minutes then release remaining using quick release. Remove lid.
4. Blend soup using an immersion blender until smooth.
5. Serve and enjoy.

Nutritional Value (Amount per Serving):
Calories 382; Fat 1.2 g; Carbohydrates 67.1 g; Sugar 4.3 g; Protein 26.1 g; Cholesterol 0 mg

Lentil Veggie Soup

Preparation Time: 10 minutes; Cooking Time: 10 minutes; Serve: 4

Ingredients:
- 1 lb mixed vegetables, chopped
- 1/4 cup lentils, soak for 30 minutes
- 1/4 tsp allspice
- 3 1/4 cups vegetable stock
- 1/2 tsp garlic, minced
- Pepper

- Salt

Directions:
1. Add all ingredients into the instant pot and stir well.
2. Seal pot with lid and cook on high for 10 minutes.
3. Once done, allow to release pressure naturally for 10 minutes then release remaining using quick release. Remove lid.
4. Blend soup using an immersion blender until smooth.
5. Serve and enjoy.

Nutritional Value (Amount per Serving):
Calories 89; Fat 0.5 g; Carbohydrates 16.3 g; Sugar 0.8 g; Protein 5.1 g; Cholesterol 0 mg

Lentil Tomato Soup

Preparation Time: 10 minutes; Cooking Time: 12 minutes; Serve: 6

Ingredients:
- 1/2 cup red lentils, soak for 30 minutes
- 1 tsp garlic, sliced
- 1 large onion, chopped
- 5 large tomatoes, chopped
- 4 cups vegetable stock
- 1/4 tsp dried mix herbs
- 2 tbsp tomato puree
- 1 large carrot, chopped
- Pepper
- Salt

Directions:
1. Add all ingredients into the instant pot and stir well.
2. Seal pot with lid and cook on high for 12 minutes.
3. Once done, allow to release pressure naturally for 10 minutes then release remaining using quick release. Remove lid.
4. Blend soup using an immersion blender until smooth.
5. Serve and enjoy.

Nutritional Value (Amount per Serving):
Calories 110; Fat 0.6 g; Carbohydrates 21.3 g; Sugar 6.8 g; Protein 6.4 g; Cholesterol 0 mg

Onion Soup

Preparation Time: 10 minutes; Cooking Time: 10 minutes; Serve: 4

Ingredients:
- 6 medium onion, diced
- 4 celery sticks, diced
- 4 carrots, peeled and diced
- 1 tsp thyme
- 1/2 tsp dried mixed herbs
- 1 1/2 tsp chives
- Pepper
- Salt

Directions:
1. Add all ingredients into the instant pot and stir well.
2. Seal pot with lid and cook on high for 10 minutes.
3. Once done, allow to release pressure naturally for 5 minutes then release remaining using quick release. Remove lid.
4. Stir well and serve.

Nutritional Value (Amount per Serving):
Calories 93; Fat 0.2 g; Carbohydrates 21.8 g; Sugar 10.1 g; Protein 2.4 g; Cholesterol 0 mg

Chicken Noodle Soup

Preparation Time: 10 minutes; Cooking Time: 10 minutes; Serve: 6

Ingredients:
- 6 cups cooked chicken, shredded
- 1 tbsp garlic, minced

- 8 oz whole wheat noodles
- 1 bell pepper, chopped
- 1 carrot, peeled and sliced
- 6 cups chicken stock
- 2 celery stalks, sliced
- 1 onion, chopped
- 3 tbsp rice vinegar
- 2 1/2 cups cabbage, shredded
- 2 tbsp fresh ginger, grated
- 2 tbsp soy sauce

Directions:
1. Add all ingredients into the inner pot of instant pot and stir well.
2. Seal pot with lid and cook on high for 10 minutes.
3. Once done, release pressure using quick release. Remove lid.
4. Stir well and serve.

Nutritional Value (Amount per Serving):
Calories 389; Fat 6.4 g; Carbohydrates 22.9 g; Sugar 4.2 g; Protein 49.3 g; Cholesterol 128 mg

Easy Cauliflower Soup

Preparation Time: 10 minutes; Cooking Time: 30 minutes; Serve: 4
Ingredients:
- 2 cups cauliflower florets
- 3 tbsp olive oil
- 1 onion, chopped
- 1 tsp pumpkin pie spice
- 5 cups chicken broth
- 1/4 tsp salt

Directions:
1. Add oil into the inner pot of instant pot and set the pot on sauté mode.
2. Add onion and sauté for 5 minutes.
3. Add remaining ingredients and stir well.
4. Seal pot with lid and cook on high for 25 minutes.
5. Once done, release pressure using quick release. Remove lid.
6. Blend soup using an immersion blender until smooth.
7. Serve and enjoy.

Nutritional Value (Amount per Serving):
Calories 163; Fat 12.3 g; Carbohydrates 6.7 g; Sugar 3.3 g; Protein 6.6 g; Cholesterol 0 mg

Cheese Kale Soup

Preparation Time: 10 minutes; Cooking Time: 5 minutes; Serve: 4
Ingredients:
- 6 cups fresh kale, chopped
- 1 tbsp olive oil
- 3/4 cup cottage cheese, cut into chunks
- 3 cups vegetable broth
- Pepper
- salt

Directions:
1. Add all ingredients except cheese into the instant pot and stir well.
2. Seal pot with lid and cook on high for 5 minutes.
3. Once done, release pressure using quick release. Remove lid.
4. Stir in cottage cheese and serve.

Nutritional Value (Amount per Serving):
Calories 147; Fat 5.4 g; Carbohydrates 12.7 g; Sugar 0.7 g; Protein 12.5 g; Cholesterol 3 mg

Chicken Kale Soup

Preparation Time: 10 minutes; Cooking Time: 15 minutes; Serve: 4
Ingredients:
- 2 cups cooked chicken, chopped
- 12 oz kale, chopped
- 2 tsp garlic, minced
- 1 onion, diced

- 4 cups vegetable broth
- Salt

Directions:
1. Add all ingredients into the instant pot and stir well.
2. Seal pot with lid and cook on high for 5 minutes.
3. Once done, allow to release pressure naturally for 5 minutes then release remaining using quick release. Remove lid.
4. Stir well and serve.

Nutritional Value (Amount per Serving):
Calories 199; Fat 3.5 g; Carbohydrates 12.8 g; Sugar 1.9 g; Protein 28.1 g; Cholesterol 54 mg

Cabbage Soup

Preparation Time: 10 minutes; Cooking Time: 7 minutes; Serve: 4
Ingredients:
- 3 cups cabbage, chopped
- 2 tbsp olive oil
- 5 oz tomato paste
- 14.5 oz can stewed tomatoes
- 1/2 onion, sliced
- 1 tbsp garlic, diced
- 14. oz can tomatoes, diced
- 4 cups vegetable stock
- Pepper
- Salt

Directions:
1. Add oil into the inner pot of instant pot and set the pot on sauté mode.
2. Add onion and garlic and sauté for 2 minutes.
3. Add cabbage, water, tomato paste, and tomatoes. Stir well.
4. Seal pot with lid and cook on high for 5 minutes.
5. Once done, allow to release pressure naturally for 5 minutes then release remaining using quick release. Remove lid.
6. Serve and enjoy.

Nutritional Value (Amount per Serving):
Calories 165; Fat 7.5 g; Carbohydrates 24.1 g; Sugar 14.3 g; Protein 4.7 g; Cholesterol 0 mg

Celery Soup

Preparation Time: 10 minutes; Cooking Time: 30 minutes; Serve: 4
Ingredients:
- 6 cups celery stalk, chopped
- 1 cup heavy cream
- 1 onion, chopped
- 2 cups vegetable broth
- 1/2 tsp dill
- Salt

Directions:
1. Add all ingredients into the instant pot and stir well.
2. Seal pot with lid and cook on high for 30 minutes.
3. Once done, release pressure using quick release. Remove lid.
4. Blend soup using an immersion blender until smooth.
5. Serve and enjoy.

Nutritional Value (Amount per Serving):
Calories 158; Fat 12.1 g; Carbohydrates 8.4 g; Sugar 3.6 g; Protein 4.4 g; Cholesterol 41 mg

Pepper Pumpkin Soup

Preparation Time: 10 minutes; Cooking Time: 6 minutes; Serve: 6
Ingredients:
- 2 cups pumpkin puree
- 1 onion, chopped
- 4 cups vegetable broth
- 1/4 tsp nutmeg
- 1/4 cup red bell pepper, chopped
- 1/8 tsp thyme, dried

- 1/2 tsp salt

Directions:
1. Add all ingredients into the instant pot and stir well.
2. Seal pot with lid and cook on high for 6 minutes.
3. Once done, allow to release pressure naturally for 5 minutes then release remaining using quick release. Remove lid.
4. Blend soup using an immersion blender until smooth.
5. Serve and enjoy.

Nutritional Value (Amount per Serving):
Calories 63; Fat 1.2 g; Carbohydrates 9.4 g; Sugar 4.2 g; Protein 4.4 g; Cholesterol 0 mg

Curried Zucchini Soup

Preparation Time: 10 minutes; Cooking Time: 10 minutes; Serve: 6

Ingredients:
- 10 cups zucchini, chopped
- 4 cups vegetable broth
- 14 oz coconut milk
- 1 tsp curry powder
- Pepper
- Salt

Directions:
1. Add all ingredients into the instant pot and stir well.
2. Seal pot with lid and cook on high for 10 minutes.
3. Once done, release pressure using quick release. Remove lid.
4. Blend soup using an immersion blender until smooth.
5. Serve and enjoy.

Nutritional Value (Amount per Serving):
Calories 209; Fat 17.1 g; Carbohydrates 10.8 g; Sugar 5.9 g; Protein 7.1 g; Cholesterol 0 mg

Chapter 5: Pasta, Grains & Beans

Delicious Chicken Pasta

Preparation Time: 10 minutes; Cooking Time: 17 minutes; Serve: 4

Ingredients:
- 3 chicken breasts, skinless, boneless, cut into pieces
- 9 oz whole-grain pasta
- 1/2 cup olives, sliced
- 1/2 cup sun-dried tomatoes
- 1 tbsp roasted red peppers, chopped
- 14 oz can tomatoes, diced
- 2 cups marinara sauce
- 1 cup chicken broth
- Pepper
- Salt

Directions:
1. Add all ingredients except whole-grain pasta into the instant pot and stir well.
2. Seal pot with lid and cook on high for 12 minutes.
3. Once done, allow to release pressure naturally. Remove lid.
4. Add pasta and stir well. Seal pot again and select manual and set timer for 5 minutes.
5. Once done, allow to release pressure naturally for 5 minutes then release remaining using quick release. Remove lid.
6. Stir well and serve.

Nutritional Value (Amount per Serving):
Calories 615; Fat 15.4 g; Carbohydrates 71 g; Sugar 17.6 g; Protein 48 g; Cholesterol 100 mg

Flavors Taco Rice Bowl

Preparation Time: 10 minutes; Cooking Time: 14 minutes; Serve: 8

Ingredients:
- 1 lb ground beef
- 8 oz cheddar cheese, shredded
- 14 oz can red beans
- 2 oz taco seasoning
- 16 oz salsa
- 2 cups of water
- 2 cups brown rice
- Pepper
- Salt

Directions:
1. Set instant pot on sauté mode.
2. Add meat to the pot and sauté until brown.
3. Add water, beans, rice, taco seasoning, pepper, and salt and stir well.
4. Top with salsa. Seal pot with lid and cook on high for 14 minutes.
5. Once done, release pressure using quick release. Remove lid.
6. Add cheddar cheese and stir until cheese is melted.
7. Serve and enjoy.

Nutritional Value (Amount per Serving):
Calories 464; Fat 15.3 g; Carbohydrates 48.9 g; Sugar 2.8 g; Protein 32.2 g; Cholesterol 83 mg

Flavorful Mac & Cheese

Preparation Time: 10 minutes; Cooking Time: 10 minutes; Serve: 6

Ingredients:
- 16 oz whole-grain elbow pasta
- 4 cups of water
- 1 cup can tomatoes, diced
- 1 tsp garlic, chopped
- 2 tbsp olive oil
- 1/4 cup green onions, chopped
- 1/2 cup parmesan cheese, grated
- 1/2 cup mozzarella cheese, grated
- 1 cup cheddar cheese, grated
- 1/4 cup passata
- 1 cup unsweetened almond milk
- 1 cup marinated artichoke, diced

- 1/2 cup sun-dried tomatoes, sliced
- 1/2 cup olives, sliced
- 1 tsp salt

Directions:
1. Add pasta, water, tomatoes, garlic, oil, and salt into the instant pot and stir well.
2. Seal pot with lid and cook on high for 4 minutes.
3. Once done, allow to release pressure naturally for 5 minutes then release remaining using quick release. Remove lid.
4. Set pot on sauté mode. Add green onion, parmesan cheese, mozzarella cheese, cheddar cheese, passata, almond milk, artichoke, sun-dried tomatoes, and olive. Mix well.
5. Stir well and cook until cheese is melted.
6. Serve and enjoy.

Nutritional Value (Amount per Serving):
Calories 519; Fat 17.1 g; Carbohydrates 66.5 g; Sugar 5.2 g; Protein 25 g; Cholesterol 26 mg

Cucumber Olive Rice

Preparation Time: 10 minutes; Cooking Time: 10 minutes; Serve: 8

Ingredients:
- 2 cups rice, rinsed
- 1/2 cup olives, pitted
- 1 cup cucumber, chopped
- 1 tbsp red wine vinegar
- 1 tsp lemon zest, grated
- 1 tbsp fresh lemon juice
- 2 tbsp olive oil
- 2 cups vegetable broth
- 1/2 tsp dried oregano
- 1 red bell pepper, chopped
- 1/2 cup onion, chopped
- 1 tbsp olive oil
- Pepper
- Salt

Directions:
1. Add oil into the inner pot of instant pot and set the pot on sauté mode.
2. Add onion and sauté for 3 minutes.
3. Add bell pepper and oregano and sauté for 1 minute.
4. Add rice and broth and stir well.
5. Seal pot with lid and cook on high for 6 minutes.
6. Once done, allow to release pressure naturally for 10 minutes then release remaining using quick release. Remove lid.
7. Add remaining ingredients and stir everything well to mix.
8. Serve immediately and enjoy it.

Nutritional Value (Amount per Serving):
Calories 229; Fat 5.1 g; Carbohydrates 40.2 g; Sugar 1.6 g; Protein 4.9 g; Cholesterol 0 mg

Flavors Herb Risotto

Preparation Time: 10 minutes; Cooking Time: 15 minutes; Serve: 4

Ingredients:
- 2 cups of rice
- 2 tbsp parmesan cheese, grated
- 3.5 oz heavy cream
- 1 tbsp fresh oregano, chopped
- 1 tbsp fresh basil, chopped
- 1/2 tbsp sage, chopped
- 1 onion, chopped
- 2 tbsp olive oil
- 1 tsp garlic, minced
- 4 cups vegetable stock
- Pepper
- Salt

Directions:
1. Add oil into the inner pot of instant pot and set the pot on sauté mode.
2. Add garlic and onion and sauté for 2-3 minutes.
3. Add remaining ingredients except for parmesan cheese and heavy cream and stir well.

4. Seal pot with lid and cook on high for 12 minutes.
5. Once done, allow to release pressure naturally for 10 minutes then release remaining using quick release. Remove lid.
6. Stir in cream and cheese and serve.

Nutritional Value (Amount per Serving):
Calories 514; Fat 17.6 g; Carbohydrates 79.4 g; Sugar 2.1 g; Protein 8.8 g; Cholesterol 36 mg

Delicious Pasta Primavera

Preparation Time: 10 minutes; Cooking Time: 4 minutes; Serve: 4
Ingredients:
- 8 oz whole wheat penne pasta
- 1 tbsp fresh lemon juice
- 2 tbsp fresh parsley, chopped
- 1/4 cup almonds slivered
- 1/4 cup parmesan cheese, grated
- 14 oz can tomatoes, diced
- 1/2 cup prunes
- 1/2 cup zucchini, chopped
- 1/2 cup asparagus, cut into 1-inch pieces
- 1/2 cup carrots, chopped
- 1/2 cup broccoli, chopped
- 1 3/4 cups vegetable stock
- Pepper
- Salt

Directions:
1. Add stock, pars, tomatoes, prunes, zucchini, asparagus, carrots, and broccoli into the instant pot and stir well.
2. Seal pot with lid and cook on high for 4 minutes.
3. Once done, release pressure using quick release. Remove lid.
4. Add remaining ingredients and stir well and serve.

Nutritional Value (Amount per Serving):
Calories 303; Fat 2.6 g; Carbohydrates 63.5 g; Sugar 13.4 g; Protein 12.8 g; Cholesterol 1 mg

Roasted Pepper Pasta

Preparation Time: 10 minutes; Cooking Time: 13 minutes; Serve: 6
Ingredients:
- 1 lb whole wheat penne pasta
- 1 tbsp Italian seasoning
- 4 cups vegetable broth
- 1 tbsp garlic, minced
- 1/2 onion, chopped
- 14 oz jar roasted red peppers
- 1 cup feta cheese, crumbled
- 1 tbsp olive oil
- Pepper
- Salt

Directions:
1. Add roasted pepper into the blender and blend until smooth.
2. Add oil into the inner pot of instant pot and set the pot on sauté mode.
3. Add garlic and onion and sauté for 2-3 minutes.
4. Add blended roasted pepper and sauté for 2 minutes.
5. Add remaining ingredients except feta cheese and stir well.
6. Seal pot with lid and cook on high for 8 minutes.
7. Once done, allow to release pressure naturally for 5 minutes then release remaining using quick release. Remove lid.
8. Top with feta cheese and serve.

Nutritional Value (Amount per Serving):
Calories 459; Fat 10.6 g; Carbohydrates 68.1 g; Sugar 2.1 g; Protein 21.3 g; Cholesterol 24 mg

Cheese Basil Tomato Rice

Preparation Time: 10 minutes; Cooking Time: 26 minutes; Serve: 8

Ingredients:
- 1 1/2 cups brown rice
- 1 cup parmesan cheese, grated
- 1/4 cup fresh basil, chopped
- 2 cups grape tomatoes, halved
- 8 oz can tomato sauce
- 1 3/4 cup vegetable broth
- 1 tbsp garlic, minced
- 1/2 cup onion, diced
- 1 tbsp olive oil
- Pepper
- Salt

Directions:
1. Add oil into the inner pot of instant pot and set the pot on sauté mode.
2. Add garlic and onion and sauté for 4 minutes.
3. Add rice, tomato sauce, broth, pepper, and salt and stir well.
4. Seal pot with lid and cook on high for 22 minutes.
5. Once done, allow to release pressure naturally for 10 minutes then release remaining using quick release. Remove lid.
6. Add remaining ingredients and stir well.
7. Serve and enjoy.

Nutritional Value (Amount per Serving):
Calories 208; Fat 5.6 g; Carbohydrates 32.1 g; Sugar 2.8 g; Protein 8.3 g; Cholesterol 8 mg

Mac & Cheese

Preparation Time: 10 minutes; Cooking Time: 4 minutes; Serve: 8

Ingredients:
- 1 lb whole grain pasta
- 1/2 cup parmesan cheese, grated
- 4 cups cheddar cheese, shredded
- 1 cup milk
- 1/4 tsp garlic powder
- 1/2 tsp ground mustard
- 2 tbsp olive oil
- 4 cups of water
- Pepper
- Salt

Directions:
1. Add pasta, garlic powder, mustard, oil, water, pepper, and salt into the instant pot.
2. Seal pot with lid and cook on high for 4 minutes.
3. Once done, release pressure using quick release. Remove lid.
4. Add remaining ingredients and stir well and serve.

Nutritional Value (Amount per Serving):
Calories 509; Fat 25.7 g; Carbohydrates 43.8 g; Sugar 3.8 g; Protein 27.3 g; Cholesterol 66 mg

Tuna Pasta

Preparation Time: 10 minutes; Cooking Time: 8 minutes; Serve: 6

Ingredients:
- 10 oz can tuna, drained
- 15 oz whole wheat rotini pasta
- 4 oz mozzarella cheese, cubed
- 1/2 cup parmesan cheese, grated
- 1 tsp dried basil
- 14 oz can tomatoes, diced
- 4 cups vegetable broth
- 1 tbsp garlic, minced
- 8 oz mushrooms, sliced
- 2 zucchini, sliced
- 1 onion, chopped
- 2 tbsp olive oil
- Pepper
- Salt

Directions:
1. Add oil into the inner pot of instant pot and set the pot on sauté mode.
2. Add mushrooms, zucchini, and onion and sauté until onion is softened.
3. Add garlic and sauté for a minute.
4. Add pasta, basil, tuna, tomatoes, and broth and stir well.

5. Seal pot with lid and cook on high for 4 minutes.
6. Once done, allow to release pressure naturally for 5 minutes then release remaining using quick release. Remove lid.
7. Add remaining ingredients and stir well and serve.

Nutritional Value (Amount per Serving):
Calories 346; Fat 11.9 g; Carbohydrates 31.3 g; Sugar 6.3 g; Protein 6.3 g; Cholesterol 30 mg

Vegan Olive Pasta

Preparation Time: 10 minutes; Cooking Time: 5 minutes; Serve: 4
Ingredients:
- 4 cups whole grain penne pasta
- 1/2 cup olives, sliced
- 1 tbsp capers
- 1/4 tsp red pepper flakes
- 3 cups of water
- 4 cups pasta sauce, homemade
- 1 tbsp garlic, minced
- Pepper
- Salt

Directions:
1. Add all ingredients into the inner pot of instant pot and stir well.
2. Seal pot with lid and cook on high for 5 minutes.
3. Once done, release pressure using quick release. Remove lid.
4. Stir and serve.

Nutritional Value (Amount per Serving):
Calories 441; Fat 10.1 g; Carbohydrates 77.3 g; Sugar 24.1 g; Protein 11.8 g; Cholesterol 5 mg

Italian Mac & Cheese

Preparation Time: 10 minutes; Cooking Time: 6 minutes; Serve: 4
Ingredients:
- 1 lb whole grain pasta
- 2 tsp Italian seasoning
- 1 1/2 tsp garlic powder
- 1 1/2 tsp onion powder
- 1 cup sour cream
- 4 cups of water
- 4 oz parmesan cheese, shredded
- 12 oz ricotta cheese
- Pepper
- Salt

Directions:
1. Add all ingredients except ricotta cheese into the inner pot of instant pot and stir well.
2. Seal pot with lid and cook on high for 6 minutes.
3. Once done, allow to release pressure naturally for 5 minutes then release remaining using quick release. Remove lid.
4. Add ricotta cheese and stir well and serve.

Nutritional Value (Amount per Serving):
Calories 388; Fat 25.8 g; Carbohydrates 18.1 g; Sugar 4 g; Protein 22.8 g; Cholesterol 74 mg

Italian Chicken Pasta

Preparation Time: 10 minutes; Cooking Time: 9 minutes; Serve: 8
Ingredients:
- 1 lb chicken breast, skinless, boneless, and cut into chunks
- 1/2 cup cream cheese
- 1 cup mozzarella cheese, shredded
- 1 1/2 tsp Italian seasoning
- 1 tsp garlic, minced
- 1 cup mushrooms, diced
- 1/2 onion, diced
- 2 tomatoes, diced
- 2 cups of water
- 16 oz whole wheat penne pasta
- Pepper
- Salt

Directions:
1. Add all ingredients except cheeses into the inner pot of instant pot and stir well.
2. Seal pot with lid and cook on high for 9 minutes.
3. Once done, allow to release pressure naturally for 5 minutes then release remaining using quick release. Remove lid.
4. Add cheeses and stir well and serve.

Nutritional Value (Amount per Serving):
Calories 328; Fat 8.5 g; Carbohydrates 42.7 g; Sugar 1.4 g; Protein 23.7 g; Cholesterol 55 mg

Delicious Greek Chicken Pasta

Preparation Time: 10 minutes; Cooking Time: 10 minutes; Serve: 6
Ingredients:
- 2 chicken breasts, skinless, boneless, and cut into chunks
- 1/2 cup olives, sliced
- 2 cups vegetable stock
- 12 oz Greek vinaigrette dressing
- 1 lb whole grain pasta
- Pepper
- Salt

Directions:
1. Add all ingredients into the inner pot of instant pot and stir well.
2. Seal pot with lid and cook on high for 10 minutes.
3. Once done, release pressure using quick release. Remove lid.
4. Stir well and serve.

Nutritional Value (Amount per Serving):
Calories 325; Fat 25.8 g; Carbohydrates 10.5 g; Sugar 4 g; Protein 15.6 g; Cholesterol 43 mg

Pesto Chicken Pasta

Preparation Time: 10 minutes; Cooking Time: 10 minutes; Serve: 6
Ingredients:
- 1 lb chicken breast, skinless, boneless, and diced
- 3 tbsp olive oil
- 1/2 cup parmesan cheese, shredded
- 1 tsp Italian seasoning
- 1/4 cup heavy cream
- 16 oz whole wheat pasta
- 6 oz basil pesto
- 3 1/2 cups water
- Pepper
- Salt

Directions:
1. Season chicken with Italian seasoning, pepper, and salt.
2. Add oil into the inner pot of instant pot and set the pot on sauté mode.
3. Add chicken to the pot and sauté until brown.
4. Add remaining ingredients except for parmesan cheese, heavy cream, and pesto and stir well.
5. Seal pot with lid and cook on high for 5 minutes.
6. Once done, release pressure using quick release. Remove lid.
7. Stir in parmesan cheese, heavy cream, and pesto and serve.

Nutritional Value (Amount per Serving):
Calories 475; Fat 14.7 g; Carbohydrates 57 g; Sugar 2.8 g; Protein 28.7 g; Cholesterol 61 mg

Spinach Pesto Pasta

Preparation Time: 10 minutes; Cooking Time: 10 minutes; Serve: 4
Ingredients:
- 8 oz whole-grain pasta
- 1/3 cup mozzarella cheese, grated
- 1/2 cup pesto
- 5 oz fresh spinach

- 1 3/4 cup water
- 8 oz mushrooms, chopped
- 1 tbsp olive oil
- Pepper
- Salt

Directions:
1. Add oil into the inner pot of instant pot and set the pot on sauté mode.
2. Add mushrooms and sauté for 5 minutes.
3. Add water and pasta and stir well.
4. Seal pot with lid and cook on high for 5 minutes.
5. Once done, release pressure using quick release. Remove lid.
6. Stir in remaining ingredients and serve.

Nutritional Value (Amount per Serving):
Calories 213; Fat 17.3 g; Carbohydrates 9.5 g; Sugar 4.5 g; Protein 7.4 g; Cholesterol 9 mg

Fiber Packed Chicken Rice

Preparation Time: 10 minutes; Cooking Time: 16 minutes; Serve: 6
Ingredients:
- 1 lb chicken breast, skinless, boneless, and cut into chunks
- 14.5 oz can cannellini beans
- 4 cups chicken broth
- 2 cups wild rice
- 1 tbsp Italian seasoning
- 1 small onion, chopped
- 1 tbsp garlic, chopped
- 1 tbsp olive oil
- Pepper
- Salt

Directions:
1. Add oil into the inner pot of instant pot and set the pot on sauté mode.
2. Add garlic and onion and sauté for 2 minutes.
3. Add chicken and cook for 2 minutes.
4. Add remaining ingredients and stir well.
5. Seal pot with lid and cook on high for 12 minutes.
6. Once done, release pressure using quick release. Remove lid.
7. Stir well and serve.

Nutritional Value (Amount per Serving):
Calories 399; Fat 6.4 g; Carbohydrates 53.4 g; Sugar 3 g; Protein 31.6 g; Cholesterol 50 mg

Tasty Greek Rice

Preparation Time: 10 minutes; Cooking Time: 10 minutes; Serve: 6
Ingredients:
- 1 3/4 cup brown rice, rinsed and drained
- 3/4 cup roasted red peppers, chopped
- 1 cup olives, chopped
- 1 tsp dried oregano
- 1 tsp Greek seasoning
- 1 3/4 cup vegetable broth
- 2 tbsp olive oil
- Salt

Directions:
1. Add oil into the inner pot of instant pot and set the pot on sauté mode.
2. Add rice and cook for 5 minutes.
3. Add remaining ingredients except for red peppers and olives and stir well.
4. Seal pot with lid and cook on high for 5 minutes.
5. Once done, allow to release pressure naturally for 10 minutes then release remaining using quick release. Remove lid.
6. Add red peppers and olives and stir well.
7. Serve and enjoy.

Nutritional Value (Amount per Serving):
Calories 285; Fat 9.1 g; Carbohydrates 45.7 g; Sugar 1.2 g; Protein 6 g; Cholesterol 0 mg

Bulgur Salad

Preparation Time: 10 minutes; Cooking Time: 1 minute; Serve: 2
Ingredients:
- 1/2 cup bulgur wheat
- 1/4 cup fresh parsley, chopped
- 1 tbsp fresh mint, chopped
- 1/3 cup feta cheese, crumbled
- 2 tbsp fresh lemon juice
- 2 tbsp olives, chopped
- 1/4 cup olive oil
- 1/2 cup tomatoes, chopped
- 1/3 cup cucumber, chopped
- 1/2 cup water
- Salt

Directions:
1. Add the bulgur wheat, water, and salt into the instant pot.
2. Seal pot with lid and cook on high for 1 minute.
3. Once done, release pressure using quick release. Remove lid.
4. Transfer bulgur wheat to the mixing bowl. Add remaining ingredients to the bowl and mix well.
5. Serve and enjoy.

Nutritional Value (Amount per Serving):
Calories 430; Fat 32.2 g; Carbohydrates 31.5 g; Sugar 3 g; Protein 8.9 g; Cholesterol 22 mg

Perfect Herb Rice

Preparation Time: 10 minutes; Cooking Time: 4 minutes; Serve: 4
Ingredients:
- 1 cup brown rice, rinsed
- 1 tbsp olive oil
- 1 1/2 cups water
- 1/2 cup fresh mix herbs, chopped
- 1 tsp salt

Directions:
1. Add all ingredients into the inner pot of instant pot and stir well.
2. Seal pot with lid and cook on high for 4 minutes.
3. Once done, allow to release pressure naturally for 10 minutes then release remaining using quick release. Remove lid.
4. Stir well and serve.

Nutritional Value (Amount per Serving):
Calories 264; Fat 9.9 g; Carbohydrates 36.7 g; Sugar 0.4 g; Protein 7.3 g; Cholesterol 0 mg

Herb Polenta

Preparation Time: 10 minutes; Cooking Time: 12 minutes; Serve: 6
Ingredients:
- 1 cup polenta
- 1/4 tsp nutmeg
- 3 tbsp fresh parsley, chopped
- 1/4 cup milk
- 1/2 cup parmesan cheese, grated
- 4 cups vegetable broth
- 2 tsp thyme, chopped
- 2 tsp rosemary, chopped
- 2 tsp sage, chopped
- 1 small onion, chopped
- 2 tbsp olive oil
- Salt

Directions:
1. Add oil into the inner pot of instant pot and set the pot on sauté mode.
2. Add onion and herbs and sauté for 4 minutes.
3. Add polenta, broth, and salt and stir well.

4. Seal pot with lid and cook on high for 8 minutes.
5. Once done, allow to release pressure naturally. Remove lid.
6. Stir in remaining ingredients and serve.

Nutritional Value (Amount per Serving):
Calories 196; Fat 7.8 g; Carbohydrates 23.5 g; Sugar 1.7 g; Protein 8.2 g; Cholesterol 6 mg

Vegetable Herb Rice

Preparation Time: 10 minutes; Cooking Time: 27 minutes; Serve: 6
Ingredients:
- 1 1/2 cups brown rice, rinsed and drained
- 1/2 cup fresh parsley, chopped
- 1 3/4 cup water
- 1/4 tsp dried oregano
- 1/2 celery, chopped
- 1/2 cup bell pepper, chopped
- 1 tbsp garlic, minced
- 1 cup onion, chopped
- 1 1/2 tbsp olive oil
- Pepper
- Salt

Directions:
1. Add oil into the inner pot of instant pot and set the pot on sauté mode.
2. Add celery, bell pepper, garlic, and onion and sauté for 5 minutes.
3. Add remaining ingredients and stir well.
4. Seal pot with lid and cook on high for 22 minutes.
5. Once done, allow to release pressure naturally. Remove lid.
6. Serve and enjoy.

Nutritional Value (Amount per Serving):
Calories 217; Fat 4.9 g; Carbohydrates 39.6 g; Sugar 1.4 g; Protein 4.1 g; Cholesterol 0 mg

Cheesy Polenta

Preparation Time: 10 minutes; Cooking Time: 20 minutes; Serve: 6
Ingredients:
- 1 cup polenta
- 1/4 cup fresh basil, chopped
- 1/4 cup fresh parsley, chopped
- 1 cup parmesan cheese, grated
- 1 cup Romano cheese, grated
- 1/2 cup heavy cream
- 2 tbsp olive oil
- 4 cups vegetable stock
- Pepper
- Salt

Directions:
1. Add polenta and stock into the instant pot and whisk well.
2. Seal pot with lid and cook on high for 20 minutes.
3. Once done, allow to release pressure naturally. Remove lid.
4. Add remaining ingredients and whisk until smooth.
5. Serve and enjoy.

Nutritional Value (Amount per Serving):
Calories 239; Fat 13.2 g; Carbohydrates 22.1 g; Sugar 0.8 g; Protein 8.8 g; Cholesterol 29 mg

Healthy Red Lentils

Preparation Time: 10 minutes; Cooking Time: 20 minutes; Serve: 4
Ingredients:
- 1 cup red lentils, rinsed and drained
- 3 cups vegetable stock
- 1/4 tsp red pepper flakes
- 1/2 tsp ground coriander
- 1 onion, chopped
- 1 tbsp olive oil
- Pepper
- salt

Directions:

1. Add oil into the inner pot of instant pot and set the pot on sauté mode.
2. Add onion and sauté for 3-5 minutes.
3. Add remaining ingredients and stir everything well.
4. Seal pot with lid and cook on high for 15 minutes.
5. Once done, allow to release pressure naturally for 10 minutes then release remaining using quick release. Remove lid.
6. Stir well and serve.

Nutritional Value (Amount per Serving):
Calories 215; Fat 4.1 g; Carbohydrates 32.2 g; Sugar 2.7 g; Protein 13 g; Cholesterol 0 mg

Quick & Easy Couscous

Preparation Time: 10 minutes; Cooking Time: 5 minutes; Serve: 4
Ingredients:
- 2 cups couscous
- 2 tbsp fresh parsley, chopped
- 2 1/2 cups vegetable stock
- Pepper
- Salt

Directions:
1. Add couscous and vegetable stock into the instant pot.
2. Seal pot with lid and cook on high for 5 minutes.
3. Once done, allow to release pressure naturally for 10 minutes then release remaining using quick release. Remove lid.
4. Stir in remaining ingredients and serve.

Nutritional Value (Amount per Serving):
Calories 330; Fat 0.6 g; Carbohydrates 67.7 g; Sugar 0.5 g; Protein 11.4 g; Cholesterol 0 mg

Healthy Green Bean Rice

Preparation Time: 10 minutes; Cooking Time: 20 minutes; Serve: 4
Ingredients:
- 2 cups brown rice, rinsed and drained
- 1 tsp Italian seasoning
- 1 tbsp garlic, minced
- 2 cups green beans, trimmed and halved
- 4 cups vegetable stock
- Pepper
- Salt

Directions:
1. Add all ingredients except green beans into the instant pot and stir well.
2. Seal pot with lid and cook on high for 15 minutes.
3. Once done, release pressure using quick release. Remove lid.
4. Add green beans. Seal pot again and cook on high for 5 minutes.
5. Once done, release pressure using quick release. Remove lid.
6. Stir well and serve.

Nutritional Value (Amount per Serving):
Calories 374; Fat 3.1 g; Carbohydrates 78 g; Sugar 1.6 g; Protein 8.7 g; Cholesterol 1 mg

Cheese Herb Rice

Preparation Time: 10 minutes; Cooking Time: 21 minutes; Serve: 4
Ingredients:
- 1 cup of rice
- 1 1/2 tbsp fresh thyme, chopped
- 2 tbsp parmesan cheese, grated
- 15 oz cream cheese
- 2 cups vegetable stock
- 1 tsp garlic, minced
- 1 tbsp olive oil
- Pepper

- Salt

Directions:
1. Add oil into the inner pot of instant pot and set the pot on sauté mode.
2. Add garlic and sauté for 1 minute.
3. Add remaining ingredients and stir everything well.
4. Seal pot with lid and cook on high for 20 minutes.
5. Once done, allow to release pressure naturally for 10 minutes then release remaining using quick release. Remove lid.
6. Stir well and serve.

Nutritional Value (Amount per Serving):
Calories 585; Fat 41.6 g; Carbohydrates 41.3 g; Sugar 0.7 g; Protein 12.5 g; Cholesterol 119 mg

Garlic Zucchini Rice

Preparation Time: 10 minutes; Cooking Time: 13 minutes; Serve: 4
Ingredients:
- 12 oz rice
- 1/2 tsp allspice
- 1 tsp thyme, chopped
- 1 zucchini, grated
- 4 cups vegetable stock
- 1 tsp garlic, minced
- 1 onion, chopped
- 2 tbsp olive oil
- Pepper
- Salt

Directions:
1. Add oil into the inner pot of instant pot and set the pot on sauté mode.
2. Add garlic and sauté for 1 minute.
3. Add remaining ingredients and stir well.
4. Seal pot with lid and cook on high for 12 minutes.
5. Once done, allow to release pressure naturally for 5 minutes then release remaining using quick release. Remove lid.
6. Serve and enjoy.

Nutritional Value (Amount per Serving):
Calories 398; Fat 7.8 g; Carbohydrates 73.7 g; Sugar 2.8 g; Protein 7.4 g; Cholesterol 0 mg

Leek Rice Pilaf

Preparation Time: 10 minutes; Cooking Time: 20 minutes; Serve: 4
Ingredients:
- 1 1/2 cups rice
- 2 tsp ground cumin
- 2 tbsp fresh parsley, chopped
- 3 cups vegetable stock
- 1 tsp chili powder
- 2 leeks, chopped
- 2 tbsp olive oil
- 1 tsp garlic, minced
- Pepper
- Salt

Directions:
1. Add oil into the inner pot of instant pot and set the pot on sauté mode.
2. Add leek and garlic and sauté for 2 minutes.
3. Add remaining ingredients and stir well.
4. Seal pot with lid and cook on high for 18 minutes.
5. Once done, allow to release pressure naturally for 10 minutes then release remaining using quick release. Remove lid.
6. Serve and enjoy.

Nutritional Value (Amount per Serving):
Calories 353; Fat 8 g; Carbohydrates 63.6 g; Sugar 2.5 g; Protein 6.3 g; Cholesterol 0 mg

Healthy Spinach Rice

Preparation Time: 10 minutes; Cooking Time: 16 minutes; Serve: 4
Ingredients:
- 1 1/2 cups rice
- 2 tbsp fresh lemon juice
- 3 1/2 cups vegetable stock
- 12 oz spinach, chopped
- 1/2 cup onion, chopped
- 2 tbsp olive oil
- 1 tsp garlic, minced
- Pepper
- Salt

Directions:
1. Add oil into the inner pot of instant pot and set the pot on sauté mode.
2. Add onion and garlic and sauté for 5 minutes.
3. Add remaining ingredients except spinach and stir well.
4. Seal pot with lid and cook on high for 8 minutes.
5. Once done, allow to release pressure naturally for 5 minutes then release remaining using quick release. Remove lid.
6. Add spinach and stir well and cook on sauté mode for 3 minutes.
7. Serve and enjoy.

Nutritional Value (Amount per Serving):
Calories 347; Fat 8 g; Carbohydrates 61.1 g; Sugar 1.8 g; Protein 8 g; Cholesterol 0 mg

Italian Pesto Pasta

Preparation Time: 10 minutes; Cooking Time: 6 minutes; Serve: 6
Ingredients:
- 16 oz whole-grain pasta
- 3/4 cup basil pesto
- 1/2 cup cherry tomatoes, halved
- 1 tbsp olive oil
- 1 tsp dried basil
- 2 1/2 cups water
- Pepper
- Salt

Directions:
1. Add pasta and water into the instant pot.
2. Seal pot with lid and cook on high for 6 minutes.
3. Once done, release pressure using quick release. Remove lid & drain excess water/
4. Add remaining ingredients and stir well and cook on sauté mode for 3 minutes.
5. Serve and enjoy.

Nutritional Value (Amount per Serving):
Calories 52; Fat 2.6 g; Carbohydrates 6.4 g; Sugar 2.3 g; Protein 1.5 g; Cholesterol 0 mg

Salsa Chicken Rice

Preparation Time: 10 minutes; Cooking Time: 12 minutes; Serve: 8
Ingredients:
- 1 lb chicken breasts, skinless, boneless, and cut into chunks
- 1 tbsp taco seasoning
- 14 oz can black beans, drained and rinsed
- 12 oz frozen corn
- 14 oz salsa
- 3 cups rice, rinsed and drained
- 3 cups vegetable broth
- 1/4 cup cheddar cheese, shredded
- Pepper
- Salt

Directions:
1. Add all ingredients except cheese into the instant pot and stir well.
2. Seal pot with lid and cook on high for 12 minutes.
3. Once done, release pressure using quick release. Remove lid.
4. Add cheese and stir well.

5. Serve and enjoy.

Nutritional Value (Amount per Serving):
Calories 693; Fat 11.9 g; Carbohydrates 114.6 g; Sugar 9.8 g; Protein 37.6 g; Cholesterol 61 mg

Salsa Avocado Rice

Preparation Time: 10 minutes; Cooking Time: 3 minutes; Serve: 3

Ingredients:
- 1 cup rice, rinsed and drained
- 1/4 cup salsa
- 1/2 cup fresh parsley, chopped
- 1/2 avocado, peeled
- 1 1/4 cup vegetable broth
- Pepper
- Salt

Directions:
1. Add rice, broth, pepper, and salt into the instant pot and stir well.
2. Seal pot with lid and cook on high for 3 minutes.
3. Once done, allow to release pressure naturally. Remove lid.
4. Transfer rice into the large bowl.
5. Add salsa, parsley, avocado, pepper, and salt into the blender and blend until smooth.
6. Pour blended salsa mixture over cooked rice and mix well.
7. Serve and enjoy.

Nutritional Value (Amount per Serving):
Calories 319; Fat 7.6 g; Carbohydrates 54.6 g; Sugar 1.3 g; Protein 7.7 g; Cholesterol 0 mg

Nutritious Rice

Preparation Time: 10 minutes; Cooking Time: 40 minutes; Serve: 6

Ingredients:
- 1 1/2 cups brown rice
- 1 1/2 cup wild rice
- 2 tbsp olive oil
- 4 1/2 cups water
- Salt

Directions:
1. Add all ingredients into the instant pot and stir well.
2. Seal pot with a lid and select multigrain mode and set timer for 40 minutes.
3. Once done, allow to release pressure naturally for 5 minutes then release remaining using quick release. Remove lid.
4. Stir well and serve.

Nutritional Value (Amount per Serving):
Calories 355; Fat 6.4 g; Carbohydrates 66.1 g; Sugar 1 g; Protein 9.5 g; Cholesterol 0 mg

Rosemary Black Beans

Preparation Time: 10 minutes; Cooking Time: 5 minutes; Serve: 8

Ingredients:
- 1 cup black beans, rinsed and soaked overnight
- 2/3 cup vegetable stock
- 1/2 tsp cumin seeds
- 1 rosemary sprig
- 1 tsp garlic, minced
- Salt

Directions:
1. Add all ingredients into the inner pot of instant pot and stir well.
2. Seal pot with lid and cook on high for 5 minutes.
3. Once done, release pressure using quick release. Remove lid.
4. Stir well and serve.

Nutritional Value (Amount per Serving):

Calories 85; Fat 0.4 g; Carbohydrates 15.5 g; Sugar 0.6 g; Protein 5.3 g; Cholesterol 0 mg

Creamy Italian Pasta

Preparation Time: 10 minutes; Cooking Time: 17 minutes; Serve: 4

Ingredients:
- 2 cups whole wheat spaghetti
- 1 3/4 cup heavy cream
- 1 tsp Italian seasoning
- 2 tbsp green onion, chopped
- 2 tbsp olive oil
- Pepper
- Salt

Directions:
1. Add oil into the inner pot of instant pot and set the pot on sauté mode.
2. Add green onion and sauté for 2 minutes.
3. Add remaining ingredients and stir well.
4. Seal pot with lid and cook on high for 15 minutes.
5. Once done, allow to release pressure naturally for 10 minutes then release remaining using quick release. Remove lid.
6. Stir well and serve.

Nutritional Value (Amount per Serving):
Calories 333; Fat 27.2 g; Carbohydrates 20.4 g; Sugar 0.8 g; Protein 4.9 g; Cholesterol 73 mg

Tasty Tomato Risotto

Preparation Time: 10 minutes; Cooking Time: 11 minutes; Serve: 2

Ingredients:
- 3/4 cup rice, rinsed and drained
- 1/2 tsp garlic powder
- 1/2 tsp cumin
- 1/3 cup tomato sauce
- 1 cup vegetable broth
- 1/2 onion, chopped
- 1 tbsp olive oil
- Salt

Directions:
1. Add oil into the inner pot of instant pot and set the pot on sauté mode.
2. Add onion and sauté for 3 minutes.
3. Add tomato sauce and broth and stir well and cook for 2 minutes.
4. Add remaining ingredients and stir well.
5. Seal pot with lid and cook on high for 6 minutes.
6. Once done, release pressure using quick release. Remove lid.
7. Stir well and serve.

Nutritional Value (Amount per Serving):
Calories 358; Fat 8.4 g; Carbohydrates 61.4 g; Sugar 3.5 g; Protein 8.4 g; Cholesterol 0 mg

Cheesy Zucchini Pasta

Preparation Time: 10 minutes; Cooking Time: 15 minutes; Serve: 4

Ingredients:
- 1 zucchini, cubed
- 8 oz whole-wheat spaghetti
- 2 tbsp pine nuts
- 4 oz mozzarella cheese, shredded
- 1/2 cup heavy cream
- 1 tbsp olive oil
- 2 tbsp green onion, chopped
- Pepper
- Salt

Directions:
1. Add oil into the inner pot of instant pot and set the pot on sauté mode.
2. Add zucchini and green onion and sauté for 2 minutes.
3. Add remaining ingredients and stir well.

4. Seal pot with lid and cook on high for 13 minutes.
   5. Once done, release pressure using quick release. Remove lid.
   6. Stir well and serve.

Nutritional Value (Amount per Serving):
Calories 270; Fat 17.4 g; Carbohydrates 18.9 g; Sugar 1.5 g; Protein 12.6 g; Cholesterol 36 mg

Kidney Bean Salad

Preparation Time: 10 minutes; Cooking Time: 17 minutes; Serve: 4
Ingredients:
- 1 lb dry kidney beans, soaked overnight
- 2 tbsp fresh parsley, chopped
- 2 tbsp green onion, minced
- 1 1/2 cups vegetable stock
- 1 tsp dried thyme
- 1 red bell pepper, chopped
- 1 tbsp garlic, chopped
- 1 onion, chopped
- 1 tsp olive oil
- Pepper
- Salt

Directions:
   1. Add oil into the inner pot of instant pot and set the pot on sauté mode.
   2. Add garlic and onion and sauté for 2 minutes.
   3. Add remaining ingredients and stir well.
   4. Seal pot with lid and cook on high for 15 minutes.
   5. Once done, allow to release pressure naturally for 10 minutes then release remaining using quick release. Remove lid.
   6. Stir well and serve.

Nutritional Value (Amount per Serving):
Calories 420; Fat 2.6 g; Carbohydrates 75.9 g; Sugar 5.4 g; Protein 26.6 g; Cholesterol 0 mg

Lentil Rice

Preparation Time: 10 minutes; Cooking Time: 20 minutes; Serve: 6
Ingredients:
- 1 1/2 cups brown rice
- 1/2 cup dry green lentils
- 3 1/2 cups vegetable stock
- 2 tbsp olive oil
- 1 tsp sea salt

Directions:
   1. Add oil into the inner pot of instant pot and set the pot on sauté mode.
   2. Add rice and sauté for 5 minutes.
   3. Add remaining ingredients and stir well.
   4. Seal pot with lid and cook on high for 15 minutes.
   5. Once done, allow to release pressure naturally for 10 minutes then release remaining using quick release. Remove lid.
   6. Serve and enjoy.

Nutritional Value (Amount per Serving):
Calories 272; Fat 6.2 g; Carbohydrates 46.3 g; Sugar 0.7 g; Protein 7.9 g; Cholesterol 0 mg

Chicken Risotto

Preparation Time: 10 minutes; Cooking Time: 12 minutes; Serve: 4
Ingredients:
- 1 lb chicken breasts, skinless, boneless, and cut into chunks
- 3 tbsp fresh parsley, chopped
- 1/3 cup parmesan cheese, grated
- 1 cup of rice
- 2 cups chicken stock
- 1 cup mushrooms, sliced
- 1 cup onion, diced

- 2 tbsp olive oil

Directions:
1. Add oil into the inner pot of instant pot and set the pot on sauté mode.
2. Add chicken and cook for 3 minutes.
3. Add mushrooms and onions and cook for 2 minutes.
4. Add remaining ingredients except for cheese and stir well.
5. Seal pot with lid and cook on high for 7 minutes.
6. Once done, release pressure using quick release. Remove lid.
7. Stir well and serve.

Nutritional Value (Amount per Serving):
Calories 490; Fat 17.7 g; Carbohydrates 41.1 g; Sugar 2 g; Protein 39.8 g; Cholesterol 106 mg

Rosemary Beans & Lentils

Preparation Time: 10 minutes; Cooking Time: 27 minutes; Serve: 8
Ingredients:
- 1 1/2 cups brown rice
- 1 tbsp garlic, minced
- 1/2 cup onion, chopped
- 1 1/2 tbsp thyme, chopped
- 2 tbsp rosemary
- 1 cup sweet potato, diced
- 1 cup navy beans, soaked overnight
- 1 cup brown lentils
- 4 cups vegetable stock
- 1 tbsp olive oil
- Pepper
- Salt

Directions:
1. Add oil into the inner pot of instant pot and set the pot on sauté mode.
2. Add garlic and onion and sauté for 4 minutes.
3. Add the rest of ingredients and stir everything well.
4. Seal pot with lid and cook on high for 23 minutes.
5. Once done, allow to release pressure naturally. Remove lid.
6. Stir well and serve.

Nutritional Value (Amount per Serving):
Calories 275; Fat 3.4 g; Carbohydrates 51.7 g; Sugar 3.4 g; Protein 10.1 g; Cholesterol 0 mg

Tasty Saucy Beans

Preparation Time: 10 minutes; Cooking Time: 30 minutes; Serve: 8
Ingredients:
- 2 cups dry pinto beans, soaked overnight
- 1 bay leaf
- 1 tsp cumin
- 1 tsp dried oregano
- 1 tbsp mustard
- 2 tbsp chili powder
- 8 oz tomato sauce
- 3 1/2 cups vegetable stock
- 1 tsp garlic, minced
- 1 jalapeno, diced
- 1 onion, diced
- 2 tbsp olive oil
- 1/2 tsp salt

Directions:
1. Add oil into the inner pot of instant pot and set the pot on sauté mode.
2. Add garlic, onion, and jalapeno and sauté for 5 minutes.
3. Add the rest of ingredients and stir everything well.
4. Seal pot with lid and cook on high for 25 minutes.
5. Once done, allow to release pressure naturally. Remove lid.
6. Stir well and serve.

Nutritional Value (Amount per Serving):
Calories 228; Fat 5 g; Carbohydrates 35.4 g; Sugar 3.4 g; Protein 11.7 g; Cholesterol 0 mg

Garlic Onion Pinto Beans

Preparation Time: 10 minutes; Cooking Time: 30 minutes; Serve: 8
Ingredients:
- 3 cups dry pinto beans, soaked overnight
- 6 cups vegetable stock
- 2 tsp dried oregano
- 1/3 cup dried onion
- 2 tbsp dried garlic
- 1 tsp sea salt

Directions:
1. Add all ingredients into the inner pot of instant pot and stir well.
2. Seal pot with lid and cook on high for 30 minutes.
3. Once done, allow to release pressure naturally. Remove lid.
4. Serve and enjoy.

Nutritional Value (Amount per Serving):
Calories 262; Fat 1 g; Carbohydrates 47.3 g; Sugar 2.3 g; Protein 16 g; Cholesterol 0 mg

Classic Greek Lentils & Rice

Preparation Time: 10 minutes; Cooking Time: 16 minutes; Serve: 6
Ingredients:
- 1/3 cup lentils, soak for 1-2 hours
- 2 cups vegetable stock
- 1/2 tsp ground coriander
- 1/4 tsp ground cumin
- 1 cup of brown rice
- 2 tbsp olive oil
- 2 cups onion, sliced
- Salt

Directions:
1. Add oil into the inner pot of instant pot and set the pot on sauté mode.
2. Add onion and sauté for 5-10 minutes.
3. Add the rest of the ingredients and stir well.
4. Seal pot with lid and cook on high for 6 minutes.
5. Once done, allow to release pressure naturally for 10 minutes then release remaining using quick release. Remove lid.
6. Serve and enjoy.

Nutritional Value (Amount per Serving):
Calories 210; Fat 5.7 g; Carbohydrates 34.5 g; Sugar 2.1 g; Protein 5.7 g; Cholesterol 0 mg

Creamy & Tasty Risotto

Preparation Time: 10 minutes; Cooking Time: 7 minutes; Serve: 4
Ingredients:
- 2 cups of rice
- 1/2 cup mozzarella cheese, shredded
- 1 cup parmesan cheese, shredded
- 4 cups vegetable stock
- 1/2 cup wine
- 1 small onion, chopped
- 2 tbsp olive oil
- Salt

Directions:
1. Add oil into the inner pot of instant pot and set the pot on sauté mode.
2. Add onion and sauté for 2 minutes.
3. Add rice, wine, stock, and salt and stir well.
4. Seal pot with lid and cook on high for 5 minutes.
5. Once done, release pressure using quick release. Remove lid.
6. Add cheeses and stir until cheese is melted.
7. Serve and enjoy.

Nutritional Value (Amount per Serving):
Calories 517; Fat 13.2 g; Carbohydrates 78.2 g; Sugar 1.8 g; Protein 15.4 g; Cholesterol 18 mg

Curried Beans

Preparation Time: 10 minutes; Cooking Time: 1 hour 30 minutes; Serve: 6
Ingredients:
- 2 cups brown rice
- 2 cups dry white beans
- 1/4 cup onion, diced
- 1 sweet potato, peeled and sliced
- 10 cups vegetable stock
- 1 tsp coriander powder
- 1 tbsp curry powder
- 1/2 tsp garlic, minced
- 1 tsp red pepper flakes
- 1 tbsp salt

Directions:
1. Add all ingredients into the inner pot of instant pot and stir well.
2. Seal pot with lid and cook on high for 1 hour 30 minutes.
3. Once done, allow to release pressure naturally. Remove lid.
4. Stir well and serve.

Nutritional Value (Amount per Serving):
Calories 487; Fat 2.7 g; Carbohydrates 95.6 g; Sugar 4.1 g; Protein 21.8 g; Cholesterol 0 mg

Tasty Salsa Beans

Preparation Time: 10 minutes; Cooking Time: 40 minutes; Serve: 6
Ingredients:
- 20 oz package ham pinto beans, rinsed
- 1 jalapeno pepper, diced
- 1 onion, diced
- 5 cups vegetable broth
- 1/4 cup parsley, chopped
- 1/2 cup salsa
- 1/2 tsp garlic, chopped
- Pepper
- Salt

Directions:
1. Add all ingredients into the inner pot of instant pot and stir well.
2. Seal pot with lid and cook on high for 40 minutes.
3. Once done, allow to release pressure naturally. Remove lid.
4. Stir well and serve.

Nutritional Value (Amount per Serving):
Calories 147; Fat 2.3 g; Carbohydrates 27.6 g; Sugar 2.1 g; Protein 12.5 g; Cholesterol 0 mg

Brown Rice Pilaf

Preparation Time: 10 minutes; Cooking Time: 27 minutes; Serve: 6
Ingredients:
- 1 1/2 cups brown rice, rinsed and drained
- 2 tbsp parsley, chopped
- 1 3/4 cups vegetable broth
- 1 tsp garlic, minced
- 1/2 cup onion, diced
- 2 tbsp olive oil
- 1/2 tsp salt

Directions:
1. Add oil into the inner pot of instant pot and set the pot on sauté mode.
2. Add onion and sauté for 5 minutes.
3. Add the rest of the ingredients except parsley and stir well.
4. Seal pot with lid and cook on high for 22 minutes.
5. Once done, allow to release pressure naturally. Remove lid.
6. Garnish with parsley and serve.

Nutritional Value (Amount per Serving):
Calories 228; Fat 6.4 g; Carbohydrates 37.6 g; Sugar 0.6 g; Protein 5.2 g; Cholesterol 0 mg

Corn Risotto

Preparation Time: 10 minutes; Cooking Time: 12 minutes; Serve: 4

Ingredients:
- 1 cup of rice
- 3 cups vegetable broth
- 1 tbsp olive oil
- 1 tsp garlic, minced
- 1 onion, chopped
- 3/4 cup sweet corn
- 1 red pepper, diced
- 1 tsp dried mix herbs
- 1/4 tsp pepper
- 1/2 tsp salt

Directions:
1. Add oil into the inner pot of instant pot and set the pot on sauté mode.
2. Add onion and garlic and sauté for 5 minutes.
3. Add the rest of the ingredients and stir well.
4. Seal pot with lid and cook on high for 8 minutes.
5. Once done, release pressure using quick release. Remove lid.
6. Stir well and serve.

Nutritional Value (Amount per Serving):
Calories 304; Fat 5.3 g; Carbohydrates 54.5 g; Sugar 4.7 g; Protein 9.5 g; Cholesterol 0 mg

Chapter 6: Vegetables

Potato Salad

Preparation Time: 10 minutes; Cooking Time: 10 minutes; Serve: 8
Ingredients:
- 5 cups potato, cubed
- 1/4 cup fresh parsley, chopped
- 1/4 tsp red pepper flakes
- 1 tbsp olive oil
- 1/3 cup mayonnaise
- 1/2 tbsp oregano
- 2 tbsp capers
- 3/4 cup feta cheese, crumbled
- 1 cup olives, halved
- 3 cups of water
- 3/4 cup onion, chopped
- Pepper
- Salt

Directions:
1. Add potatoes, onion, and salt into the instant pot.
2. Seal pot with lid and cook on high for 3 minutes.
3. Once done, release pressure using quick release. Remove lid.
4. Remove potatoes from pot and place in a large mixing bowl.
5. Add remaining ingredients and stir everything well.
6. Serve and enjoy.

Nutritional Value (Amount per Serving):
Calories 152; Fat 9.9 g; Carbohydrates 13.6 g; Sugar 2.1 g; Protein 3.5 g; Cholesterol 15 mg

Greek Green Beans

Preparation Time: 10 minutes; Cooking Time: 15 minutes; Serve: 4
Ingredients:
- 1 lb green beans, remove stems
- 2 potatoes, quartered
- 1 1/2 onion, sliced
- 1 tsp dried oregano
- 1/4 cup dill, chopped
- 1/4 cup fresh parsley, chopped
- 1 zucchini, quartered
- 1/2 cup olive oil
- 1 cup of water
- 14.5 oz can tomatoes, diced
- Pepper
- Salt

Directions:
1. Add all ingredients into the inner pot of instant pot and stir everything well.
2. Seal pot with lid and cook on high for 15 minutes.
3. Once done, release pressure using quick release. Remove lid.
4. Stir well and serve.

Nutritional Value (Amount per Serving):
Calories 381; Fat 25.8 g; Carbohydrates 37.7 g; Sugar 9 g; Protein 6.6 g; Cholesterol 0 mg

Healthy Vegetable Medley

Preparation Time: 10 minutes; Cooking Time: 17 minutes; Serve: 6
Ingredients:
- 3 cups broccoli florets
- 1 sweet potato, chopped
- 1 tsp garlic, minced
- 14 oz coconut milk
- 28 oz can tomatoes, chopped
- 14 oz can chickpeas, drained and rinsed
- 1 onion, chopped
- 1 tbsp olive oil
- 1 tsp Italian seasoning
- Pepper
- Salt

Directions:

1. Add oil into the inner pot of instant pot and set the pot on sauté mode.
2. Add garlic and onion and sauté until onion is softened.
3. Add remaining ingredients and stir everything well.
4. Seal pot with lid and cook on high for 12 minutes.
5. Once done, allow to release pressure naturally for 10 minutes then release remaining using quick release. Remove lid.
6. Stir well and serve.

Nutritional Value (Amount per Serving):
Calories 322; Fat 19.3 g; Carbohydrates 34.3 g; Sugar 9.6 g; Protein 7.9 g; Cholesterol 1 mg

Spicy Zucchini

Preparation Time: 10 minutes; Cooking Time: 5 minutes; Serve: 4
Ingredients:
- 4 zucchini, cut into 1/2-inch pieces
- 1 cup of water
- 1/2 tsp Italian seasoning
- 1/2 tsp red pepper flakes
- 1 tsp garlic, minced
- 1 tbsp olive oil
- 1/2 cup can tomato, crushed
- Salt

Directions:
1. Add water and zucchini into the instant pot.
2. Seal pot with lid and cook on high for 2 minutes.
3. Once done, release pressure using quick release. Remove lid.
4. Drain zucchini well and clean the instant pot.
5. Add oil into the inner pot of instant pot and set the pot on sauté mode.
6. Add garlic and sauté for 30 seconds.
7. Add remaining ingredients and stir well and cook for 2-3 minutes.
8. Serve and enjoy.

Nutritional Value (Amount per Serving):
Calories 69; Fat 4.1 g; Carbohydrates 7.9 g; Sugar 3.5 g; Protein 2.7 g; Cholesterol 0 mg

Healthy Garlic Eggplant

Preparation Time: 10 minutes; Cooking Time: 10 minutes; Serve: 4
Ingredients:
- 1 eggplant, cut into 1-inch pieces
- 1/2 cup water
- 1/4 cup can tomato, crushed
- 1/2 tsp Italian seasoning
- 1 tsp paprika
- 1/2 tsp chili powder
- 1 tsp garlic powder
- 2 tbsp olive oil
- Salt

Directions:
1. Add water and eggplant into the instant pot.
2. Seal pot with lid and cook on high for 5 minutes.
3. Once done, release pressure using quick release. Remove lid.
4. Drain eggplant well and clean the instant pot.
5. Add oil into the inner pot of instant pot and set the pot on sauté mode.
6. Add eggplant along with remaining ingredients and stir well and cook for 5 minutes.
7. Serve and enjoy.

Nutritional Value (Amount per Serving):
Calories 97; Fat 7.5 g; Carbohydrates 8.2 g; Sugar 3.7 g; Protein 1.5 g; Cholesterol 0 mg

Carrot Potato Medley

Preparation Time: 10 minutes; Cooking Time: 15 minutes; Serve: 6

Ingredients:
- 4 lbs baby potatoes, clean and cut in half
- 1 1/2 lbs carrots, cut into chunks
- 1 tsp Italian seasoning
- 1 1/2 cups vegetable broth
- 1 tbsp garlic, chopped
- 1 onion, chopped
- 2 tbsp olive oil
- Pepper
- Salt

Directions:
1. Add oil into the inner pot of instant pot and set the pot on sauté mode.
2. Add onion and sauté for 5 minutes.
3. Add carrots and cook for 5 minutes.
4. Add remaining ingredients and stir well.
5. Seal pot with lid and cook on high for 5 minutes.
6. Once done, allow to release pressure naturally for 10 minutes then release remaining using quick release. Remove lid.
7. Stir and serve.

Nutritional Value (Amount per Serving):
Calories 283; Fat 5.6 g; Carbohydrates 51.3 g; Sugar 6.6 g; Protein 10.2 g; Cholesterol 1 mg

Lemon Herb Potatoes

Preparation Time: 10 minutes; Cooking Time: 11 minutes; Serve: 6

Ingredients:
- 1 1/2 lbs baby potatoes, rinsed and pat dry
- 1/2 fresh lemon juice
- 1 tsp dried oregano
- 1/2 tsp garlic, minced
- 1 tbsp olive oil
- 1 cup vegetable broth
- 1/2 tsp sea salt

Directions:
1. Add broth and potatoes into the instant pot.
2. Seal pot with lid and cook on high for 8 minutes.
3. Once done, release pressure using quick release. Remove lid.
4. Drain potatoes well and clean the instant pot.
5. Add oil into the inner pot of instant pot and set the pot on sauté mode.
6. Add potatoes, garlic, oregano, lemon juice, and salt and cook for 3 minutes.
7. Serve and enjoy.

Nutritional Value (Amount per Serving):
Calories 94; Fat 2.7 g; Carbohydrates 14.6 g; Sugar 0.2 g; Protein 3.8 g; Cholesterol 0 mg

Flavors Basil Lemon Ratatouille

Preparation Time: 10 minutes; Cooking Time: 10 minutes; Serve: 8

Ingredients:
- 1 small eggplant, cut into cubes
- 1 cup fresh basil
- 2 cups grape tomatoes
- 1 onion, chopped
- 2 summer squash, sliced
- 2 zucchini, sliced
- 2 tbsp vinegar
- 2 tbsp tomato paste
- 1 tbsp garlic, minced
- 1 fresh lemon juice
- 1/4 cup olive oil
- Salt

Directions:
1. Add basil, vinegar, tomato paste, garlic, lemon juice, oil, and salt into the blender and blend until smooth.
2. Add eggplant, tomatoes, onion, squash, and zucchini into the instant pot.
3. Pour blended basil mixture over vegetables and stir well.

4. Seal pot with lid and cook on high for 10 minutes.
5. Once done, allow to release pressure naturally. Remove lid.
6. Stir well and serve.

Nutritional Value (Amount per Serving):
Calories 103; Fat 6.8 g; Carbohydrates 10.6 g; Sugar 6.1 g; Protein 2.4 g; Cholesterol 0 mg

Garlic Basil Zucchini

Preparation Time: 10 minutes; Cooking Time: 8 minutes; Serve: 4

Ingredients:
- 14 oz zucchini, sliced
- 1/4 cup fresh basil, chopped
- 1/2 tsp red pepper flakes
- 14 oz can tomatoes, chopped
- 1 tsp garlic, minced
- 1/2 onion, chopped
- 1/4 cup feta cheese, crumbled
- 1 tbsp olive oil
- Salt

Directions:
1. Add oil into the inner pot of instant pot and set the pot on sauté mode.
2. Add onion and garlic and sauté for 2 minutes.
3. Add remaining ingredients except feta cheese and stir well.
4. Seal pot with lid and cook on high for 6 minutes.
5. Once done, allow to release pressure naturally. Remove lid.
6. Top with feta cheese and serve.

Nutritional Value (Amount per Serving):
Calories 99; Fat 5.7 g; Carbohydrates 10.4 g; Sugar 6.1 g; Protein 3.7 g; Cholesterol 8 mg

Feta Green Beans

Preparation Time: 10 minutes; Cooking Time: 15 minutes; Serve: 4

Ingredients:
- 1 1/2 lbs green beans, trimmed
- 1/4 cup feta cheese, crumbled
- 28 oz can tomatoes, crushed
- 2 tsp oregano
- 1 tsp cumin
- 1/2 cup water
- 1 tbsp olive oil
- 1 tbsp garlic, minced
- 1 onion, chopped
- 1 lb baby potatoes, clean and cut into chunks
- Pepper
- Salt

Directions:
1. Add oil into the inner pot of instant pot and set the pot on sauté mode.
2. Add onion and garlic and sauté for 3-5 minutes.
3. Add remaining ingredients except feta cheese and stir well.
4. Seal pot with lid and cook on high for 10 minutes.
5. Once done, allow to release pressure naturally for 5 minutes then release remaining using quick release. Remove lid.
6. Top with feta cheese and serve.

Nutritional Value (Amount per Serving):
Calories 234; Fat 6.1 g; Carbohydrates 40.7 g; Sugar 10.7 g; Protein 9.7 g; Cholesterol 8 mg

Garlic Parmesan Artichokes

Preparation Time: 10 minutes; Cooking Time: 10 minutes; Serve: 4

Ingredients:
- 4 artichokes, wash, trim, and cut top
- 1/2 cup vegetable broth
- 1/4 cup parmesan cheese, grated
- 1 tbsp olive oil

- 2 tsp garlic, minced
- Salt

Directions:
1. Pour broth into the instant pot then place steamer rack in the pot.
2. Place artichoke steam side down on steamer rack into the pot.
3. Sprinkle garlic and grated cheese on top of artichokes and season with salt. Drizzle oil over artichokes.
4. Seal pot with lid and cook on high for 10 minutes.
5. Once done, release pressure using quick release. Remove lid.
6. Serve and enjoy.

Nutritional Value (Amount per Serving):
Calories 132; Fat 5.2 g; Carbohydrates 17.8 g; Sugar 1.7 g; Protein 7.9 g; Cholesterol 4 mg

Delicious Pepper Zucchini

Preparation Time: 10 minutes; Cooking Time: 10 minutes; Serve: 6
Ingredients:
- 1 zucchini, sliced
- 2 poblano peppers, sliced
- 1 tbsp sour cream
- 1/2 tsp ground cumin
- 1 yellow squash, sliced
- 1 tbsp garlic, minced
- 1/2 onion, sliced
- 1 tbsp olive oil
- Salt

Directions:
1. Add oil into the inner pot of instant pot and set the pot on sauté mode.
2. Add poblano peppers and sauté for 5 minutes
3. Add onion and garlic and sauté for 3 minutes.
4. Add remaining ingredients except for sour cream and stir well.
5. Seal pot with lid and cook on high for 2 minutes.
6. Once done, release pressure using quick release. Remove lid.
7. Add sour cream and stir well and serve.

Nutritional Value (Amount per Serving):
Calories 42; Fat 2.9 g; Carbohydrates 4 g; Sugar 1.7 g; Protein 1 g; Cholesterol 1 mg

Celery Carrot Brown Lentils

Preparation Time: 10 minutes; Cooking Time: 25 minutes; Serve: 6
Ingredients:
- 2 cups dry brown lentils, rinsed and drained
- 2 1/2 cups vegetable stock
- 2 tomatoes, chopped
- 1/2 tsp red pepper flakes
- 1/2 tsp ground cinnamon
- 1 bay leaf
- 1 tbsp tomato paste
- 2 celery stalks, diced
- 2 carrots, grated
- 1 tbsp garlic, minced
- 2 onions, chopped
- 1/4 cup olive oil
- Pepper
- Salt

Directions:
1. Add oil into the inner pot of instant pot and set the pot on sauté mode.
2. Add celery, carrot, garlic, onion, pepper, and salt and sauté for 3 minutes.
3. Add remaining ingredients and stir everything well.
4. Seal pot with lid and cook on high for 22 minutes.
5. Once done, release pressure using quick release. Remove lid.
6. Stir well and serve.

Nutritional Value (Amount per Serving):

Calories 137; Fat 8.8 g; Carbohydrates 12.3 g; Sugar 4.7 g; Protein 3.1 g; Cholesterol 0 mg

Lemon Artichokes

Preparation Time: 10 minutes; Cooking Time: 20 minutes; Serve: 4

Ingredients:
- 4 artichokes, trim and cut the top
- 1/4 cup fresh lemon juice
- 2 cups vegetable stock
- 1 tsp lemon zest, grated
- Pepper
- Salt

Directions:
1. Pour the stock into the instant pot then place steamer rack in the pot.
2. Place artichoke steam side down on steamer rack into the pot.
3. Sprinkle lemon zest over artichokes. Season with pepper and salt.
4. Pour lemon juice over artichokes.
5. Seal pot with lid and cook on high for 20 minutes.
6. Once done, allow to release pressure naturally for 5 minutes then release remaining using quick release. Remove lid.
7. Serve and enjoy.

Nutritional Value (Amount per Serving):
Calories 83; Fat 0.4 g; Carbohydrates 17.9 g; Sugar 2.3 g; Protein 5.6 g; Cholesterol 0 mg

Easy Chili Pepper Zucchinis

Preparation Time: 10 minutes; Cooking Time: 10 minutes; Serve: 4

Ingredients:
- 4 zucchinis, cut into cubes
- 1/2 tsp red pepper flakes
- 1/2 tsp cayenne
- 1 tbsp chili powder
- 1/4 cup vegetable stock
- Salt

Directions:
1. Add all ingredients into the inner pot of instant pot and stir well.
2. Seal pot with lid and cook on high for 10 minutes.
3. Once done, allow to release pressure naturally for 10 minutes then release remaining using quick release. Remove lid.
4. Stir and serve.

Nutritional Value (Amount per Serving):
Calories 38; Fat 0.7 g; Carbohydrates 8.8 g; Sugar 3.6 g; Protein 2.7 g; Cholesterol 0 mg

Delicious Okra

Preparation Time: 10 minutes; Cooking Time: 10 minutes; Serve: 4

Ingredients:
- 2 cups okra, chopped
- 2 tbsp fresh dill, chopped
- 1 tbsp paprika
- 1 cup can tomato, crushed
- Pepper
- Salt

Directions:
1. Add all ingredients into the inner pot of instant pot and stir well.
2. Seal pot with lid and cook on high for 10 minutes.
3. Once done, allow to release pressure naturally for 5 minutes then release remaining using quick release. Remove lid.
4. Stir well and serve.

Nutritional Value (Amount per Serving):
Calories 37; Fat 0.5 g; Carbohydrates 7.4 g; Sugar 0.9 g; Protein 2 g; Cholesterol 0 mg

Tomato Dill Cauliflower

Preparation Time: 10 minutes; Cooking Time: 12 minutes; Serve: 4
Ingredients:
- 1 lb cauliflower florets, chopped
- 1 tbsp fresh dill, chopped
- 1/4 tsp Italian seasoning
- 1 tbsp vinegar
- 1 cup can tomatoes, crushed
- 1 cup vegetable stock
- 1 tsp garlic, minced
- Pepper
- Salt

Directions:
1. Add all ingredients except dill into the instant pot and stir well.
2. Seal pot with lid and cook on high for 12 minutes.
3. Once done, allow to release pressure naturally for 10 minutes then release remaining using quick release. Remove lid.
4. Garnish with dill and serve.

Nutritional Value (Amount per Serving):
Calories 47; Fat 0.3 g; Carbohydrates 10 g; Sugar 5 g; Protein 3.1 g; Cholesterol 0 mg

Parsnips with Eggplant

Preparation Time: 10 minutes; Cooking Time: 12 minutes; Serve: 4
Ingredients:
- 2 parsnips, sliced
- 1 cup can tomatoes, crushed
- 1/2 tsp ground cumin
- 1 tbsp paprika
- 1 tsp garlic, minced
- 1 eggplant, cut into chunks
- 1/4 tsp dried basil
- Pepper
- Salt

Directions:
1. Add all ingredients into the instant pot and stir well.
2. Seal pot with lid and cook on high for 12 minutes.
3. Once done, release pressure using quick release. Remove lid.
4. Stir and serve.

Nutritional Value (Amount per Serving):
Calories 98; Fat 0.7 g; Carbohydrates 23 g; Sugar 8.8 g; Protein 2.8 g; Cholesterol 0 mg

Easy Garlic Beans

Preparation Time: 10 minutes; Cooking Time: 5 minutes; Serve: 4
Ingredients:
- 1 lb green beans, trimmed
- 1 1/2 cup vegetable stock
- 1 tsp garlic, minced
- 1 tbsp olive oil
- Pepper
- Salt

Directions:
1. Add all ingredients into the instant pot and stir well.
2. Seal pot with lid and cook on high for 5 minutes.
3. Once done, release pressure using quick release. Remove lid.
4. Stir and serve.

Nutritional Value (Amount per Serving):
Calories 69; Fat 3.7 g; Carbohydrates 8.7 g; Sugar 1.9 g; Protein 2.3 g; Cholesterol 0 mg

Eggplant with Olives

Preparation Time: 10 minutes; Cooking Time: 12 minutes; Serve: 4
Ingredients:

- 4 cups eggplants, cut into cubes
- 1/2 cup vegetable stock
- 1 tsp chili powder
- 1 cup olives, pitted and sliced
- 1 onion, chopped
- 1 tbsp olive oil
- 1/4 cup grape tomatoes
- Pepper
- Salt

Directions:
1. Add oil into the inner pot of instant pot and set the pot on sauté mode.
2. Add onion and sauté for 2 minutes.
3. Add remaining ingredients and stir everything well.
4. Seal pot with lid and cook on high for 12 minutes.
5. Once done, allow to release pressure naturally for 10 minutes then release remaining using quick release. Remove lid.
6. Stir and serve.

Nutritional Value (Amount per Serving):
Calories 105; Fat 7.4 g; Carbohydrates 10.4 g; Sugar 4.1 g; Protein 1.6 g; Cholesterol 0 mg

Vegan Carrots & Broccoli

Preparation Time: 10 minutes; Cooking Time: 5 minutes; Serve: 6
Ingredients:
- 4 cups broccoli florets
- 2 carrots, peeled and sliced
- 1/4 cup water
- 1/2 lemon juice
- 1 tsp garlic, minced
- 1 tbsp olive oil
- 1/4 cup vegetable stock
- 1/4 tsp Italian seasoning
- Salt

Directions:
1. Add oil into the inner pot of instant pot and set the pot on sauté mode.
2. Add garlic and sauté for 30 seconds.
3. Add carrots and broccoli and cook for 2 minutes.
4. Add remaining ingredients and stir everything well.
5. Seal pot with lid and cook on high for 3 minutes.
6. Once done, release pressure using quick release. Remove lid.
7. Stir well and serve.

Nutritional Value (Amount per Serving):
Calories 51; Fat 2.6 g; Carbohydrates 6.3 g; Sugar 2.2 g; Protein 2 g; Cholesterol 0 mg

Zucchini Tomato Potato Ratatouille

Preparation Time: 10 minutes; Cooking Time: 10 minutes; Serve: 6
Ingredients:
- 1 1/2 lbs potatoes, cut into cubes
- 1/2 cup fresh basil
- 28 oz fire-roasted tomatoes, chopped
- 1 onion, chopped
- 4 mushrooms, sliced
- 1 bell pepper, diced
- 12 oz eggplant, diced
- 8 oz zucchini, diced
- 8 oz yellow squash, diced
- Pepper
- Salt

Directions:
1. Add all ingredients except basil into the instant pot and stir well.
2. Seal pot with lid and cook on high for 10 minutes.
3. Once done, release pressure using quick release. Remove lid.
4. Add basil and stir well and serve.

Nutritional Value (Amount per Serving):

Calories 175; Fat 1.9 g; Carbohydrates 36 g; Sugar 11.5 g; Protein 5.9 g; Cholesterol 0 mg

Easy Curried Spinach Chickpeas

Preparation Time: 10 minutes; Cooking Time: 35 minutes; Serve: 6

Ingredients:
- 1 cup dry chickpeas, rinsed
- 2 cups spinach, chopped
- 1/8 tsp ground nutmeg
- 1 tbsp curry powder
- 1/2 tsp garlic powder
- 14 oz can tomatoes, crushed
- 4 cup vegetable stock
- Pepper
- Salt

Directions:
1. Add chickpeas and stock into the instant pot.
2. Seal pot with lid and cook on high for 30 minutes.
3. Once done, allow to release pressure naturally for 10 minutes then release remaining using quick release. Remove lid.
4. Drain excess liquid from chickpeas. Set pot on sauté mode.
5. Add remaining ingredients and stir well and cook for 5 minutes.
6. Stir well and serve.

Nutritional Value (Amount per Serving):
Calories 146; Fat 2.3 g; Carbohydrates 25.4 g; Sugar 6.4 g; Protein 7.8 g; Cholesterol 0 mg

Vegan Sweet Potato Hummus

Preparation Time: 10 minutes; Cooking Time: 5 minutes; Serve: 8

Ingredients:
- 14 oz can chickpeas, rinsed and drained
- 1 tsp ground cumin
- 1/4 cup tahini
- 1 fresh lemon juice
- 1 tbsp garlic, minced
- 1 sweet potato, peeled and diced
- 2 tbsp olive oil
- 1/2 tsp salt

Directions:
1. Add oil into the inner pot of instant pot and set the pot on sauté mode.
2. Add sweet potato, garlic, and salt and sauté for 3 minutes.
3. Add lemon juice and stir well.
4. Seal pot with lid and cook on high for 2 minutes.
5. Once done, release pressure using quick release. Remove lid.
6. Transfer sweet potatoes into the food processor along with remaining ingredients and process until smooth.
7. Serve and enjoy.

Nutritional Value (Amount per Serving):
Calories 151; Fat 8.2 g; Carbohydrates 16.4 g; Sugar 1.1 g; Protein 4.2 g; Cholesterol 0 mg

Quinoa Veggie Ratatouille

Preparation Time: 10 minutes; Cooking Time: 10 minutes; Serve: 2

Ingredients:
- 1 eggplant, cut into chunks
- 1/4 cup fresh basil
- 1/2 cup olives, pitted and sliced
- 1/2 cup cooked quinoa
- 14 oz can tomatoes, diced
- 1 tbsp vinegar
- 2 zucchinis, cut into 1-inch pieces
- 1 bell pepper, cut into 1-inch pieces
- 1 tsp garlic, minced
- 1/2 onion, sliced
- 1 tbsp olive oil
- Pepper

- Salt

Directions:
1. Add oil into the inner pot of instant pot and set the pot on sauté mode.
2. Add eggplant and sauté until browned. Transfer eggplant on a plate.
3. Add onion, zucchini, bell pepper, and garlic and cook for 3 minutes.
4. Add vinegar and stir well and cook for a minute.
5. Add tomatoes and stir. Seal pot with lid and cook on high for 3 minutes.
6. Once done, release pressure using quick release. Remove lid.
7. Add eggplant, quinoa, basil, pepper, and salt and stir well.
8. Serve and enjoy.

Nutritional Value (Amount per Serving):
Calories 421; Fat 14.1 g; Carbohydrates 67.2 g; Sugar 21.2 g; Protein 13.8 g; Cholesterol 0 mg

Vegetable Chili

Preparation Time: 10 minutes; Cooking Time: 8 minutes; Serve: 6
Ingredients:
- 1 1/2 lbs butternut squash, cubed
- 4 cups tomatoes, diced
- 14 oz can black beans, rinsed and drained
- 1 cup vegetable stock
- 1 tbsp chili powder
- 1 tsp garlic, minced
- 1 jalapeno pepper, chopped
- 1 small onion, diced
- 1 tbsp olive oil
- Pepper
- Salt

Directions:
1. Add oil into the inner pot of instant pot and set the pot on sauté mode.
2. Add jalapeno and onion and sauté for 2-4 minutes.
3. Add chili powder and garlic and sauté for a minute.
4. Add remaining ingredients and stir everything well.
5. Seal pot with lid and cook on high for 3 minutes.
6. Once done, release pressure using quick release. Remove lid.
7. Serve and enjoy.

Nutritional Value (Amount per Serving):
Calories 165; Fat 3.2 g; Carbohydrates 31.9 g; Sugar 6.9 g; Protein 6.2 g; Cholesterol 0 mg

Vegan Basil Artichoke Olive

Preparation Time: 10 minutes; Cooking Time: 12 minutes; Serve: 6
Ingredients:
- 28 oz can tomatoes, crushed
- 1/4 tsp dried oregano
- 1 tbsp tomato paste
- 1/4 cup fresh basil, chopped
- 1/4 cup olives, pitted
- 16 oz can artichoke hearts, drained and chopped
- 1 tsp garlic, minced
- 1 onion, chopped
- 1/4 cup olive oil
- Pepper
- Salt

Directions:
1. Add oil into the inner pot of instant pot and set the pot on sauté mode.
2. Add garlic and onion and sauté for a minute.
3. Add basil, olives, and artichokes and cook for 1 minute.
4. Add remaining ingredients and stir well.
5. Seal pot with lid and cook on high for 10 minutes.
6. Once done, release pressure using quick release. Remove lid.

7. Stir and serve.

Nutritional Value (Amount per Serving):
Calories 139; Fat 9.1 g; Carbohydrates 13.3 g; Sugar 6.2 g; Protein 2.9 g; Cholesterol 0 mg

Lemon Basil Eggplants

Preparation Time: 10 minutes; Cooking Time: 10 minutes; Serve: 4

Ingredients:
- 1 lb eggplant, cut into chunks
- 1 tbsp fresh chives, chopped
- 1/4 cup fresh lemon juice
- 1/2 cup vegetable stock
- 1 tsp ground coriander
- 1 1/2 tbsp paprika
- 1/2 tsp dried basil
- Pepper
- Salt

Directions:
1. Add all ingredients except chives into the instant pot and stir well.
2. Seal pot with lid and cook on high for 10 minutes.
3. Once done, allow to release pressure naturally for 10 minutes then release remaining using quick release. Remove lid.
4. Garnish with chives and serve.

Nutritional Value (Amount per Serving):
Calories 41; Fat 0.7 g; Carbohydrates 8.6 g; Sugar 4.1 g; Protein 1.7 g; Cholesterol 0 mg

Delicious Cauliflower Rice

Preparation Time: 10 minutes; Cooking Time: 15 minutes; Serve: 4

Ingredients:
- 1 1/2 cups cauliflower rice
- 1/2 tsp dried thyme
- 1 tsp paprika
- 2 eggplant, cut into chunks
- 1 tbsp olive oil
- 2 cups vegetable stock
- 1 onion, chopped
- 1/2 cup grape tomatoes
- Pepper
- Salt

Directions:
1. Add oil into the inner pot of instant pot and set the pot on sauté mode.
2. Add onion and sauté for 3 minutes.
3. Add remaining ingredients and stir everything well.
4. Seal pot with lid and cook on high for 12 minutes.
5. Once done, allow to release pressure naturally for 10 minutes then release remaining using quick release. Remove lid.
6. Stir well and serve.

Nutritional Value (Amount per Serving):
Calories 128; Fat 4.8 g; Carbohydrates 20.3 g; Sugar 10.5 g; Protein 4.5 g; Cholesterol 0 mg

Spicy Mushrooms

Preparation Time: 10 minutes; Cooking Time: 5 minutes; Serve: 4

Ingredients:
- 1 lb mushrooms, sliced
- 1 tbsp fresh lemon juice
- 1 tbsp balsamic vinegar
- 1/4 tsp paprika
- 1/4 tsp ground cumin
- 1/4 tsp dried oregano
- 1 chipotle chili in adobo sauce
- 1 tbsp garlic, minced
- 2 tbsp olive oil
- Salt

Directions:
1. Add oil into the inner pot of instant pot and set the pot on sauté mode.

2. Add garlic and mushrooms and sauté for 2 minutes.
3. Add remaining ingredients and stir everything well.
4. Seal pot with lid and cook on high for 3 minutes.
5. Once done, release pressure using quick release. Remove lid.
6. Stir well and serve.

Nutritional Value (Amount per Serving):
Calories 97; Fat 7.7 g; Carbohydrates 5.5 g; Sugar 2.6 g; Protein 3.8 g; Cholesterol 0 mg

Delicious Baby Carrots

Preparation Time: 10 minutes; Cooking Time: 20 minutes; Serve: 8
Ingredients:
- 2 1/2 lbs baby carrots
- 1 tsp Italian seasoning
- 1/4 cup vegetable broth
- 1 tbsp garlic, chopped
- 1/2 onion, chopped
- 1 tbsp olive oil

Directions:
1. Add oil into the inner pot of instant pot and set the pot on sauté mode.
2. Add garlic and onion and sauté for 5 minutes.
3. Add carrots and sauté for 5 minutes.
4. Add remaining ingredients and stir well.
5. Seal pot with lid and cook on high for 10 minutes.
6. Once done, release pressure using quick release. Remove lid.
7. Stir and serve.

Nutritional Value (Amount per Serving):
Calories 74; Fat 2.2 g; Carbohydrates 12.8 g; Sugar 7.1 g; Protein 1.1 g; Cholesterol 0 mg

Easy Bell Pepper Gumbo

Preparation Time: 10 minutes; Cooking Time: 2 minutes; Serve: 4
Ingredients:
- 4 bell peppers, cut into strips
- 1 tbsp fresh lime juice
- 1/4 cup vegetable stock
- 1/4 tsp turmeric
- 1/2 tsp chili powder
- 1/2 tsp ground cumin
- 1 tbsp garlic, minced
- 1 tbsp olive oil
- Pepper
- Salt

Directions:
1. Add oil into the inner pot of instant pot and set the pot on sauté mode.
2. Add garlic and sauté for 30 seconds.
3. Add remaining ingredients except for lime juice and stir well.
4. Seal pot with lid and cook on high for 2 minutes.
5. Once done, release pressure using quick release. Remove lid.
6. Add lime juice and stir well and serve.

Nutritional Value (Amount per Serving):
Calories 64; Fat 3.7 g; Carbohydrates 8.1 g; Sugar 4.3 g; Protein 1.3 g; Cholesterol 0 mg

Healthy Chickpea & Broccoli

Preparation Time: 10 minutes; Cooking Time: 5 minutes; Serve: 2
Ingredients:
- 14 oz can chickpeas, rinsed and drained
- 1 tbsp olive oil
- 4 cups broccoli florets, chopped
- 1 tbsp garlic, chopped
- 1/4 cup vegetable stock
- 1/4 tsp red pepper flakes
- Pepper

- Salt

Directions:
1. Add oil into the inner pot of instant pot and set the pot on sauté mode.
2. Add garlic and sauté for 30 seconds.
3. Add remaining ingredients and stir well.
4. Seal pot with lid and cook on high for 5 minutes.
5. Once done, allow to release pressure naturally for 10 minutes then release remaining using quick release. Remove lid.
6. Stir and serve.

Nutritional Value (Amount per Serving):
Calories 366; Fat 9.9 g; Carbohydrates 58.6 g; Sugar 3.2 g; Protein 15.3 g; Cholesterol 0 mg

Nutritious Potato Lentils

Preparation Time: 10 minutes; Cooking Time: 5 minutes; Serve: 2
Ingredients:
- 1 sweet potato, peeled and chopped
- 1/2 cup red lentils, rinsed and drained
- 1 1/2 cups water
- 2 tbsp vinegar
- 1/4 tsp chili powder
- 1/4 tsp garlic powder
- 1/4 tsp cinnamon
- 1 small onion, chopped

Directions:
1. Add all ingredients into the inner pot of instant pot and stir well.
2. Seal pot with lid and cook on high for 5 minutes.
3. Once done, allow to release pressure naturally for 10 minutes then release remaining using quick release. Remove lid.
4. Serve over cooked brown rice.

Nutritional Value (Amount per Serving):
Calories 241; Fat 0.7 g; Carbohydrates 44.7 g; Sugar 6.3 g; Protein 14 g; Cholesterol 0 mg

Rosemary Potatoes

Preparation Time: 10 minutes; Cooking Time: 20 minutes; Serve: 6
Ingredients:
- 2 lbs baby potatoes
- 1 fresh rosemary sprig
- 1 cup vegetable stock
- 1/4 cup olive oil
- 2 garlic cloves
- Pepper
- Salt

Directions:
1. Add oil into the inner pot of instant pot and set the pot on sauté mode.
2. Add garlic, potatoes, and rosemary and cook for 10 minutes.
3. Add stock, pepper, and salt and stir well.
4. Seal pot with lid and cook on high for 10 minutes.
5. Once done, release pressure using quick release. Remove lid.
6. Serve and enjoy.

Nutritional Value (Amount per Serving):
Calories 163; Fat 8.6 g; Carbohydrates 19.4 g; Sugar 0.1 g; Protein 4 g; Cholesterol 0 mg

Delicious Italian Bell Pepper

Preparation Time: 10 minutes; Cooking Time: 13 minutes; Serve: 4
Ingredients:
- 5 bell peppers, cut into strips
- 2 tbsp fresh parsley, chopped
- 1 tbsp garlic, chopped
- 2 tomatoes, chopped

- 1 onion, sliced
- 1 tbsp olive oil
- Pepper
- Salt

Directions:
1. Add oil into the inner pot of instant pot and set the pot on sauté mode.
2. Add onion and sauté for 3 minutes.
3. Add garlic and bell peppers and cook for 5 minutes.
4. Add remaining ingredients and stir well.
5. Seal pot with lid and cook on high for 5 minutes.
6. Once done, release pressure using quick release. Remove lid.
7. Stir well and serve.

Nutritional Value (Amount per Serving):
Calories 103; Fat 4.1 g; Carbohydrates 17 g; Sugar 10.3 g; Protein 2.5 g; Cholesterol 0 mg

Pesto Zucchini

Preparation Time: 10 minutes; Cooking Time: 8 minutes; Serve: 4
Ingredients:
- 2 zucchinis, sliced
- 1 cup vegetable stock
- 1 tsp Italian seasoning
- 2 tbsp olive oil
- 1 cup mozzarella cheese, shredded
- 1 eggplant, sliced
- 1 bell pepper, cut into strips
- 1/4 cup basil pesto
- Pepper
- Salt

Directions:
1. Add all ingredients except pesto into the instant pot and stir well.
2. Seal pot with lid and cook on high for 8 minutes.
3. Once done, release pressure using quick release. Remove lid.
4. Stir well. Top with basil pesto and serve.

Nutritional Value (Amount per Serving):
Calories 139; Fat 9.1 g; Carbohydrates 12.9 g; Sugar 6.9 g; Protein 4.8 g; Cholesterol 5 mg

Pesto Cauliflower

Preparation Time: 10 minutes; Cooking Time: 8 minutes; Serve: 2
Ingredients:
- 2 cups cauliflower florets
- 1 tbsp olive oil
- 1 tbsp fresh lemon juice
- 1/4 cup pine nuts
- 2 tbsp cream cheese
- 1/2 cup spinach, chopped
- 1 avocado, sliced
- 1/2 tsp red pepper flakes
- 1/4 tsp dried mint
- 1/4 tsp dried thyme
- 1/4 tsp dried rosemary
- 1 tsp sea salt

Directions:
1. Add cauliflower into the instant pot. Add water to cover the cauliflower.
2. Seal pot with lid and cook on high for 5 minutes.
3. Once done, release pressure using quick release. Remove lid.
4. Drain cauliflower well and set aside. Clean the instant pot.
5. Add avocado, spinach, cream cheese, pine nuts, lemon juice, rosemary, thyme, mint, and salt into the blender and blend until smooth.
6. Add oil into the inner pot of instant pot and set the pot on sauté mode.
7. Add cauliflower and blended avocado mixture into the pot and stir well and cook for 2 minutes.
8. Serve and enjoy.

Nutritional Value (Amount per Serving):

Calories 445; Fat 42 g; Carbohydrates 17.3 g; Sugar 3.8 g; Protein 7.3 g; Cholesterol 11 mg

Italian Tomato Mushrooms

Preparation Time: 10 minutes; Cooking Time: 13 minutes; Serve: 2

Ingredients:
- 1 cup tomatoes, chopped
- 2 cups mushrooms, sliced
- 1 tbsp olive oil
- 1/2 cup zucchini, chopped
- 1/4 cup green onions, chopped
- 1 cup cream cheese
- 1/2 tsp mint, chopped
- 1/2 tsp dried rosemary
- 1/2 tsp dried oregano
- Salt

Directions:
1. Add tomatoes, rosemary, oregano, mint, and salt into the blender and blend until smooth.
2. Add oil into the inner pot of instant pot and set the pot on sauté mode.
3. Add green onion and zucchini and sauté for 5 minutes. Transfer zucchini and onion mixture on a plate.
4. Add 1 cup water and mushrooms into the pot and stir well.
5. Seal pot with lid and cook on high for 3 minutes.
6. Once done, release pressure using quick release. Remove lid.
7. Add blended tomato mixture, zucchini, and cream cheese and cook on sauté mode for 5 minutes.
8. Stir well and serve.

Nutritional Value (Amount per Serving):
Calories 507; Fat 48 g; Carbohydrates 11.2 g; Sugar 4.6 g; Protein 12.4 g; Cholesterol 128 mg

Chickpea & Potato

Preparation Time: 10 minutes; Cooking Time: 8 minutes; Serve: 2

Ingredients:
- 1 cup cooked chickpeas
- 1/2 tsp ground cumin
- 1 tsp ground coriander
- 1/4 tsp ginger
- 2 potatoes, peeled and cubed
- 1 cup tomatoes, diced
- 1 onion, chopped
- 1 tbsp olive oil
- 1/4 cup vegetable stock
- 1 tsp turmeric
- 1/2 tsp salt

Directions:
1. Add oil into the inner pot of instant pot and set the pot on sauté mode.
2. Add onion and potatoes and cook for 2-3 minutes.
3. Add remaining ingredients and stir everything well.
4. Seal pot with lid and cook on high for 5 minutes.
5. Once done, allow to release pressure naturally for 10 minutes then release remaining using quick release. Remove lid.
6. Serve and enjoy.

Nutritional Value (Amount per Serving):
Calories 617; Fat 13.7 g; Carbohydrates 104 g; Sugar 18 g; Protein 24.5 g; Cholesterol 0 mg

Zesty Green Beans

Preparation Time: 10 minutes; Cooking Time: 15 minutes; Serve: 4

Ingredients:
- 1 lb green beans, trimmed
- 1 cup vegetable stock
- 1 lemon juice
- 1 tsp lemon zest, grated

- Pepper
- Salt

Directions:
1. Pour the stock into the instant pot.
2. Add green beans, lemon juice, lemon zest, pepper, and salt into the bowl and toss well.
3. Transfer green beans into the steamer basket. Place a steamer basket in the pot.
4. Seal pot with lid and cook on high for 15 minutes.
5. Once done, allow to release pressure naturally for 5 minutes then release remaining using quick release. Remove lid.
6. Serve and enjoy.

Nutritional Value (Amount per Serving):
Calories 40; Fat 0.3 g; Carbohydrates 8.7 g; Sugar 2.1 g; Protein 2.3 g; Cholesterol 0 mg

Rosemary Garlic Zucchini

Preparation Time: 10 minutes; Cooking Time: 3 minutes; Serve: 2
Ingredients:
- 2 zucchini, cut into lengthwise
- 3 tbsp parmesan cheese, grated
- 1/2 cup water
- 1/2 tsp dried basil
- 1/4 tsp dried rosemary
- 2 tbsp olive oil
- 1/4 tsp garlic powder
- Pepper
- Salt

Directions:
1. Pout water into the instant pot.
2. Toss zucchini with oil, basil, rosemary, garlic, pepper, and salt.
3. Transfer zucchini into the steamer basket and place basket in the pot.
4. Seal pot with lid and cook on high for 3 minutes.
5. Once done, release pressure using quick release. Remove lid.
6. Transfer zucchini on a plate.
7. Top with cheese and serve.

Nutritional Value (Amount per Serving):
Calories 177; Fat 16 g; Carbohydrates 7.2 g; Sugar 3.5 g; Protein 4.9 g; Cholesterol 5 mg

Healthy Baby Carrots

Preparation Time: 10 minutes; Cooking Time: 20 minutes; Serve: 4
Ingredients:
- 1 lb baby carrots
- 1 tsp Italian seasoning
- 1 tbsp balsamic vinegar
- 2 tbsp olive oil
- 1/4 cup vegetable stock
- Pepper
- Salt

Directions:
1. Add all ingredients into the inner pot of instant pot and stir well.
2. Seal pot with lid and cook on high for 20 minutes.
3. Once done, allow to release pressure naturally for 5 minutes then release remaining using quick release. Remove lid.
4. Serve and enjoy.

Nutritional Value (Amount per Serving):
Calories 105; Fat 7.5 g; Carbohydrates 9.6 g; Sugar 5.6 g; Protein 0.8 g; Cholesterol 1 mg

Greek Cauliflower Rice

Preparation Time: 10 minutes; Cooking Time: 12 minutes; Serve: 2
Ingredients:

- 1/2 cup cauliflower rice
- 1 tbsp pecans, toasted and chopped
- 1/2 tbsp fresh lime juice
- 1 1/3 cup vegetable stock
- 3 oz spinach, chopped
- 1/4 cup water
- 1 tbsp olive oil
- 1/2 small onion, chopped
- 1/2 tsp garlic, minced
- 1/4 cup grape tomatoes, halved
- 2 tbsp feta cheese, crumbled
- Salt

Directions:
1. Add oil into the inner pot of instant pot and set the pot on sauté mode.
2. Add garlic and onion and sauté for 5 minutes.
3. Add cauliflower rice, water, and stock and stir well.
4. Seal pot with lid and cook on high for 4 minutes.
5. Once done, release pressure using quick release. Remove lid.
6. Add spinach and tomatoes and cook on sauté mode for 3 minutes.
7. Add remaining ingredients and stir well and serve.

Nutritional Value (Amount per Serving):
Calories 176; Fat 14.8 g; Carbohydrates 8.9 g; Sugar 3.8 g; Protein 5 g; Cholesterol 8 mg

Tomato & Cheese Mix

Preparation Time: 10 minutes; Cooking Time: 15 minutes; Serve: 4
Ingredients:
- 1 lb grape tomatoes, halved
- 1 cup feta cheese, crumbled
- 1 cup heavy cream
- 1 onion, chopped
- 1 tbsp olive oil
- 1/4 tsp Italian seasoning
- Pepper
- Salt

Directions:
1. Add oil into the inner pot of instant pot and set the pot on sauté mode.
2. Add onion and sauté for 3 minutes.
3. Add remaining ingredients and stir well.
4. Seal pot with lid and cook on high for 12 minutes.
5. Once done, release pressure using quick release. Remove lid.
6. Stir and serve.

Nutritional Value (Amount per Serving):
Calories 265; Fat 22.9 g; Carbohydrates 9.4 g; Sugar 5.7 g; Protein 7.3 g; Cholesterol 75 mg

Beans & Mushrooms

Preparation Time: 10 minutes; Cooking Time: 8 minutes; Serve: 2
Ingredients:
- 1/2 lb green beans, trimmed
- 1 tbsp olive oil
- 1 tbsp balsamic vinegar
- 4 oz mushrooms, sliced
- 1/2 tsp garlic, minced
- 1/2 onion, chopped
- 1 cup of water
- Pepper
- Salt

Directions:
1. Add water and beans into the instant pot.
2. Seal pot with lid and cook on high for 3 minutes.
3. Once done, release pressure using quick release. Remove lid.
4. Drain beans well and clean the instant pot.
5. Add oil into the inner pot of instant pot and set the pot on sauté mode.
6. Add garlic and onion and sauté for 2 minutes.
7. Add mushrooms and cook for 2-3 minutes.

8. Add green beans, vinegar, pepper, and salt and stir well.
9. Serve and enjoy.

Nutritional Value (Amount per Serving):
Calories 121; Fat 7.3 g; Carbohydrates 12.9 g; Sugar 3.8 g; Protein 4.2 g; Cholesterol 0 mg

Radish & Asparagus

Preparation Time: 10 minutes; Cooking Time: 8 minutes; Serve: 4

Ingredients:
- 3/4 cup radishes, halved
- 1 lb asparagus, trimmed & cut in half
- 1 tsp chili powder
- 1 tsp lemon zest, grated
- 2 tbsp green onion, chopped
- 2 tbsp olive oil
- Pepper
- Salt

Directions:
1. Add all ingredients into the inner pot of instant pot and stir well.
2. Seal pot with lid and cook on high for 8 minutes.
3. Once done, allow to release pressure naturally for 5 minutes then release remaining using quick release. Remove lid.
4. Stir and serve.

Nutritional Value (Amount per Serving):
Calories 90; Fat 7.3 g; Carbohydrates 5.8 g; Sugar 2.7 g; Protein 2.8 g; Cholesterol 0 mg

Spicy Cauliflower

Preparation Time: 10 minutes; Cooking Time: 6 minutes; Serve: 2

Ingredients:
- 1/2 small cauliflower head, cut into florets
- 1 tbsp fresh parsley, chopped
- 1/2 cup water
- 1/4 tsp paprika
- 1/4 tsp turmeric
- 1/2 tsp ground cumin
- 1 tbsp olive oil
- 1/4 tsp chili powder
- 1/4 small onion, chopped
- 1 tomato, chopped
- Pepper
- Salt

Directions:
1. Add tomato, onion, and chili powder into the blender and blend until smooth.
2. Add oil into the inner pot of instant pot and set the pot on sauté mode.
3. Add blended tomato mixture into the pot and cook for 2-3 minutes.
4. Add paprika, cumin, turmeric, and pepper and stir for a minute.
5. Add remaining ingredients and stir well.
6. Seal pot with lid and cook on high for 3 minutes.
7. Once done, release pressure using quick release. Remove lid.
8. Stir and serve.

Nutritional Value (Amount per Serving):
Calories 97; Fat 7.5 g; Carbohydrates 7.6 g; Sugar 3.7 g; Protein 2.2 g; Cholesterol 0 mg

Creamy Lemon Bell Peppers

Preparation Time: 10 minutes; Cooking Time: 15 minutes; Serve: 4

Ingredients:
- 1 lb bell peppers, cut into strips
- 1 tbsp chives, chopped
- 1 tbsp fresh lime juice
- 1/2 cup heavy cream
- 1/4 tsp dried mix herbs
- Pepper
- Salt

Directions:
1. Add all ingredients into the inner pot of instant pot and stir well.
2. Seal pot with lid and cook on high for 15 minutes.
3. Once done, allow to release pressure naturally for 5 minutes then release remaining using quick release. Remove lid.
4. Stir and serve.

Nutritional Value (Amount per Serving):
Calories 72; Fat 5.7 g; Carbohydrates 5.2 g; Sugar 1.8 g; Protein 0.9 g; Cholesterol 21 mg

Creamy Dill Potatoes

Preparation Time: 10 minutes; Cooking Time: 20 minutes; Serve: 4

Ingredients:
- 2 lbs potatoes, peeled and cut into chunks
- 1 tbsp fresh dill, chopped
- 1 cup vegetable stock
- 3/4 cup heavy cream
- Pepper
- Salt

Directions:
1. Add all ingredients into the inner pot of instant pot and stir well.
2. Seal pot with lid and cook on high for 20 minutes.
3. Once done, allow to release pressure naturally for 10 minutes then release remaining using quick release. Remove lid.
4. Stir and serve.

Nutritional Value (Amount per Serving):
Calories 238; Fat 8.6 g; Carbohydrates 37 g; Sugar 2.8 g; Protein 4.5 g; Cholesterol 31 mg

Chapter 7: Appetizers

Spicy Pepper Eggplant Spread

Preparation Time: 10 minutes; Cooking Time: 9 minutes; Serve: 4
Ingredients:
- 3 cups Italian eggplants, cut into 1/-inch chunks
- 1/2 cup tomatoes, diced
- 1 cup red pepper, diced
- 1/2 tsp red pepper flakes
- 1 tbsp vinegar
- 2 tbsp garlic, minced
- 1/2 cup onion, diced
- 2 tbsp olive oil
- 1/4 cup water
- 1 tsp kosher salt

Directions:
1. Add oil into the inner pot of instant pot and set the pot on sauté mode.
2. Add red pepper and eggplant and sauté for 5 minutes.
3. Add remaining ingredients and stir everything well.
4. Seal pot with lid and cook on high for 4 minutes.
5. Once done, release pressure using quick release. Remove lid.
6. Mash the spread mixture using the spatula and serve.

Nutritional Value (Amount per Serving):
Calories 237; Fat 19.2 g; Carbohydrates 18 g; Sugar 2.8 g; Protein 1 g; Cholesterol 0 mg

Pinto Bean Dip

Preparation Time: 10 minutes; Cooking Time: 45 minutes; Serve: 6
Ingredients:
- 1 cup dry pinto beans
- 2 tsp chili powder
- 3 chilies de Arbol, remove the stem
- 4 cups of water
- 1 tsp salt

Directions:
1. Add beans, chilies, and water into the instant pot and stir well.
2. Seal pot with lid and cook on high for 45 minutes.
3. Once done, allow to release pressure naturally for 10 minutes then release remaining using quick release. Remove lid.
4. Transfer instant pot bean mixture into the blender along with chili powder and salt and blend until smooth.
5. Serve and enjoy.

Nutritional Value (Amount per Serving):
Calories 139; Fat 0.6 g; Carbohydrates 24.6 g; Sugar 4.2 g; Protein 8 g; Cholesterol 0 mg

Spicy Jalapeno Spinach Artichoke Dip

Preparation Time: 10 minutes; Cooking Time: 3 minutes; Serve: 15
Ingredients:
- 10 oz spinach, chopped
- 1/2 cup parmesan cheese, grated
- 8 oz Italian cheese, shredded
- 1/4 cup fresh parsley, chopped
- 2 tbsp jalapeno, diced
- 1 1/2 tbsp garlic, minced
- 2 tbsp green onion, chopped
- 14 oz cream cheese, cubed
- 18 oz jar marinated artichoke hearts, chopped
- 1 1/2 tbsp fresh lemon juice
- 1/2 cup vegetable stock

Directions:
1. Add all ingredients except parmesan cheese and Italian cheese into the instant pot and stir well.

2. Seal pot with lid and cook on high for 3 minutes.
3. Once done, allow to release pressure naturally for 5 minutes then release remaining using quick release. Remove lid.
4. Set pot on sauté mode. Add parmesan cheese and Italian cheese and stir well and cook until cheese is melted.
5. Serve and enjoy.

Nutritional Value (Amount per Serving):
Calories 195; Fat 16.3 g; Carbohydrates 3.7 g; Sugar 0.6 g; Protein 6.7 g; Cholesterol 42 mg

Perfect Black Bean Dip

Preparation Time: 10 minutes; Cooking Time: 30 minutes; Serve: 24

Ingredients:
- 1 1/2 cup dry black beans, rinsed and drained
- 1/2 tsp ground coriander
- 1/2 tsp chili powder
- 1 tsp paprika
- 2 tsp ground cumin
- 1 fresh lime juice
- 1 1/2 tbsp olive oil
- 1 3/4 cup chicken broth
- 14 oz can tomatoes, diced
- 2 jalapenos, chopped
- 1 tbsp garlic, minced
- 1 onion, diced
- 1/2 tsp salt

Directions:
1. Add all ingredients into the instant pot and stir everything well.
2. Seal pot with lid and cook on high for 30 minutes.
3. Once done, allow to release pressure naturally for 10 minutes then release remaining using quick release. Remove lid.
4. Blend bean mixture using an immersion blender until smooth.
5. Serve and enjoy.

Nutritional Value (Amount per Serving):
Calories 59; Fat 1.2 g; Carbohydrates 9.4 g; Sugar 1.1 g; Protein 3.3 g; Cholesterol 143 mg

Flavorful Italian Peppers

Preparation Time: 10 minutes; Cooking Time: 3 minutes; Serve: 4

Ingredients:
- 4 red bell peppers, cut into strips and remove seeds
- 1/2 tsp Italian seasoning
- 1/2 tsp garlic powder
- 1 tbsp vinegar
- 3 tbsp olive oil
- 1 cup of water
- Pepper
- Salt

Directions:
1. Add bell peppers and water into the instant pot.
2. Seal pot with lid and cook on high for 3 minutes.
3. Once done, release pressure using quick release. Remove lid.
4. In a small bowl, mix together oil, vinegar, garlic powder, Italian seasoning, pepper, and salt.
5. Once bell peppers are cooked then pour oil mixture over bell peppers and mix well.
6. Serve warm and enjoy.

Nutritional Value (Amount per Serving):
Calories 132; Fat 11 g; Carbohydrates 9.4 g; Sugar 6.2 g; Protein 1.3 g; Cholesterol 0 mg

Cheese Stuff Artichokes

Preparation Time: 10 minutes; Cooking Time: 20 minutes; Serve: 2

Ingredients:
- 2 artichokes, trimmed and cut the 1/2-inch top
- 1/4 cup sour cream
- 1 tbsp olive oil
- 1/4 cup fresh lemon juice
- 1 1/2 tsp garlic, minced
- 1 tsp Italian seasoning
- 1/2 cup parmesan cheese, grated
- 1 cup whole wheat breadcrumbs, homemade

Directions:
1. Spread artichoke leaves and clean the central core.
2. In a bowl, mix together breadcrumbs, garlic, parmesan cheese, sour cream, oil, lemon juice, and Italian seasoning.
3. Stuff breadcrumbs mixture into the artichokes.
4. Pour 1 1/2 cups of water into the instant pot then place the trivet in the pot.
5. Place artichokes on top of the trivet.
6. Seal pot with lid and cook on high for 20 minutes.
7. Once done, release pressure using quick release. Remove lid.
8. Serve and enjoy.

Nutritional Value (Amount per Serving):
Calories 428; Fat 20 g; Carbohydrates 48.7 g; Sugar 3.5 g; Protein 19.8 g; Cholesterol 30 mg

Sausage Queso Dip

Preparation Time: 10 minutes; Cooking Time: 18 minutes; Serve: 8

Ingredients:
- 1 lb Italian sausage, crumbled
- 4 cups Monterey jack cheese, shredded
- 12 oz milk
- 1/4 cup pickles peppers, diced
- 3.5 oz can olives, drained and sliced
- 14.5 oz can tomatoes, diced
- 1 small onion, chopped

Directions:
1. Set instant pot on sauté mode. Add sausage to the pot and cook for 3 minutes.
2. Add onion and sauté for 5 minutes.
3. Add remaining ingredients except for cheese and stir well and cook for 5 minutes.
4. Add shredded cheese and cook for 5 minutes or until cheese is melted.
5. Stir everything well and serve.

Nutritional Value (Amount per Serving):
Calories 458; Fat 35.8 g; Carbohydrates 6.8 g; Sugar 4.4 g; Protein 27.1 g; Cholesterol 102 mg

Chocolate Hummus

Preparation Time: 10 minutes; Cooking Time: 25 minutes; Serve: 10

Ingredients:
- 3/4 cup dried chickpeas, soaked overnight and drained
- 1 tsp vanilla
- 1/2 cup unsweetened cocoa powder
- 1/4 cup maple syrup
- 1/4 cup peanut butter
- 2 1/2 cups water
- Pinch of salt

Directions:
1. Add water and chickpeas into the instant pot.
2. Seal pot with lid and cook on high for 25 minutes.
3. Once done, release pressure using quick release. Remove lid.
4. Drain chickpeas well and reserved half cup of chickpea liquid.
5. Transfer chickpeas, reserved liquid, and remaining ingredients into the food processor and process until smooth.
6. Serve and enjoy.

Nutritional Value (Amount per Serving):
Calories 124; Fat 4.8 g; Carbohydrates 18 g; Sugar 7 g; Protein 5.4 g; Cholesterol 0 mg

Tasty Spinach Artichoke Dip

Preparation Time: 10 minutes; Cooking Time: 4 minutes; Serve: 10
Ingredients:
- 15 oz can artichoke hearts, drained
- 1/2 tsp onion powder
- 1 tsp garlic, chopped
- 1/2 cup mayonnaise
- 1/2 cup sour cream
- 1/2 cup vegetable broth
- 8 oz mozzarella cheese, shredded
- 15 oz parmesan cheese, shredded
- 10 oz spinach
- 8 oz cream cheese

Directions:
1. Add all ingredients except parmesan cheese and mozzarella cheese into the instant pot and stir well.
2. Seal pot with lid and cook on high for 4 minutes.
3. Once done, release pressure using quick release. Remove lid.
4. Add parmesan cheese and mozzarella cheese and stir until cheese is melted.
5. Serve and enjoy.

Nutritional Value (Amount per Serving):
Calories 372; Fat 27.5 g; Carbohydrates 9.6 g; Sugar 1.4 g; Protein 24 g; Cholesterol 75 mg

Rosemary Hummus

Preparation Time: 10 minutes; Cooking Time: 35 minutes; Serve: 10
Ingredients:
- 1 1/2 cups dry chickpeas
- 5 tbsp rosemary garlic olive oil
- 1/2 tsp smoked paprika
- 2 tbsp fresh lemon juice
- 2 tbsp tahini
- 6 cups of water
- 1 tsp salt

Directions:
1. Add water and chickpeas into the instant pot.
2. Seal pot with lid and cook on high for 35 minutes.
3. Once done, allow to release pressure naturally for 10 minutes then release remaining using quick release. Remove lid.
4. Drain chickpeas well and transfer into the food processor along with remaining ingredients and process until smooth.
5. Serve and enjoy.

Nutritional Value (Amount per Serving):
Calories 183; Fat 5 g; Carbohydrates 28 g; Sugar 3.5 g; Protein 7.3 g; Cholesterol 0 mg

Homemade Salsa

Preparation Time: 10 minutes; Cooking Time: 30 minutes; Serve: 12
Ingredients:
- 12 cups fresh tomatoes, peel and diced
- 1/4 cup fresh parsley, chopped
- 1 1/2 tbsp cayenne
- 2 tbsp fresh lemon juice
- 1 1/2 tbsp garlic, minced
- 1/2 cup white vinegar
- 12 oz tomato paste
- 3 jalapeno peppers, chopped
- 1 1/2 cups onion, chopped
- 2 green peppers, diced
- 1 tbsp salt

Directions:
1. Add all ingredients into the instant pot and stir well.

2. Seal pot with lid and cook on high for 30 minutes.
3. Once done, allow to release pressure naturally for 10 minutes then release remaining using quick release. Remove lid.
4. Stir well and serve. Store leftover in an air-tight container.

Nutritional Value (Amount per Serving):
Calories 74; Fat 0.7 g; Carbohydrates 15.8 g; Sugar 9.6 g; Protein 3.4 g; Cholesterol 0 mg

Cheesy Corn Dip

Preparation Time: 10 minutes; Cooking Time: 10 minutes; Serve: 6
Ingredients:
- 4 ears corn
- 1/4 cup fresh basil, minced
- 1/4 cup fresh cilantro, minced
- 1 tbsp fresh lime juice
- 1/4 tsp cayenne
- 1/2 tsp cumin
- 1/2 tsp garlic powder
- 1 tsp paprika
- 1 1/2 tsp chili powder
- 1/4 cup mayonnaise
- 4 oz cream cheese
- 1 cup of water
- Pepper
- Salt

Directions:
1. Pour water into the instant pot then place the trivet in the pot.
2. Place corn on top of the trivet.
3. Seal pot with lid and cook on high for 5 minutes.
4. Once done, release pressure using quick release. Remove lid.
5. Remove corn and drain water from instant pot and clean the pot.
6. Cut corn from the cob. Add corn kernels, cayenne, cumin, garlic, paprika, chili powder, mayonnaise, cream cheese, pepper, and salt into the instant pot and stir well.
7. Seal pot with lid and cook on high for 5 minutes.
8. Once done, release pressure using quick release. Remove lid.
9. Add basil, cilantro, and lime juice and stir well.
10. Serve and enjoy.

Nutritional Value (Amount per Serving):
Calories 199; Fat 11.3 g; Carbohydrates 23.7 g; Sugar 4.3 g; Protein 5.1 g; Cholesterol 23 mg

Light & Creamy Garlic Hummus

Preparation Time: 10 minutes; Cooking Time: 40 minutes; Serve: 12
Ingredients:
- 1 1/2 cups dry chickpeas, rinsed
- 2 1/2 tbsp fresh lemon juice
- 1 tbsp garlic, minced
- 1/2 cup tahini
- 6 cups of water
- Pepper
- Salt

Directions:
1. Add water and chickpeas into the instant pot.
2. Seal pot with a lid and select manual and set timer for 40 minutes.
3. Once done, allow to release pressure naturally. Remove lid.
4. Drain chickpeas well and reserved 1/2 cup chickpeas liquid.
5. Transfer chickpeas, reserved liquid, lemon juice, garlic, tahini, pepper, and salt into the food processor and process until smooth.
6. Serve and enjoy.

Nutritional Value (Amount per Serving):
Calories 152; Fat 6.9 g; Carbohydrates 17.6 g; Sugar 2.8 g; Protein 6.6 g; Cholesterol 0 mg

Perfect Queso

Preparation Time: 10 minutes; Cooking Time: 15 minutes; Serve: 16

Ingredients:
- 1 lb ground beef
- 32 oz Velveeta cheese, cut into cubes
- 10 oz can tomatoes, diced
- 1 1/2 tbsp taco seasoning
- 1 tsp chili powder
- 1 onion, diced
- Pepper
- Salt

Directions:
1. Set instant pot on sauté mode.
2. Add meat, onion, taco seasoning, chili powder, pepper, and salt into the pot and cook until meat is no longer pink.
3. Add tomatoes and stir well. Top with cheese and do not stir.
4. Seal pot with lid and cook on high for 4 minutes.
5. Once done, release pressure using quick release. Remove lid.
6. Stir everything well and serve.

Nutritional Value (Amount per Serving):
Calories 257; Fat 15.9 g; Carbohydrates 10.2 g; Sugar 4.9 g; Protein 21 g; Cholesterol 71 mg

Creamy Potato Spread

Preparation Time: 10 minutes; Cooking Time: 15 minutes; Serve: 6

Ingredients:
- 1 lb sweet potatoes, peeled and chopped
- 3/4 tbsp fresh chives, chopped
- 1/2 tsp paprika
- 1 tbsp garlic, minced
- 1 cup tomato puree
- Pepper
- Salt

Directions:
1. Add all ingredients except chives into the inner pot of instant pot and stir well.
2. Seal pot with lid and cook on high for 15 minutes.
3. Once done, allow to release pressure naturally for 10 minutes then release remaining using quick release. Remove lid.
4. Transfer instant pot sweet potato mixture into the food processor and process until smooth.
5. Garnish with chives and serve.

Nutritional Value (Amount per Serving):
Calories 108; Fat 0.3 g; Carbohydrates 25.4 g; Sugar 2.4 g; Protein 2 g; Cholesterol 0 mg

Cucumber Tomato Okra Salsa

Preparation Time: 10 minutes; Cooking Time: 15 minutes; Serve: 4

Ingredients:
- 1 lb tomatoes, chopped
- 1/4 tsp red pepper flakes
- 1/4 cup fresh lemon juice
- 1 cucumber, chopped
- 1 tbsp fresh oregano, chopped
- 1 tbsp fresh basil, chopped
- 1 tbsp olive oil
- 1 onion, chopped
- 1 tbsp garlic, chopped
- 1 1/2 cups okra, chopped
- Pepper
- Salt

Directions:
1. Add oil into the inner pot of instant pot and set the pot on sauté mode.
2. Add onion, garlic, pepper, and salt and sauté for 3 minutes.
3. Add remaining ingredients except for cucumber and stir well.
4. Seal pot with lid and cook on high for 12 minutes.

5. Once done, allow to release pressure naturally for 10 minutes then release remaining using quick release. Remove lid.
   6. Once the salsa mixture is cool then add cucumber and mix well.
   7. Serve and enjoy.

Nutritional Value (Amount per Serving):
Calories 99; Fat 4.2 g; Carbohydrates 14.3 g; Sugar 6.4 g; Protein 2.9 g; Cholesterol 0 mg

Parmesan Potatoes

Preparation Time: 10 minutes; Cooking Time: 6 minutes; Serve: 4

Ingredients:
- 2 lb potatoes, rinsed and cut into chunks
- 2 tbsp parmesan cheese, grated
- 2 tbsp olive oil
- 1/2 tsp parsley
- 1/2 tsp Italian seasoning
- 1 tsp garlic, minced
- 1 cup vegetable broth
- 1/2 tsp salt

Directions:
1. Add all ingredients except cheese into the instant pot and stir well.
2. Seal pot with lid and cook on high for 6 minutes.
3. Once done, release pressure using quick release. Remove lid.
4. Add parmesan cheese and stir until cheese is melted.
5. Serve and enjoy.

Nutritional Value (Amount per Serving):
Calories 237; Fat 8.3 g; Carbohydrates 36.3 g; Sugar 2.8 g; Protein 5.9 g; Cholesterol 2 mg

Creamy Artichoke Dip

Preparation Time: 10 minutes; Cooking Time: 5 minutes; Serve: 8

Ingredients:
- 28 oz can artichoke hearts, drain and quartered
- 1 1/2 cups parmesan cheese, shredded
- 1 cup sour cream
- 1 cup mayonnaise
- 3.5 oz can green chilies
- 1 cup of water
- Pepper
- Salt

Directions:
1. Add artichokes, water, and green chilis into the instant pot.
2. Seal pot with the lid and select manual and set timer for 1 minute.
3. Once done, release pressure using quick release. Remove lid. Drain excess water.
4. Set instant pot on sauté mode. Add remaining ingredients and stir well and cook until cheese is melted.
5. Serve and enjoy.

Nutritional Value (Amount per Serving):
Calories 262; Fat 7.6 g; Carbohydrates 14.4 g; Sugar 2.8 g; Protein 8.4 g; Cholesterol 32 mg

Homemade Salsa

Preparation Time: 10 minutes; Cooking Time: 5 minutes; Serve: 8

Ingredients:
- 12 oz grape tomatoes, halved
- 1/4 cup fresh cilantro, chopped
- 1 fresh lime juice
- 28 oz tomatoes, crushed
- 1 tbsp garlic, minced
- 1 green bell pepper, chopped
- 1 red bell pepper, chopped
- 2 onions, chopped
- 6 whole tomatoes
- Salt

Directions:
1. Add whole tomatoes into the instant pot and gently smash the tomatoes.
2. Add remaining ingredients except cilantro, lime juice, and salt and stir well.
3. Seal pot with lid and cook on high for 5 minutes.
4. Once done, allow to release pressure naturally for 10 minutes then release remaining using quick release. Remove lid.
5. Add cilantro, lime juice, and salt and stir well.
6. Serve and enjoy.

Nutritional Value (Amount per Serving):
Calories 146; Fat 1.2 g; Carbohydrates 33.2 g; Sugar 4 g; Protein 6.9 g; Cholesterol 0 mg

Delicious Eggplant Caponata

Preparation Time: 10 minutes; Cooking Time: 5 minutes; Serve: 8
Ingredients:
- 1 eggplant, cut into 1/2-inch chunks
- 1 lb tomatoes, diced
- 1/2 cup tomato puree
- 1/4 cup dates, chopped
- 2 tbsp vinegar
- 1/2 cup fresh parsley, chopped
- 2 celery stalks, chopped
- 1 small onion, chopped
- 2 zucchini, cut into 1/2-inch chunks
- Pepper
- Salt

Directions:
1. Add all ingredients into the inner pot of instant pot and stir well.
2. Seal pot with lid and cook on high for 5 minutes.
3. Once done, release pressure using quick release. Remove lid.
4. Stir well and serve.

Nutritional Value (Amount per Serving):
Calories 60; Fat 0.4 g; Carbohydrates 14 g; Sugar 8.8 g; Protein 2.3 g; Cholesterol 0.4 mg

Flavorful Roasted Baby Potatoes

Preparation Time: 10 minutes; Cooking Time: 10 minutes; Serve: 4
Ingredients:
- 2 lbs baby potatoes, clean and cut in half
- 1/2 cup vegetable stock
- 1 tsp paprika
- 3/4 tsp garlic powder
- 1 tsp onion powder
- 2 tsp Italian seasoning
- 1 tbsp olive oil
- Pepper
- Salt

Directions:
1. Add oil into the inner pot of instant pot and set the pot on sauté mode.
2. Add potatoes and sauté for 5 minutes. Add remaining ingredients and stir well.
3. Seal pot with lid and cook on high for 5 minutes.
4. Once done, release pressure using quick release. Remove lid.
5. Stir well and serve.

Nutritional Value (Amount per Serving):
Calories 175; Fat 4.5 g; Carbohydrates 29.8 g; Sugar 0.7 g; Protein 6.1 g; Cholesterol 2 mg

Perfect Italian Potatoes

Preparation Time: 10 minutes; Cooking Time: 7 minutes; Serve: 6
Ingredients:
- 2 lbs baby potatoes, clean and cut in half
- 3/4 cup vegetable broth
- 6 oz Italian dry dressing mix

Directions:
1. Add all ingredients into the inner pot of instant pot and stir well.
2. Seal pot with lid and cook on high for 7 minutes.
3. Once done, allow to release pressure naturally for 3 minutes then release remaining using quick release. Remove lid.
4. Stir well and serve.

Nutritional Value (Amount per Serving):
Calories 149; Fat 0.3 g; Carbohydrates 41.6 g; Sugar 11.4 g; Protein 4.5 g; Cholesterol 0 mg

Garlic Pinto Bean Dip

Preparation Time: 10 minutes; Cooking Time: 43 minutes; Serve: 6
Ingredients:
- 1 cup dry pinto beans, rinsed
- 1/2 tsp cumin
- 1/2 cup salsa
- 2 garlic cloves
- 2 chipotle peppers in adobo sauce
- 5 cups vegetable stock
- Pepper
- Salt

Directions:
1. Add beans, stock, garlic, and chipotle peppers into the instant pot.
2. Seal pot with lid and cook on high for 43 minutes.
3. Once done, release pressure using quick release. Remove lid.
4. Drain beans well and reserve 1/2 cup of stock.
5. Transfer beans, reserve stock, and remaining ingredients into the food processor and process until smooth.
6. Serve and enjoy.

Nutritional Value (Amount per Serving):
Calories 129; Fat 0.9 g; Carbohydrates 23 g; Sugar 1.9 g; Protein 8 g; Cholesterol 2 mg

Creamy Eggplant Dip

Preparation Time: 10 minutes; Cooking Time: 20 minutes; Serve: 4
Ingredients:
- 1 eggplant
- 1/2 tsp paprika
- 1 tbsp olive oil
- 1 tbsp fresh lime juice
- 2 tbsp tahini
- 1 garlic clove
- 1 cup of water
- Pepper
- Salt

Directions:
1. Add water and eggplant into the instant pot.
2. Seal pot with the lid and select manual and set timer for 20 minutes.
3. Once done, release pressure using quick release. Remove lid.
4. Drain eggplant and let it cool.
5. Once the eggplant is cool then remove eggplant skin and transfer eggplant flesh into the food processor.
6. Add remaining ingredients into the food processor and process until smooth.
7. Serve and enjoy.

Nutritional Value (Amount per Serving):
Calories 108; Fat 7.8 g; Carbohydrates 9.7 g; Sugar 3.7 g; Protein 2.5 g; Cholesterol 0 mg

Jalapeno Chickpea Hummus

Preparation Time: 10 minutes; Cooking Time: 25 minutes; Serve: 4
Ingredients:

- 1 cup dry chickpeas, soaked overnight and drained
- 1 tsp ground cumin
- 1/4 cup jalapenos, diced
- 1/2 cup fresh cilantro
- 1 tbsp tahini
- 1/2 cup olive oil
- Pepper
- Salt

Directions:
1. Add chickpeas into the instant pot and cover with vegetable stock.
2. Seal pot with lid and cook on high for 25 minutes.
3. Once done, allow to release pressure naturally. Remove lid.
4. Drain chickpeas well and transfer into the food processor along with remaining ingredients and process until smooth.
5. Serve and enjoy.

Nutritional Value (Amount per Serving):
Calories 425; Fat 30.4 g; Carbohydrates 31.8 g; Sugar 5.6 g; Protein 10.5 g; Cholesterol 0 mg

Tasty Black Bean Dip

Preparation Time: 10 minutes; Cooking Time: 18 minutes; Serve: 6
Ingredients:
- 2 cups dry black beans, soaked overnight and drained
- 1 1/2 cups cheese, shredded
- 1 tsp dried oregano
- 1 1/2 tsp chili powder
- 2 cups tomatoes, chopped
- 2 tbsp olive oil
- 1 1/2 tbsp garlic, minced
- 1 medium onion, sliced
- 4 cups vegetable stock
- Pepper
- Salt

Directions:
1. Add all ingredients except cheese into the instant pot.
2. Seal pot with lid and cook on high for 18 minutes.
3. Once done, allow to release pressure naturally. Remove lid. Drain excess water.
4. Add cheese and stir until cheese is melted.
5. Blend bean mixture using an immersion blender until smooth.
6. Serve and enjoy.

Nutritional Value (Amount per Serving):
Calories 402; Fat 15.3 g; Carbohydrates 46.6 g; Sugar 4.4 g; Protein 22.2 g; Cholesterol 30 mg

Healthy Kidney Bean Dip

Preparation Time: 10 minutes; Cooking Time: 10 minutes; Serve: 6
Ingredients:
- 1 cup dry white kidney beans, soaked overnight and drained
- 1 tbsp fresh lemon juice
- 2 tbsp water
- 1/2 cup coconut yogurt
- 1 roasted garlic clove
- 1 tbsp olive oil
- 1/4 tsp cayenne
- 1 tsp dried parsley
- Pepper
- Salt

Directions:
1. Add soaked beans and 1 3/4 cups of water into the instant pot.
2. Seal pot with lid and cook on high for 10 minutes.
3. Once done, allow to release pressure naturally. Remove lid.
4. Drain beans well and transfer them into the food processor.
5. Add remaining ingredients into the food processor and process until smooth.
6. Serve and enjoy.

Nutritional Value (Amount per Serving):
Calories 136; Fat 3.2 g; Carbohydrates 20 g; Sugar 2.1 g; Protein 7.7 g; Cholesterol 0 mg

Creamy Pepper Spread

Preparation Time: 10 minutes; Cooking Time: 15 minutes; Serve: 4

Ingredients:
- 1 lb red bell peppers, chopped and remove seeds
- 1 1/2 tbsp fresh basil
- 1 tbsp olive oil
- 1 tbsp fresh lime juice
- 1 tsp garlic, minced
- Pepper
- Salt

Directions:
1. Add all ingredients into the inner pot of instant pot and stir well.
2. Seal pot with lid and cook on high for 15 minutes.
3. Once done, allow to release pressure naturally for 10 minutes then release remaining using quick release. Remove lid.
4. Transfer bell pepper mixture into the food processor and process until smooth.
5. Serve and enjoy.

Nutritional Value (Amount per Serving):
Calories 41; Fat 3.6 g; Carbohydrates 3.5 g; Sugar 1.7 g; Protein 0.4 g; Cholesterol 0 mg

Healthy Spinach Dip

Preparation Time: 10 minutes; Cooking Time: 8 minutes; Serve: 4

Ingredients:
- 14 oz spinach
- 2 tbsp fresh lime juice
- 1 tbsp garlic, minced
- 2 tbsp olive oil
- 2 tbsp coconut cream
- Pepper
- Salt

Directions:
1. Add all ingredients except coconut cream into the instant pot and stir well.
2. Seal pot with lid and cook on low pressure for 8 minutes.
3. Once done, allow to release pressure naturally for 5 minutes then release remaining using quick release. Remove lid.
4. Add coconut cream and stir well and blend spinach mixture using a blender until smooth.
5. Serve and enjoy.

Nutritional Value (Amount per Serving):
Calories 109; Fat 9.2 g; Carbohydrates 6.6 g; Sugar 1.1 g; Protein 3.2 g; Cholesterol 0 mg

Kidney Bean Spread

Preparation Time: 10 minutes; Cooking Time: 18 minutes; Serve: 4

Ingredients:
- 1 lb dry kidney beans, soaked overnight and drained
- 1 tsp garlic, minced
- 2 tbsp olive oil
- 1 tbsp fresh lemon juice
- 1 tbsp paprika
- 4 cups vegetable stock
- 1/2 cup onion, chopped
- Pepper
- Salt

Directions:
1. Add beans and stock into the instant pot.
2. Seal pot with lid and cook on high for 18 minutes.
3. Once done, allow to release pressure naturally. Remove lid.
4. Drain beans well and reserve 1/2 cup stock.

5. Transfer beans, reserve stock, and remaining ingredients into the food processor and process until smooth.
   6. Serve and enjoy.

Nutritional Value (Amount per Serving):
Calories 461; Fat 8.6 g; Carbohydrates 73 g; Sugar 4 g; Protein 26.4 g; Cholesterol 0 mg

Tomato Cucumber Salsa

Preparation Time: 10 minutes; Cooking Time: 5 minutes; Serve: 4

Ingredients:
- 1 cucumber, chopped
- 1 1/2 lbs grape tomatoes, chopped
- 1 tbsp fresh chives, chopped
- 1 tbsp fresh parsley, chopped
- 1 tbsp fresh basil, chopped
- 2 onion, chopped
- 1/4 cup vinegar
- 2 tbsp olive oil
- 1/4 cup vegetable stock
- 2 chili peppers, chopped
- Pepper
- Salt

Directions:
1. Add tomatoes, stock, and chili peppers into the instant pot and stir well.
2. Seal pot with lid and cook on low pressure for 5 minutes.
3. Once done, allow to release pressure naturally for 5 minutes then release remaining using quick release. Remove lid.
4. Transfer tomato mixture into the mixing bowl.
5. Add remaining ingredients into the bowl and mix well.
6. Serve and enjoy.

Nutritional Value (Amount per Serving):
Calories 129; Fat 7.5 g; Carbohydrates 15 g; Sugar 8.3 g; Protein 2.7 g; Cholesterol 0 mg

Spicy Berry Dip

Preparation Time: 10 minutes; Cooking Time: 15 minutes; Serve: 4

Ingredients:
- 10 oz cranberries
- 1/4 cup fresh orange juice
- 3/4 tsp paprika
- 1/2 tsp chili powder
- 1 tsp lemon zest
- 1 tbsp lemon juice

Directions:
1. Add all ingredients into the inner pot of instant pot and stir well.
2. Seal pot with lid and cook on high for 15 minutes.
3. Once done, allow to release pressure naturally for 5 minutes then release remaining using quick release. Remove lid.
4. Blend cranberry mixture using a blender until getting the desired consistency.
5. Serve and enjoy.

Nutritional Value (Amount per Serving):
Calories 49; Fat 0.2 g; Carbohydrates 8.6 g; Sugar 4.1 g; Protein 0.3 g; Cholesterol 0 mg

Rosemary Cauliflower Dip

Preparation Time: 10 minutes; Cooking Time: 15 minutes; Serve: 4

Ingredients:
- 1 lb cauliflower florets
- 1 tbsp fresh parsley, chopped
- 1/2 cup heavy cream
- 1/2 cup vegetable stock
- 1 tbsp garlic, minced
- 1 tbsp rosemary, chopped
- 1 tbsp olive oil
- 1 onion, chopped
- Pepper
- Salt

Directions:
1. Add oil into the inner pot of instant pot and set the pot on sauté mode.
2. Add onion and sauté for 5 minutes.
3. Add remaining ingredients except for parsley and heavy cream and stir well.
4. Seal pot with lid and cook on high for 10 minutes.
5. Once done, allow to release pressure naturally for 10 minutes then release remaining using quick release. Remove lid.
6. Add cream and stir well. Blend cauliflower mixture using immersion blender until smooth.
7. Garnish with parsley and serve.

Nutritional Value (Amount per Serving):
Calories 128; Fat 9.4 g; Carbohydrates 10.4 g; Sugar 4 g; Protein 3.1 g; Cholesterol 21 mg

Tomato Olive Salsa

Preparation Time: 10 minutes; Cooking Time: 5 minutes; Serve: 4

Ingredients:
- 2 cups olives, pitted and chopped
- 1/4 cup fresh parsley, chopped
- 1/4 cup fresh basil, chopped
- 2 tbsp green onion, chopped
- 1 cup grape tomatoes, halved
- 1 tbsp olive oil
- 1 tbsp vinegar
- Pepper
- Salt

Directions:
1. Add all ingredients into the inner pot of instant pot and stir well.
2. Seal pot with lid and cook on high for 5 minutes.
3. Once done, allow to release pressure naturally for 5 minutes then release remaining using quick release. Remove lid.
4. Stir well and serve.

Nutritional Value (Amount per Serving):
Calories 119; Fat 10.8 g; Carbohydrates 6.5 g; Sugar 1.3 g; Protein 1.2 g; Cholesterol 0 mg

Easy Tomato Dip

Preparation Time: 10 minutes; Cooking Time: 13 minutes; Serve: 4

Ingredients:
- 2 cups tomato puree
- 1/2 tsp ground cumin
- 1 tsp garlic, minced
- 1/4 cup vinegar
- 1 onion, chopped
- 1 tbsp olive oil
- Pepper
- Salt

Directions:
1. Add oil into the inner pot of instant pot and set the pot on sauté mode.
2. Add onion and sauté for 3 minutes.
3. Add remaining ingredients and stir well.
4. Seal pot with lid and cook on high for 10 minutes.
5. Once done, allow to release pressure naturally for 10 minutes then release remaining using quick release. Remove lid.
6. Blend tomato mixture using an immersion blender until smooth.
7. Serve and enjoy.

Nutritional Value (Amount per Serving):
Calories 94; Fat 3.9 g; Carbohydrates 14.3 g; Sugar 7.3 g; Protein 2.5 g; Cholesterol 0 mg

Balsamic Bell Pepper Salsa

Preparation Time: 10 minutes; Cooking Time: 6 minutes; Serve: 2

Ingredients:
- 2 red bell peppers, chopped and seeds removed
- 1 cup grape tomatoes, halved
- 1/2 tbsp cayenne
- 1 tbsp balsamic vinegar
- 2 cup vegetable broth
- 1/2 cup sour cream
- 1/2 tsp garlic powder
- 1/2 onion, chopped
- Salt

Directions:
1. Add all ingredients except cream into the instant pot and stir well.
2. Seal pot with lid and cook on high for 6 minutes.
3. Once done, release pressure using quick release. Remove lid.
4. Add sour cream and stir well.
5. Blend the salsa mixture using an immersion blender until smooth.
6. Serve and enjoy.

Nutritional Value (Amount per Serving):
Calories 235; Fat 14.2 g; Carbohydrates 19.8 g; Sugar 10.7 g; Protein 9.2 g; Cholesterol 25 mg

Spicy Chicken Dip

Preparation Time: 10 minutes; Cooking Time: 15 minutes; Serve: 10

Ingredients:
- 1 lb chicken breast, skinless and boneless
- 1/2 cup sour cream
- 8 oz cheddar cheese, shredded
- 1/2 cup chicken stock
- 2 jalapeno pepper, sliced
- 8 oz cream cheese
- Pepper
- Salt

Directions:
1. Add chicken, stock, jalapenos, and cream cheese into the instant pot.
2. Seal pot with lid and cook on high for 12 minutes.
3. Once done, release pressure using quick release. Remove lid.
4. Shred chicken using a fork.
5. Set pot on sauté mode. Add remaining ingredients and stir well and cook until cheese is melted.
6. Serve and enjoy.

Nutritional Value (Amount per Serving):
Calories 248; Fat 19 g; Carbohydrates 1.6 g; Sugar 0.3 g; Protein 17.4 g; Cholesterol 83 mg

Slow Cooked Cheesy Artichoke Dip

Preparation Time: 10 minutes; Cooking Time: 60 minutes; Serve: 6

Ingredients:
- 10 oz can artichoke hearts, drained and chopped
- 4 cups spinach, chopped
- 8 oz cream cheese
- 3 tbsp sour cream
- 1/4 cup mayonnaise
- 3/4 cup mozzarella cheese, shredded
- 1/4 cup parmesan cheese, grated
- 3 garlic cloves, minced
- 1/2 tsp dried parsley
- Pepper
- Salt

Directions:
1. Add all ingredients into the inner pot of instant pot and stir well.
2. Seal the pot with the lid and select slow cook mode and set the timer for 60 minutes. Stir once while cooking.

3. Serve and enjoy.

Nutritional Value (Amount per Serving):
Calories 226; Fat 19.3 g; Carbohydrates 7.5 g; Sugar 1.2 g; Protein 6.8 g; Cholesterol 51 mg

Olive Eggplant Spread

Preparation Time: 10 minutes; Cooking Time: 8 minutes; Serve: 12

Ingredients:
- 1 3/4 lbs eggplant, chopped
- 1/2 tbsp dried oregano
- 1/4 cup olives, pitted and chopped
- 1 tbsp tahini
- 1/4 cup fresh lime juice
- 1/2 cup water
- 2 garlic cloves
- 1/4 cup olive oil
- Salt

Directions:
1. Add oil into the inner pot of instant pot and set the pot on sauté mode.
2. Add eggplant and cook for 3-5 minutes. Turn off sauté mode.
3. Add water and salt and stir well.
4. Seal pot with lid and cook on high for 3 minutes.
5. Once done, release pressure using quick release. Remove lid.
6. Drain eggplant well and transfer into the food processor.
7. Add remaining ingredients into the food processor and process until smooth.
8. Serve and enjoy.

Nutritional Value (Amount per Serving):
Calories 65; Fat 5.3 g; Carbohydrates 4.7 g; Sugar 2 g; Protein 0.9 g; Cholesterol 0 mg

Pepper Tomato Eggplant Spread

Preparation Time: 10 minutes; Cooking Time: 10 minutes; Serve: 3

Ingredients:
- 2 cups eggplant, chopped
- 1/4 cup vegetable broth
- 2 tbsp tomato paste
- 1/4 cup sun-dried tomatoes, minced
- 1 cup bell pepper, chopped
- 1 tsp garlic, minced
- 1 cup onion, chopped
- 3 tbsp olive oil
- Salt

Directions:
1. Add oil into the inner pot of instant pot and set the pot on sauté mode.
2. Add onion and sauté for 3 minutes.
3. Add eggplant, bell pepper, and garlic and sauté for 2 minutes.
4. Add remaining ingredients and stir well.
5. Seal pot with lid and cook on high for 5 minutes.
6. Once done, release pressure using quick release. Remove lid.
7. Lightly mash the eggplant mixture using a potato masher.
8. Stir well and serve.

Nutritional Value (Amount per Serving):
Calories 178; Fat 14.4 g; Carbohydrates 12.8 g; Sugar 7 g; Protein 2.4 g; Cholesterol 0 mg

Chapter 8: Poultry

Flavorful Mediterranean Chicken

Preparation Time: 10 minutes; Cooking Time: 20 minutes; Serve: 8
Ingredients:
- 2 lbs chicken thighs
- 1/2 cup olives
- 28 oz can tomatoes, diced
- 1 1/2 tsp dried oregano
- 2 tsp dried parsley
- 1/2 tsp ground coriander powder
- 1/4 tsp chili pepper
- 1 tsp onion powder
- 1 sp paprika
- 2 cups onion, chopped
- 2 tbsp olive oil
- Pepper
- Salt

Directions:
1. Add oil into the inner pot of instant pot and set the pot on sauté mode.
2. Add chicken and cook until browned. Transfer chicken on a plate.
3. Add onion and sauté for 5 minutes.
4. Add all spices, tomatoes, and salt and cook for 2-3 minutes.
5. Return chicken to the pot and stir everything well.
6. Seal pot with lid and cook on high for 8 minutes.
7. Once done, release pressure using quick release. Remove lid.
8. Add olives and stir well.
9. Serve and enjoy.

Nutritional Value (Amount per Serving):
Calories 292; Fat 13 g; Carbohydrates 8.9 g; Sugar 4.8 g; Protein 34.3 g; Cholesterol 101 mg

Artichoke Olive Chicken

Preparation Time: 10 minutes; Cooking Time: 8 minutes; Serve: 6
Ingredients:
- 2 1/2 lbs chicken breasts, skinless and boneless
- 14 oz can artichokes
- 1/2 cup olives, pitted
- 3/4 cup prunes
- 1 tbsp capers
- 1 1/2 tbsp garlic, chopped
- 3 tbsp red wine vinegar
- 2 tsp dried oregano
- 1/3 cup wine
- Pepper
- Salt

Directions:
1. Add all ingredients except chicken into the instant pot and stir well.
2. Add chicken and mix well. Seal pot with lid and cook on high for 8 minutes.
3. Once done, allow to release pressure naturally for 10 minutes then release remaining using quick release. Remove lid.
4. Serve and enjoy.

Nutritional Value (Amount per Serving):
Calories 472; Fat 15.5 g; Carbohydrates 22.7 g; Sugar 8.9 g; Protein 57.6 g; Cholesterol 168 mg

Easy Chicken Piccata

Preparation Time: 10 minutes; Cooking Time: 41 minutes; Serve: 6
Ingredients:
- 8 chicken thighs, bone-in, and skin-on
- 2 tbsp fresh parsley, chopped
- 1 tbsp olive oil
- 3 tbsp capers
- 2 tbsp fresh lemon juice
- 1/2 cup chicken broth
- 1/4 cup dry white wine
- 1 tbsp garlic, minced

Directions:
1. Add oil into the inner pot of instant pot and set the pot on sauté mode.
2. Add garlic and sauté for 1 minute.
3. Add wine and cook for 5 minutes or until wine reduced by half.
4. Add lemon juice and broth and stir well.
5. Add chicken and seal pot with the lid and select manual and set a timer for 30 minutes.
6. Once done, release pressure using quick release. Remove lid.
7. Remove chicken from pot and place on a baking tray. Broil chicken for 5 minutes.
8. Add capers and stir well.
9. Garnish with parsley and serve.

Nutritional Value (Amount per Serving):
Calories 406; Fat 17 g; Carbohydrates 1.2 g; Sugar 0.3 g; Protein 57 g; Cholesterol 173 mg

Garlic Thyme Chicken Drumsticks

Preparation Time: 10 minutes; Cooking Time: 18 minutes; Serve: 4

Ingredients:
- 8 chicken drumsticks, skin-on
- 2 tbsp balsamic vinegar
- 2/3 cup can tomatoes, diced
- 6 garlic cloves
- 1 tsp lemon zest, grated
- 1 tsp dried thyme
- 1/4 tsp red pepper flakes
- 1 1/2 onions, cut into wedges
- 1 tbsp olive oil
- Pepper
- Salt

Directions:
1. Add oil into the inner pot of instant pot and set the pot on sauté mode.
2. Add onion and 1/2 tsp salt and sauté for 2-3 minutes.
3. Add chicken, garlic, lemon zest, red pepper flakes, and thyme and mix well.
4. Add vinegar and tomatoes and stir well.
5. Seal pot with lid and cook on high for 15 minutes.
6. Once done, release pressure using quick release. Remove lid.
7. Stir well and serve.

Nutritional Value (Amount per Serving):
Calories 220; Fat 8.9 g; Carbohydrates 7.8 g; Sugar 3.2 g; Protein 26.4 g; Cholesterol 81 mg

Tender Chicken & Mushrooms

Preparation Time: 10 minutes; Cooking Time: 21 minutes; Serve: 6

Ingredients:
- 1 lb chicken breasts, skinless, boneless, & cut into 1-inch pieces
- 1/4 cup olives, sliced
- 2 oz feta cheese, crumbled
- 1/4 cup sherry
- 1 cup chicken broth
- 1 tsp Italian seasoning
- 12 oz mushrooms, sliced
- 2 celery stalks, diced
- 1 tsp garlic, minced
- 1/2 cup onion, chopped
- 2 tbsp olive oil
- Pepper
- Salt

Directions:
1. Add oil into the inner pot of instant pot and set the pot on sauté mode.
2. Add mushrooms, celery, garlic, and onion and sauté for 5-7 minutes.
3. Add chicken, Italian seasoning, pepper, and salt and stir well and cook for 4 minutes.
4. Add sherry and broth and stir well.
5. Seal pot with lid and cook on high for 10 minutes.

6. Once done, allow to release pressure naturally for 10 minutes then release remaining using quick release. Remove lid.
7. Add olives and feta cheese and stir well.
8. Serve and enjoy.

Nutritional Value (Amount per Serving):
Calories 244; Fat 13.5 g; Carbohydrates 4.1 g; Sugar 2 g; Protein 26 g; Cholesterol 76 mg

Delicious Chicken Casserole

Preparation Time: 10 minutes; Cooking Time: 20 minutes; Serve: 4

Ingredients:
- 1 lb chicken breasts, skinless, boneless, & cubed
- 2 tsp paprika
- 3 tbsp tomato paste
- 1 cup chicken stock
- 4 tomatoes, chopped
- 1 small eggplant, chopped
- 1 tbsp Italian seasoning
- 2 bell pepper, sliced
- 1 onion, sliced
- 1 tbsp garlic, minced
- 1 tbsp olive oil
- Pepper
- Salt

Directions:
1. Add oil into the inner pot of instant pot and set the pot on sauté mode.
2. Season chicken with pepper and salt and add into the instant pot. Cook chicken until lightly golden brown.
3. Remove chicken from pot and place on a plate.
4. Add garlic and onion and sauté until onion is softened about 3-5 minutes.
5. Return chicken to the pot. Pour remaining ingredients over chicken and stir well.
6. Seal pot with lid and cook on high for 10 minutes.
7. Once done, release pressure using quick release. Remove lid.
8. Stir well and serve.

Nutritional Value (Amount per Serving):
Calories 356; Fat 13.9 g; Carbohydrates 22.7 g; Sugar 12.9 g; Protein 36.9 g; Cholesterol 103 mg

Perfect Chicken & Rice

Preparation Time: 10 minutes; Cooking Time: 25 minutes; Serve: 4

Ingredients:
- 1 lb chicken breasts, skinless and boneless
- 1 tsp olive oil
- 1 cup onion, diced
- 1 tsp garlic minced
- 4 carrots, peeled and sliced
- 1 tbsp Mediterranean spice mix
- 2 cups brown rice, rinsed
- 2 cups chicken stock
- Pepper
- Salt

Directions:
1. Add oil into the inner pot of instant pot and set the pot on sauté mode.
2. Add garlic and onion and sauté until onion is softened.
3. Add stock, carrot, rice, and Mediterranean spice mix and stir well.
4. Place chicken on top of rice mixture and season with pepper and salt. Do not mix.
5. Seal pot with a lid and select manual and set timer for 20 minutes.
6. Once done, allow to release pressure naturally for 10 minutes then release remaining using quick release. Remove lid.
7. Remove chicken from pot and shred using a fork.
8. Return shredded chicken to the pot and stir well.
9. Serve and enjoy.

Nutritional Value (Amount per Serving):
Calories 612; Fat 12.4 g; Carbohydrates 81.7 g; Sugar 4.6 g; Protein 41.1 g; Cholesterol 101 mg

Moroccan Chicken

Preparation Time: 10 minutes; Cooking Time: 25 minutes; Serve: 6
Ingredients:
- 2 lbs chicken breasts, cut into chunks
- 1/2 tsp cinnamon
- 1 tsp turmeric
- 1/2 tsp ginger
- 1 tsp cumin
- 2 tbsp Dijon mustard
- 1 tbsp molasses
- 1 tbsp honey
- 2 tbsp tomato paste
- 5 garlic cloves, chopped
- 2 onions, cut into quarters
- 2 green bell peppers, cut into strips
- 2 red bell peppers, cut into strips
- 2 cups olives, pitted
- 1 lemon, peeled and sliced
- 2 tbsp olive oil
- Pepper
- Salt

Directions:
1. Add oil into the inner pot of instant pot and set the pot on sauté mode.
2. Add chicken and sauté for 5 minutes.
3. Add remaining ingredients and stir everything well.
4. Seal pot with a lid and select manual and set timer for 20 minutes.
5. Once done, release pressure using quick release. Remove lid.
6. Stir well and serve.

Nutritional Value (Amount per Serving):
Calories 446; Fat 21.2 g; Carbohydrates 18.5 g; Sugar 9.7 g; Protein 45.8 g; Cholesterol 135 mg

Flavorful Cafe Rio Chicken

Preparation Time: 10 minutes; Cooking Time: 12 minutes; Serve: 6
Ingredients:
- 2 lbs chicken breasts, skinless and boneless
- 1/2 cup chicken stock
- 2 1/2 tbsp ranch seasoning
- 1/2 tbsp ground cumin
- 1/2 tbsp chili powder
- 1/2 tbsp garlic, minced
- 2/3 cup Italian dressing
- Pepper
- Salt

Directions:
1. Add chicken into the instant pot.
2. Mix together remaining ingredients and pour over chicken.
3. Seal pot with a lid and select manual and set timer for 12 minutes.
4. Once done, allow to release pressure naturally for 10 minutes then release remaining using quick release. Remove lid.
5. Shred the chicken using a fork and serve.

Nutritional Value (Amount per Serving):
Calories 382; Fat 18.9 g; Carbohydrates 3.6 g; Sugar 2.3 g; Protein 44.1 g; Cholesterol 152 mg

Zesty Veggie Chicken

Preparation Time: 10 minutes; Cooking Time: 5 minutes; Serve: 4
Ingredients:
- 1 lb chicken tender, skinless, boneless and cut into chunks
- 10 oz of frozen vegetables
- 1/3 cup zesty Italian dressing
- 1/2 tsp Italian seasoning
- 1 cup fried onions
- 2/3 cup rice
- 1 cup chicken broth

- Pepper
- Salt

Directions:
1. Add all ingredients except vegetables into the instant pot.
2. Meanwhile, cook frozen vegetables in microwave according to packet instructions.
3. Seal pot with lid and cook on high for 5 minutes.
4. Once done, allow to release pressure naturally for 10 minutes then release remaining using quick release. Remove lid.
5. Add cooked vegetables and stir well.
6. Serve and enjoy.

Nutritional Value (Amount per Serving):
Calories 482; Fat 15.9 g; Carbohydrates 40.5 g; Sugar 2.6 g; Protein 38.3 g; Cholesterol 101 mg

Creamy Chicken Breasts

Preparation Time: 10 minutes; Cooking Time: 12 minutes; Serve: 4

Ingredients:
- 4 chicken breasts, skinless and boneless
- 1 tbsp basil pesto
- 1 1/2 tbsp cornstarch
- 1/4 cup roasted red peppers, chopped
- 1/3 cup heavy cream
- 1 tsp Italian seasoning
- 1 tsp garlic, minced
- 1 cup chicken broth
- Pepper
- Salt

Directions:
1. Add chicken into the instant pot. Season chicken with Italian seasoning, pepper, and salt. Sprinkle with garlic.
2. Pour broth over chicken. Seal pot with lid and cook on high for 8 minutes.
3. Once done, allow to release pressure naturally for 5 minutes then release remaining using quick release. Remove lid.
4. Transfer chicken on a plate and clean the instant pot.
5. Set instant pot on sauté mode. Add heavy cream, pesto, cornstarch, and red pepper to the pot and stir well and cook for 3-4 minutes.
6. Return chicken to the pot and coat well with the sauce.
7. Serve and enjoy.

Nutritional Value (Amount per Serving):
Calories 341; Fat 15.2 g; Carbohydrates 4.4 g; Sugar 0.8 g; Protein 43.8 g; Cholesterol 144 mg

Cheese Garlic Chicken & Potatoes

Preparation Time: 10 minutes; Cooking Time: 13 minutes; Serve: 4

Ingredients:
- 2 lbs chicken breasts, skinless, boneless, cut into chunks
- 1 tbsp olive oil
- 3/4 cup chicken broth
- 1 tbsp Italian seasoning
- 1 tbsp garlic powder
- 1 tsp garlic, minced
- 1 1/2 cup parmesan cheese, shredded
- 1 lb potatoes, chopped
- Pepper
- Salt

Directions:
1. Add oil into the inner pot of instant pot and set the pot on sauté mode.
2. Add chicken and cook until browned.
3. Add remaining ingredients except for cheese and stir well.
4. Seal pot with lid and cook on high for 8 minutes.
5. Once done, release pressure using quick release. Remove lid.

6. Top with cheese and cover with lid for 5 minutes or until cheese is melted.
7. Serve and enjoy.

Nutritional Value (Amount per Serving):
Calories 674; Fat 29 g; Carbohydrates 21.4 g; Sugar 2.3 g; Protein 79.7 g; Cholesterol 228 mg

Easy Chicken Scampi

Preparation Time: 10 minutes; Cooking Time: 25 minutes; Serve: 4

Ingredients:
- 3 chicken breasts, skinless, boneless, and sliced
- 1 tsp garlic, minced
- 1 tbsp Italian seasoning
- 2 cups chicken broth
- 1 bell pepper, sliced
- 1/2 onion, sliced
- Pepper
- Salt

Directions:
1. Add chicken into the instant pot and top with remaining ingredients.
2. Seal pot with lid and cook on high for 25 minutes.
3. Once done, release pressure using quick release. Remove lid.
4. Remove chicken from pot and shred using a fork. Return shredded chicken to the pot and stir well.
5. Serve over cooked whole grain pasta and top with cheese.

Nutritional Value (Amount per Serving):
Calories 254; Fat 9.9 g; Carbohydrates 4.6 g; Sugar 2.8 g; Protein 34.6 g; Cholesterol 100 mg

Protein Packed Chicken Bean Rice

Preparation Time: 10 minutes; Cooking Time: 15 minutes; Serve: 6

Ingredients:
- 1 lb chicken breasts, skinless, boneless, and cut into chunks
- 14 oz can cannellini beans, rinsed and drained
- 4 cups chicken broth
- 2 cups brown rice
- 1 tbsp Italian seasoning
- 1 small onion, chopped
- 1 tbsp garlic, chopped
- 1 tbsp olive oil
- Pepper
- Salt

Directions:
1. Add oil into the inner pot of instant pot and set the pot on sauté mode.
2. Add garlic and onion and sauté for 3 minutes.
3. Add remaining ingredients and stir everything well.
4. Seal pot with a lid and select manual and set timer for 12 minutes.
5. Once done, release pressure using quick release. Remove lid.
6. Stir well and serve.

Nutritional Value (Amount per Serving):
Calories 494; Fat 11.3 g; Carbohydrates 61.4 g; Sugar 1.7 g; Protein 34.2 g; Cholesterol 69 mg

Pesto Vegetable Chicken

Preparation Time: 10 minutes; Cooking Time: 25 minutes; Serve: 4

Ingredients:
- 1 1/2 lbs chicken thighs, skinless, boneless, and cut into pieces
- 1/2 cup chicken broth
- 1/4 cup fresh parsley, chopped
- 2 cups cherry tomatoes, halved
- 1 cup basil pesto
- 3/4 lb asparagus, trimmed and cut in half
- 2/3 cup sun-dried tomatoes, drained and chopped

- 2 tbsp olive oil
- Pepper
- Salt

Directions:
1. Add oil into the inner pot of instant pot and set the pot on sauté mode.
2. Add chicken and sauté for 5 minutes.
3. Add remaining ingredients except for tomatoes and stir well.
4. Seal pot with a lid and select manual and set timer for 15 minutes.
5. Once done, release pressure using quick release. Remove lid.
6. Add tomatoes and stir well. Again seal the pot and select manual and set timer for 5 minutes.
7. Release pressure using quick release. Remove lid.
8. Stir well and serve.

Nutritional Value (Amount per Serving):
Calories 459; Fat 20.5 g; Carbohydrates 14.9 g; Sugar 9.2 g; Protein 9.2 g; Cholesterol 151 mg

Greek Chicken Rice

Preparation Time: 10 minutes; Cooking Time: 14 minutes; Serve: 4

Ingredients:
- 3 chicken breasts, skinless, boneless, and cut into chunks
- 1/4 fresh parsley, chopped
- 1 zucchini, sliced
- 2 bell peppers, chopped
- 1 cup rice, rinsed and drained
- 1 1/2 cup chicken broth
- 1 tbsp oregano
- 3 tbsp fresh lemon juice
- 1 tbsp garlic, minced
- 1 onion, diced
- 2 tbsp olive oil
- Pepper
- Salt

Directions:
1. Add oil into the inner pot of instant pot and set the pot on sauté mode.
2. Add onion and chicken and cook for 5 minutes.
3. Add rice, oregano, lemon juice, garlic, broth, pepper, and salt and stir everything well.
4. Seal pot with lid and cook on high for 4 minutes.
5. Once done, release pressure using quick release. Remove lid.
6. Add parsley, zucchini, and bell peppers and stir well.
7. Seal pot again with lid and select manual and set timer for 5 minutes.
8. Release pressure using quick release. Remove lid.
9. Stir well and serve.

Nutritional Value (Amount per Serving):
Calories 500; Fat 16.5 g; Carbohydrates 48 g; Sugar 5.7 g; Protein 38.7 g; Cholesterol 97 mg

Flavorful Chicken Tacos

Preparation Time: 10 minutes; Cooking Time: 10 minutes; Serve: 3

Ingredients:
- 2 chicken breasts, skinless and boneless
- 1 tbsp chili powder
- 1/2 tsp ground cumin
- 1/2 tsp garlic powder
- 1/4 tsp onion powder
- 1/2 tsp paprika
- 4 oz can green chilis, diced
- 1/4 cup chicken broth
- 14 oz can tomatoes, diced
- Pepper
- Salt

Directions:
1. Add all ingredients except chicken into the instant pot and stir well.
2. Add chicken and stir. Seal pot with lid and cook on high for 10 minutes.

3. Once done, allow to release pressure naturally for 5 minutes then release remaining using quick release. Remove lid.
4. Remove chicken from pot and shred using a fork.
5. Return shredded chicken to the pot and stir well.
6. Serve and enjoy.

Nutritional Value (Amount per Serving):
Calories 237; Fat 8 g; Carbohydrates 10.8 g; Sugar 5 g; Protein 30.5 g; Cholesterol 87 mg

Quinoa Chicken Bowls

Preparation Time: 10 minutes; Cooking Time: 6 minutes; Serve: 4

Ingredients:
- 1 lb chicken breasts, skinless, boneless, and cut into chunks
- 14 oz can chickpeas, drained and rinsed
- 1 cup olives, pitted and sliced
- 1 cup cherry tomatoes, halved
- 1 cucumber, sliced
- 2 tsp Greek seasoning
- 1 1/2 cups chicken broth
- 1 cup quinoa, rinsed and drained
- Pepper
- Salt

Directions:
1. Add broth and quinoa into the instant pot and stir well.
2. Season chicken with greek seasoning, pepper, and salt and place into the instant pot.
3. Seal pot with lid and cook on high for 6 minutes.
4. Once done, release pressure using quick release. Remove lid.
5. Stir quinoa and chicken mixture well.
6. Add remaining ingredients and stir everything well.
7. Serve immediately and enjoy it.

Nutritional Value (Amount per Serving):
Calories 566; Fat 16.4 g; Carbohydrates 57.4 g; Sugar 2.7 g; Protein 46.8 g; Cholesterol 101 mg

Quick Chicken with Mushrooms

Preparation Time: 10 minutes; Cooking Time: 22 minutes; Serve: 6

Ingredients:
- 2 lbs chicken breasts, skinless and boneless
- 1/2 cup heavy cream
- 1/3 cup water
- 3/4 lb mushrooms, sliced
- 3 tbsp olive oil
- 1 tsp Italian seasoning
- Pepper
- Salt

Directions:
1. Add oil into the inner pot of instant pot and set the pot on sauté mode.
2. Season chicken with Italian seasoning, pepper, and salt.
3. Add chicken to the pot and sauté for 5 minutes. Remove chicken from pot and set aside.
4. Add mushrooms and sauté for 5 minutes or until mushrooms are lightly brown.
5. Return chicken to the pot. Add water and stir well.
6. Seal pot with a lid and select manual and set timer for 12 minutes.
7. Once done, release pressure using quick release. Remove lid.
8. Remove chicken from pot and place on a plate.
9. Set pot on sauté mode. Add heavy cream and stir well and cook for 5 minutes.
10. Pour mushroom sauce over chicken and serve.

Nutritional Value (Amount per Serving):
Calories 396; Fat 22.3 g; Carbohydrates 2.2 g; Sugar 1.1 g; Protein 45.7 g; Cholesterol 149 mg

Herb Garlic Chicken

Preparation Time: 10 minutes; Cooking Time: 12 minutes; Serve: 8
Ingredients:
- 4 lbs chicken breasts, skinless and boneless
- 1 tbsp garlic powder
- 2 tbsp dried Italian herb mix
- 2 tbsp olive oil
- 1/4 cup chicken stock
- Pepper
- Salt

Directions:
1. Coat chicken with oil and season with dried herb, garlic powder, pepper, and salt.
2. Place chicken into the instant pot. Pour stock over the chicken.
3. Seal pot with a lid and select manual and set timer for 12 minutes.
4. Once done, allow to release pressure naturally for 5 minutes then release remaining using quick release. Remove lid.
5. Shred chicken using a fork and serve.

Nutritional Value (Amount per Serving):
Calories 502; Fat 20.8 g; Carbohydrates 7.8 g; Sugar 1 g; Protein 66.8 g; Cholesterol 202 mg

Delicious Chicken Cacciatore

Preparation Time: 10 minutes; Cooking Time: 18 minutes; Serve: 6
Ingredients:
- 6 chicken thighs, skinless and boneless
- 1 tbsp fresh parsley, chopped
- 1 tbsp fresh basil, chopped
- 1/4 cup olives, pitted
- 1/2 tsp dried oregano
- 1/4 tsp dried thyme
- 1 1/2 tbsp garlic, minced
- 1 carrot, sliced
- 1 bell pepper, chopped
- 2 tbsp tomato paste
- 28 oz fire-roasted tomatoes, crushed
- 1/2 onion, chopped
- 1 tbsp olive oil
- Pepper
- Salt

Directions:
1. Add oil into the inner pot of instant pot and set the pot on sauté mode.
2. Add onion and sauté for 3 minutes.
3. Add chicken and sauté for 3-5 minutes.
4. Add remaining ingredients except for olives, parsley, and basil and stir well.
5. Seal pot with lid and cook on high for 10 minutes.
6. Once done, allow to release pressure naturally. Remove lid.
7. Add olives, parsley, and basil and stir well.
8. Serve and enjoy.

Nutritional Value (Amount per Serving):
Calories 375; Fat 13.9 g; Carbohydrates 15.2 g; Sugar 8.4 g; Protein 43.1 g; Cholesterol 130 mg

Pesto Chicken

Preparation Time: 10 minutes; Cooking Time: 5 minutes; Serve: 4
Ingredients:
- 1 lb chicken thighs, skinless and boneless
- 1/4 cup water
- 1 tsp Italian seasoning
- 2 tbsp basil pesto
- 1/4 cup heavy cream
- 1 tbsp garlic, minced
- 1 cup tomatoes, chopped
- 1 cup onion, diced
- Pepper
- Salt

Directions:

1. Add all ingredients except heavy cream into the instant pot and stir well.
2. Seal pot with lid and cook on high for 5 minutes.
3. Once done, allow to release pressure naturally for 10 minutes then release remaining using quick release. Remove lid.
4. Remove chicken from pot.
5. Add heavy cream into the pot and stir well. Using immersion blender blend pot mixture until smooth and creamy.
6. Pour sauce over chicken and serve.

Nutritional Value (Amount per Serving):
Calories 268; Fat 11.7 g; Carbohydrates 5.5 g; Sugar 2.5 g; Protein 33.9 g; Cholesterol 112 mg

One Pot Chicken & Potatoes

Preparation Time: 10 minutes; Cooking Time: 13 minutes; Serve: 6
Ingredients:
- 6 chicken thighs, bone-in, and skin-on
- 1 tsp oregano
- 1 lb potatoes, halved
- 2 tbsp honey
- 1 fresh lemon juice
- 1 tsp garlic, minced
- 1 cup chicken stock
- 1 tsp paprika
- 1/2 tsp allspice
- 2 tbsp olive oil
- Pepper
- Salt

Directions:
1. In a small bowl, mix together 1 tablespoon oil, allspice, paprika, pepper, and salt and rub over chicken.
2. Add remaining oil into the instant pot and set the pot on sauté mode.
3. Add chicken to the pot and sauté until brown, about 5 minutes.
4. Add remaining ingredients and stir everything well.
5. Seal pot with lid and cook on high for 8 minutes.
6. Once done, allow to release pressure naturally for 5 minutes then release remaining using quick release. Remove lid.
7. Stir well and serve.

Nutritional Value (Amount per Serving):
Calories 397; Fat 15.8 g; Carbohydrates 18.6 g; Sugar 7 g; Protein 43.8 g; Cholesterol 130 mg

Lemon Olive Chicken

Preparation Time: 10 minutes; Cooking Time: 11 minutes; Serve: 8
Ingredients:
- 2 lbs chicken breasts, skinless and boneless
- 4 oz olives, pitted
- 2 lemons, quartered and remove seeds
- 1 cinnamon stick
- 1 tsp turmeric powder
- 1 tsp ground coriander
- 1 tsp ground ginger
- 1 tsp ground cumin
- 1 1/2 tsp paprika
- 1/2 cup chicken broth
- 1 tbsp garlic, minced
- 1 tbsp olive oil
- 2 onions, sliced
- Pepper
- Salt

Directions:
1. Add chicken, lemon, cinnamon, turmeric, coriander, ginger, cumin, paprika, pepper, and salt into the zip-lock bag. Seal bag shake well and place in refrigerator overnight.
2. Add oil into the inner pot of instant pot and set the pot on sauté mode.
3. Add garlic and onion and sauté for 5 minutes.
4. Add marinated chicken, broth, and olives and stir well.

5. Seal pot with lid and cook on high for 6 minutes.
6. Once done, allow to release pressure naturally for 10 minutes then release remaining using quick release. Remove lid.
7. Stir and serve.

Nutritional Value (Amount per Serving):
Calories 271; Fat 12 g; Carbohydrates 6.1 g; Sugar 1.7 g; Protein 33.9 g; Cholesterol 101 mg

Shredded Greek Chicken

Preparation Time: 10 minutes; Cooking Time: 9 minutes; Serve: 4
Ingredients:
- 1 1/2 lbs chicken breasts, skinless and boneless
- 12 oz jar marinated artichoke hearts, drained and chopped
- 12 oz jar roasted red peppers, drained and chopped
- 1 cup chicken broth
- 1/2 lemon juice
- 1/2 tsp dill
- 1/2 tbsp basil
- 1 tbsp oregano
- 1 tbsp garlic, minced
- 1 onion, diced
- 1 tbsp olive oil
- Pepper
- Salt

Directions:
1. Add oil into the inner pot of instant pot and set the pot on sauté mode.
2. Add garlic and onion and sauté for 2-3 minutes.
3. Add chicken, lemon juice, broth, and all seasonings. Stir well.
4. Seal pot with lid and cook on high for 6 minutes.
5. Once done, allow to release pressure naturally for 5 minutes then release remaining using quick release. Remove lid.
6. Remove chicken from pot and shred using a fork.
7. Return shredded chicken to the pot along with roasted peppers and artichoke and stir well.
8. Serve over rice.

Nutritional Value (Amount per Serving):
Calories 543; Fat 29.5 g; Carbohydrates 14.7 g; Sugar 5.4 g; Protein 53.4 g; Cholesterol 151 mg

Creamy Greek Chicken

Preparation Time: 10 minutes; Cooking Time: 12 minutes; Serve: 8
Ingredients:
- 2 lbs chicken breasts, skinless and boneless
- 8 oz cream cheese
- 1/4 cup fresh lemon juice
- 1/8 tsp nutmeg
- 1/8 tsp cinnamon
- 1/4 tsp rosemary
- 1/4 tsp parsley
- 1/4 tsp dill
- 1/2 tsp garlic powder
- 1/2 tsp onion powder
- 1/8 tsp thyme
- 1/2 tsp oregano
- 1/4 tsp basil
- 1 cup chicken broth
- 1 onion, diced
- Pepper
- Salt

Directions:
1. Add all ingredients except cream cheese and lemon juice into the instant pot and stir well.
2. Seal pot with lid and cook on high for 12 minutes.
3. Once done, allow to release pressure naturally for 10 minutes then release remaining using quick release. Remove lid.
4. Remove chicken from pot and shred using a fork. Return shredded chicken to the pot.

5. Set pot on sauté mode. Add lemon juice and cream cheese and stir well and cook until cheese is melted.
6. Serve and enjoy.

Nutritional Value (Amount per Serving):
Calories 329; Fat 18.6 g; Carbohydrates 2.7 g; Sugar 1 g; Protein 35.8 g; Cholesterol 132 mg

Delicious Gyro Chicken

Preparation Time: 10 minutes; Cooking Time: 12 minutes; Serve: 3

Ingredients:
- 1 lb chicken thighs
- 1 cup chicken broth
- 1 tsp garlic, minced
- 1 tbsp fresh lemon juice
- 1 tbsp olive oil
- 2 tbsp fresh cilantro, chopped
- 1 tbsp green onion, chopped
- 1/2 tsp oregano
- 1/2 tsp cumin powder
- 1/2 tsp ground cinnamon
- 1/2 tsp paprika
- 1/2 tsp Adobo seasoning
- 1 onion, sliced
- Pepper
- Salt

Directions:
1. Season chicken with oregano, cinnamon, cumin, paprika, adobo seasoning, pepper, and salt and place into the instant pot.
2. Pour remaining ingredients over chicken.
3. Seal pot with lid and cook on high for 12 minutes.
4. Once done, release pressure using quick release. Remove lid.
5. Stir well and serve.

Nutritional Value (Amount per Serving):
Calories 362; Fat 16.6 g; Carbohydrates 5.2 g; Sugar 2 g; Protein 46.1 g; Cholesterol 135 mg

Moroccan Spiced Chicken

Preparation Time: 10 minutes; Cooking Time: 20 minutes; Serve: 4

Ingredients:
- 1 lb chicken thighs, boneless and cut into chunks
- 1 cup can tomato, crushed
- 1/2 tsp red pepper flakes
- 1 tsp dried parsley
- 1/2 tsp coriander
- 1 tsp cumin
- 14 oz can chickpeas, drained and rinsed
- 2 tomatoes, chopped
- 1 tbsp garlic, minced
- 1 onion, sliced
- 2 red peppers, diced
- 1 tbsp olive oil
- Pepper
- Salt

Directions:
1. Add oil into the inner pot of instant pot and set the pot on sauté mode.
2. Add onion and garlic and sauté for 5 minutes.
3. Add chicken and cook for 5 minutes.
4. Add remaining ingredients and stir well.
5. Seal pot with lid and cook on high for 10 minutes.
6. Once done, release pressure using quick release. Remove lid.
7. Stir well and serve.

Nutritional Value (Amount per Serving):
Calories 416; Fat 21.3 g; Carbohydrates 32.3 g; Sugar 4 g; Protein 26.1 g; Cholesterol 96 mg

Moist & Tender Turkey Breast

Preparation Time: 10 minutes; Cooking Time: 25 minutes; Serve: 8
Ingredients:
- 4 lbs turkey breast, bone-in
- 1 tsp Italian seasoning
- 2 tbsp olive oil
- 14 oz chicken broth
- 1 celery ribs, chopped
- 1 large onion, cut into wedges
- 3/4 lbs carrots, cut into pieces
- Pepper
- Salt

Directions:
1. Add carrots, celery, onion, and broth into the instant pot and stir well.
2. Coat turkey breast with oil and season with Italian seasoning, pepper, and salt and place on top of vegetables into the instant pot.
3. Seal pot with lid and cook on high for 25 minutes.
4. Once done, allow to release pressure naturally for 10 minutes then release remaining using quick release. Remove lid.
5. Slice and serve.

Nutritional Value (Amount per Serving):
Calories 301; Fat 7.7 g; Carbohydrates 15.9 g; Sugar 11.1 g; Protein 40.3 g; Cholesterol 98 mg

Tasty Turkey Chili

Preparation Time: 10 minutes; Cooking Time: 25 minutes; Serve: 4
Ingredients:
- 1 lb cooked turkey, shredded
- 2 cups chicken broth
- 1 tsp tomato paste
- 1 small onion, chopped
- 1 tbsp Italian seasoning
- 1 tsp garlic powder
- 1 tbsp cumin, roasted
- 1 tbsp chili powder
- 2 cups tomatoes, crushed
- 1 tsp garlic, minced
- 14 oz can red beans, drained
- 14 oz can chickpeas, drained
- 1/2 cup corn
- 2 carrots, peeled and chopped
- 1/2 cup celery, chopped
- 1/4 cup edamame
- 2 tbsp olive oil
- Pepper
- Salt

Directions:
1. Add all ingredients into the instant pot and stir everything well.
2. Seal pot with lid and cook on high for 15 minutes.
3. Once done, allow to release pressure naturally. Remove lid.
4. Set pot on sauté mode and cook for 5-10 minutes or until chili thicken.
5. Stir well and serve.

Nutritional Value (Amount per Serving):
Calories 593; Fat 18.1 g; Carbohydrates 56 g; Sugar 7.3 g; Protein 50.9 g; Cholesterol 88 mg

Chapter 9: Beef

Moist Shredded Beef

Preparation Time: 10 minutes; Cooking Time: 20 minutes; Serve: 8

Ingredients:
- 2 lbs beef chuck roast, cut into chunks
- 1/2 tbsp dried red pepper
- 1 tbsp Italian seasoning
- 1 tbsp garlic, minced
- 2 tbsp vinegar
- 14 oz can fire-roasted tomatoes
- 1/2 cup bell pepper, chopped
- 1/2 cup carrots, chopped
- 1 cup onion, chopped
- 1 tsp salt

Directions:
1. Add all ingredients into the inner pot of instant pot and set the pot on sauté mode.
2. Seal pot with lid and cook on high for 20 minutes.
3. Once done, release pressure using quick release. Remove lid.
4. Shred the meat using a fork.
5. Stir well and serve.

Nutritional Value (Amount per Serving):
Calories 456; Fat 32.7 g; Carbohydrates 7.7 g; Sugar 4.1 g; Protein 31 g; Cholesterol 118 mg

Hearty Beef Ragu

Preparation Time: 10 minutes; Cooking Time: 50 minutes; Serve: 4

Ingredients:
- 1 1/2 lbs beef steak, diced
- 1 1/2 cup beef stock
- 1 tbsp coconut amino
- 14 oz can tomatoes, chopped
- 1/2 tsp ground cinnamon
- 1 tsp dried oregano
- 1 tsp dried thyme
- 1 tsp dried basil
- 1 tsp paprika
- 1 bay leaf
- 1 tbsp garlic, chopped
- 1/2 tsp cayenne pepper
- 1 celery stick, diced
- 1 carrot, diced
- 1 onion, diced
- 2 tbsp olive oil
- 1/4 tsp pepper
- 1 1/2 tsp sea salt

Directions:
1. Add oil into the instant pot and set the pot on sauté mode.
2. Add celery, carrots, onion, and salt and sauté for 5 minutes.
3. Add meat and remaining ingredients and stir everything well.
4. Seal pot with lid and cook on high for 30 minutes.
5. Once done, allow to release pressure naturally for 10 minutes then release remaining using quick release. Remove lid.
6. Shred meat using a fork. Set pot on sauté mode and cook for 10 minutes. Stir every 2-3 minutes.
7. Serve and enjoy.

Nutritional Value (Amount per Serving):
Calories 435; Fat 18.1 g; Carbohydrates 12.3 g; Sugar 5.5 g; Protein 54.4 g; Cholesterol 152 mg

Dill Beef Brisket

Preparation Time: 10 minutes; Cooking Time: 50 minutes; Serve: 4

Ingredients:
- 2 1/2 lbs beef brisket, cut into cubes
- 2 1/2 cups beef stock
- 2 tbsp dill, chopped
- 1 celery stalk, chopped
- 1 onion, sliced
- 1 tbsp garlic, minced

- Pepper
- Salt

Directions:
1. Add all ingredients into the inner pot of instant pot and stir well.
2. Seal pot with lid and cook on high for 50 minutes.
3. Once done, allow to release pressure naturally for 10 minutes then release remaining using quick release. Remove lid.
4. Serve and enjoy.

Nutritional Value (Amount per Serving):
Calories 556; Fat 18.1 g; Carbohydrates 4.3 g; Sugar 1.3 g; Protein 88.5 g; Cholesterol 253 mg

Tasty Beef Stew

Preparation Time: 10 minutes; Cooking Time: 30 minutes; Serve: 4
Ingredients:
- 2 1/2 lbs beef roast, cut into chunks
- 1 cup beef broth
- 1/2 cup balsamic vinegar
- 1 tbsp honey
- 1/2 tsp red pepper flakes
- 1 tbsp garlic, minced
- Pepper
- Salt

Directions:
1. Add all ingredients into the inner pot of instant pot and stir well.
2. Seal pot with lid and cook on high for 30 minutes.
3. Once done, allow to release pressure naturally. Remove lid.
4. Stir well and serve.

Nutritional Value (Amount per Serving):
Calories 562; Fat 18.1 g; Carbohydrates 5.7 g; Sugar 4.6 g; Protein 87.4 g; Cholesterol 253 mg

Meatloaf

Preparation Time: 10 minutes; Cooking Time: 35 minutes; Serve: 6
Ingredients:
- 2 lbs ground beef
- 2 eggs, lightly beaten
- 1/4 tsp dried basil
- 3 tbsp olive oil
- 1/2 tsp dried sage
- 1 1/2 tsp dried parsley
- 1 tsp oregano
- 2 tsp thyme
- 1 tsp rosemary
- Pepper
- Salt

Directions:
1. Pour 1 1/2 cups of water into the instant pot then place the trivet in the pot.
2. Spray loaf pan with cooking spray.
3. Add all ingredients into the mixing bowl and mix until well combined.
4. Transfer meat mixture into the prepared loaf pan and place loaf pan on top of the trivet in the pot.
5. Seal pot with lid and cook on high for 35 minutes.
6. Once done, allow to release pressure naturally for 10 minutes then release remaining using quick release. Remove lid.
7. Serve and enjoy.

Nutritional Value (Amount per Serving):
Calories 365; Fat 18 g; Carbohydrates 0.7 g; Sugar 0.1 g; Protein 47.8 g; Cholesterol 190 mg

Flavorful Beef Bourguignon

Preparation Time: 10 minutes; Cooking Time: 20 minutes; Serve: 4
Ingredients:

- 1 1/2 lbs beef chuck roast, cut into chunks
- 2/3 cup beef stock
- 2 tbsp fresh thyme
- 1 bay leaf
- 1 tsp garlic, minced
- 8 oz mushrooms, sliced
- 2 tbsp tomato paste
- 2/3 cup dry red wine
- 1 onion, sliced
- 4 carrots, cut into chunks
- 1 tbsp olive oil
- Pepper
- Salt

Directions:
1. Add oil into the instant pot and set the pot on sauté mode.
2. Add meat and sauté until brown. Add onion and sauté until softened.
3. Add remaining ingredients and stir well.
4. Seal pot with lid and cook on high for 12 minutes.
5. Once done, allow to release pressure naturally. Remove lid.
6. Stir well and serve.

Nutritional Value (Amount per Serving):
Calories 744; Fat 51.3 g; Carbohydrates 14.5 g; Sugar 6.5 g; Protein 48.1 g; Cholesterol 175 mg

Delicious Beef Chili

Preparation Time: 10 minutes; Cooking Time: 35 minutes; Serve: 8
Ingredients:
- 2 lbs ground beef
- 1 tsp olive oil
- 1 tsp garlic, minced
- 1 small onion, chopped
- 2 tbsp chili powder
- 1 tsp oregano
- 1/2 tsp thyme
- 28 oz can tomatoes, crushed
- 2 cups beef stock
- 2 carrots, chopped
- 3 sweet potatoes, peeled and cubed
- Pepper
- Salt

Directions:
1. Add oil into the instant pot and set the pot on sauté mode.
2. Add meat and cook until brown.
3. Add remaining ingredients and stir well.
4. Seal pot with lid and cook on high for 35 minutes.
5. Once done, allow to release pressure naturally. Remove lid.
6. Stir well and serve.

Nutritional Value (Amount per Serving):
Calories 302; Fat 8.2 g; Carbohydrates 19.2 g; Sugar 4.8 g; Protein 37.1 g; Cholesterol 101 mg

Rosemary Creamy Beef

Preparation Time: 10 minutes; Cooking Time: 40 minutes; Serve: 4
Ingredients:
- 2 lbs beef stew meat, cubed
- 2 tbsp fresh parsley, chopped
- 1 tsp garlic, minced
- 1/2 tsp dried rosemary
- 1 tsp chili powder
- 1 cup beef stock
- 1 cup heavy cream
- 1 onion, chopped
- 1 tbsp olive oil
- Pepper
- Salt

Directions:
1. Add oil into the instant pot and set the pot on sauté mode.
2. Add rosemary, garlic, onion, and chili powder and sauté for 5 minutes.
3. Add meat and cook for 5 minutes.

4. Add remaining ingredients and stir well.
5. Seal pot with lid and cook on high for 30 minutes.
6. Once done, allow to release pressure naturally for 10 minutes then release remaining using quick release. Remove lid.
7. Serve and enjoy.

Nutritional Value (Amount per Serving):
Calories 574; Fat 29 g; Carbohydrates 4.3 g; Sugar 1.3 g; Protein 70.6 g; Cholesterol 244 mg

Spicy Beef Chili Verde

Preparation Time: 10 minutes; Cooking Time: 23 minutes; Serve: 2
Ingredients:
- 1/2 lb beef stew meat, cut into cubes
- 1/4 tsp chili powder
- 1 tbsp olive oil
- 1 cup chicken broth
- 1 Serrano pepper, chopped
- 1 tsp garlic, minced
- 1 small onion, chopped
- 1/4 cup grape tomatoes, chopped
- 1/4 cup tomatillos, chopped
- Pepper
- Salt

Directions:
1. Add oil into the instant pot and set the pot on sauté mode.
2. Add garlic and onion and sauté for 3 minutes.
3. Add remaining ingredients and stir well.
4. Seal pot with lid and cook on high for 20 minutes.
5. Once done, allow to release pressure naturally. Remove lid.
6. Stir well and serve.

Nutritional Value (Amount per Serving):
Calories 317; Fat 15.1 g; Carbohydrates 6.4 g; Sugar 2.6 g; Protein 37.8 g; Cholesterol 101 mg

Carrot Mushroom Beef Roast

Preparation Time: 10 minutes; Cooking Time: 40 minutes; Serve: 4
Ingredients:
- 1 1/2 lbs beef roast
- 1 tsp paprika
- 1/4 tsp dried rosemary
- 1 tsp garlic, minced
- 1/2 lb mushrooms, sliced
- 1/2 cup chicken stock
- 2 carrots, sliced
- Pepper
- Salt

Directions:
1. Add all ingredients into the inner pot of instant pot and stir well.
2. Seal pot with lid and cook on high for 40 minutes.
3. Once done, allow to release pressure naturally for 10 minutes then release remaining using quick release. Remove lid.
4. Slice and serve.

Nutritional Value (Amount per Serving):
Calories 345; Fat 10.9 g; Carbohydrates 5.6 g; Sugar 2.6 g; Protein 53.8 g; Cholesterol 152 mg

Italian Beef Roast

Preparation Time: 10 minutes; Cooking Time: 50 minutes; Serve: 6
Ingredients:
- 2 1/2 lbs beef roast, cut into chunks
- 1 cup chicken broth
- 1 cup red wine
- 2 tbsp Italian seasoning
- 2 tbsp olive oil
- 1 bell pepper, chopped

- 2 celery stalks, chopped
- 1 tsp garlic, minced
- 1 onion, sliced
- Pepper
- Salt

Directions:
1. Add oil into the instant pot and set the pot on sauté mode.
2. Add the meat into the pot and sauté until brown.
3. Add onion, bell pepper, and celery and sauté for 5 minutes.
4. Add remaining ingredients and stir well.
5. Seal pot with lid and cook on high for 40 minutes.
6. Once done, allow to release pressure naturally. Remove lid.
7. Stir well and serve.

Nutritional Value (Amount per Serving):
Calories 460; Fat 18.2 g; Carbohydrates 5.3 g; Sugar 2.7 g; Protein 58.7 g; Cholesterol 172 mg

Thyme Beef Round Roast

Preparation Time: 10 minutes; Cooking Time: 55 minutes; Serve: 8

Ingredients:
- 4 lbs beef bottom round roast, cut into pieces
- 2 tbsp honey
- 5 fresh thyme sprigs
- 2 cups red wine
- 1 lb carrots, cut into chunks
- 2 cups chicken broth
- 6 garlic cloves, smashed
- 1 onion, diced
- 1/4 cup olive oil
- 2 lbs potatoes, peeled and cut into chunks
- Pepper
- Salt

Directions:
1. Add all ingredients except carrots and potatoes into the instant pot.
2. Seal pot with lid and cook on high for 45 minutes.
3. Once done, release pressure using quick release. Remove lid.
4. Add carrots and potatoes and stir well.
5. Seal pot again with lid and cook on high for 10 minutes.
6. Once done, allow to release pressure naturally. Remove lid.
7. Stir well and serve.

Nutritional Value (Amount per Serving):
Calories 648; Fat 21.7 g; Carbohydrates 33.3 g; Sugar 9.7 g; Protein 67.1 g; Cholesterol 200 mg

Jalapeno Beef Chili

Preparation Time: 10 minutes; Cooking Time: 40 minutes; Serve: 8

Ingredients:
- 1 lb ground beef
- 1 tsp garlic powder
- 1 jalapeno pepper, chopped
- 1 tbsp ground cumin
- 1 tbsp chili powder
- 1 lb ground pork
- 4 tomatillos, chopped
- 1/2 onion, chopped
- 5 oz tomato paste
- Pepper
- Salt

Directions:
1. Add oil into the instant pot and set the pot on sauté mode.
2. Add beef and pork and cook until brown.
3. Add remaining ingredients and stir well.
4. Seal pot with lid and cook on high for 35 minutes.
5. Once done, allow to release pressure naturally. Remove lid.

6. Stir well and serve.

Nutritional Value (Amount per Serving):
Calories 217; Fat 6.1 g; Carbohydrates 6.2 g; Sugar 2.7 g; Protein 33.4 g; Cholesterol 92 mg

Beef with Tomatoes

Preparation Time: 10 minutes; Cooking Time: 40 minutes; Serve: 4

Ingredients:
- 2 lb beef roast, sliced
- 1 tbsp chives, chopped
- 1 tsp garlic, minced
- 1/2 tsp chili powder
- 2 tbsp olive oil
- 1 onion, chopped
- 1 cup beef stock
- 1 tbsp oregano, chopped
- 1 cup tomatoes, chopped
- Pepper
- Salt

Directions:
1. Add oil into the instant pot and set the pot on sauté mode.
2. Add garlic, onion, and chili powder and sauté for 5 minutes.
3. Add meat and cook for 5 minutes.
4. Add remaining ingredients and stir well.
5. Seal pot with lid and cook on high for 30 minutes.
6. Once done, allow to release pressure naturally for 10 minutes then release remaining using quick release. Remove lid.
7. Stir well and serve.

Nutritional Value (Amount per Serving):
Calories 511; Fat 21.6 g; Carbohydrates 5.6 g; Sugar 2.5 g; Protein 70.4 g; Cholesterol 203 mg

Tasty Beef Goulash

Preparation Time: 10 minutes; Cooking Time: 30 minutes; Serve: 2

Ingredients:
- 1/2 lb beef stew meat, cubed
- 1 tbsp olive oil
- 1/2 onion, chopped
- 1/2 cup sun-dried tomatoes, chopped
- 1/4 zucchini, chopped
- 1/2 cabbage, sliced
- 1 1/2 tbsp olive oil
- 2 cups chicken broth
- Pepper
- Salt

Directions:
1. Add oil into the instant pot and set the pot on sauté mode.
2. Add onion and sauté for 3-5 minutes.
3. Add tomatoes and cook for 5 minutes.
4. Add remaining ingredients and stir well.
5. Seal pot with lid and cook on high for 20 minutes.
6. Once done, allow to release pressure naturally for 10 minutes then release remaining using quick release. Remove lid.
7. Stir well and serve.

Nutritional Value (Amount per Serving):
Calories 389; Fat 15.8 g; Carbohydrates 19.3 g; Sugar 10.7 g; Protein 43.2 g; Cholesterol 101 mg

Beef & Beans

Preparation Time: 10 minutes; Cooking Time: 30 minutes; Serve: 4

Ingredients:
- 1 1/2 lbs beef, cubed
- 8 oz can tomatoes, chopped
- 8 oz red beans, soaked overnight and rinsed

- 1 tsp garlic, minced
- 1 1/2 cups beef stock
- 1/2 tsp chili powder
- 1 tbsp paprika
- 2 tbsp olive oil
- 1 onion, chopped
- Pepper
- Salt

Directions:
1. Add oil into the instant pot and set the pot on sauté mode.
2. Add meat and cook for 5 minutes.
3. Add garlic and onion and sauté for 5 minutes.
4. Add remaining ingredients and stir well.
5. Seal pot with lid and cook on high for 25 minutes.
6. Once done, allow to release pressure naturally. Remove lid.
7. Stir well and serve.

Nutritional Value (Amount per Serving):
Calories 604; Fat 18.7 g; Carbohydrates 41.6 g; Sugar 4.5 g; Protein 66.6 g; Cholesterol 152 mg

Delicious Ground Beef

Preparation Time: 10 minutes; Cooking Time: 10 minutes; Serve: 4

Ingredients:
- 1 lb ground beef
- 1 tbsp olive oil
- 2 tbsp tomato paste
- 1 cup chicken broth
- 12 oz cheddar cheese, shredded
- 1 tbsp Italian seasoning
- Pepper
- Salt

Directions:
1. Add oil into the instant pot and set the pot on sauté mode.
2. Add meat and cook until browned.
3. Add remaining ingredients except for cheese and stir well.
4. Seal pot with lid and cook on high for 7 minutes.
5. Once done, release pressure using quick release. Remove lid.
6. Add cheese and stir well and cook on sauté mode until cheese is melted.
7. Serve and enjoy.

Nutritional Value (Amount per Serving):
Calories 610; Fat 40.2 g; Carbohydrates 3.2 g; Sugar 1.9 g; Protein 57.2 g; Cholesterol 193 mg

Bean Beef Chili

Preparation Time: 10 minutes; Cooking Time: 40 minutes; Serve: 4

Ingredients:
- 1 lb ground beef
- 1/2 onion, diced
- 1/2 jalapeno pepper, minced
- 1 tsp chili powder
- 1/2 bell pepper, chopped
- 1 tsp garlic, chopped
- 1 cup chicken broth
- 14 oz can black beans, rinsed and drained
- 14 oz can red beans, rinsed and drained
- Pepper
- Salt

Directions:
1. Set instant pot on sauté mode.
2. Add meat and sauté until brown.
3. Add remaining ingredients and stir well.
4. Seal pot with lid and cook on high for 35 minutes.
5. Once done, release pressure using quick release. Remove lid.
6. Stir well and serve.

Nutritional Value (Amount per Serving):
Calories 409; Fat 8.3 g; Carbohydrates 36.3 g; Sugar 4.2 g; Protein 46.6 g; Cholesterol 101 mg

Garlic Caper Beef Roast

Preparation Time: 10 minutes; Cooking Time: 40 minutes; Serve: 4
Ingredients:
- 2 lbs beef roast, cubed
- 1 tbsp fresh parsley, chopped
- 1 tbsp capers, chopped
- 1 tbsp garlic, minced
- 1 cup chicken stock
- 1/2 tsp dried rosemary
- 1/2 tsp ground cumin
- 1 onion, chopped
- 1 tbsp olive oil
- Pepper
- Salt

Directions:
1. Add oil into the instant pot and set the pot on sauté mode.
2. Add garlic and onion and sauté for 5 minutes.
3. Add meat and cook until brown.
4. Add remaining ingredients and stir well.
5. Seal pot with lid and cook on high for 30 minutes.
6. Once done, allow to release pressure naturally. Remove lid.
7. Stir well and serve.

Nutritional Value (Amount per Serving):
Calories 470; Fat 17.9 g; Carbohydrates 3.9 g; Sugar 1.4 g; Protein 69.5 g; Cholesterol 203 mg

Cauliflower Tomato Beef

Preparation Time: 10 minutes; Cooking Time: 25 minutes; Serve: 2
Ingredients:
- 1/2 lb beef stew meat, chopped
- 1 tsp paprika
- 1 tbsp balsamic vinegar
- 1 celery stalk, chopped
- 1/4 cup grape tomatoes, chopped
- 1 onion, chopped
- 1 tbsp olive oil
- 1/4 cup cauliflower, chopped
- Pepper
- Salt

Directions:
1. Add oil into the instant pot and set the pot on sauté mode.
2. Add meat and sauté for 5 minutes.
3. Add remaining ingredients and stir well.
4. Seal pot with lid and cook on high for 20 minutes.
5. Once done, allow to release pressure naturally. Remove lid.
6. Stir and serve.

Nutritional Value (Amount per Serving):
Calories 306; Fat 14.3 g; Carbohydrates 7.6 g; Sugar 3.5 g; Protein 35.7 g; Cholesterol 101 mg

Artichoke Beef Roast

Preparation Time: 10 minutes; Cooking Time: 45 minutes; Serve: 6
Ingredients:
- 2 lbs beef roast, cubed
- 1 tbsp garlic, minced
- 1 onion, chopped
- 1/2 tsp paprika
- 1 tbsp parsley, chopped
- 2 tomatoes, chopped
- 1 tbsp capers, chopped
- 10 oz can artichokes, drained and chopped
- 2 cups chicken stock
- 1 tbsp olive oil
- Pepper

- Salt

Directions:
1. Add oil into the instant pot and set the pot on sauté mode.
2. Add garlic and onion and sauté for 5 minutes.
3. Add meat and cook until brown.
4. Add remaining ingredients and stir well.
5. Seal pot with lid and cook on high for 35 minutes.
6. Once done, allow to release pressure naturally. Remove lid.
7. Serve and enjoy.

Nutritional Value (Amount per Serving):
Calories 344; Fat 12.2 g; Carbohydrates 9.2 g; Sugar 2.6 g; Protein 48.4 g; Cholesterol 135 mg

Italian Beef

Preparation Time: 10 minutes; Cooking Time: 35 minutes; Serve: 4
Ingredients:
- 1 lb ground beef
- 1 tbsp olive oil
- 1/2 cup mozzarella cheese, shredded
- 1/2 cup tomato puree
- 1 tsp basil
- 1 tsp oregano
- 1/2 onion, chopped
- 1 carrot, chopped
- 14 oz can tomatoes, diced
- Pepper
- Salt

Directions:
1. Add oil into the instant pot and set the pot on sauté mode.
2. Add onion and sauté for 2 minutes.
3. Add meat and sauté until browned.
4. Add remaining ingredients except for cheese and stir well.
5. Seal pot with lid and cook on high for 35 minutes.
6. Once done, release pressure using quick release. Remove lid.
7. Add cheese and stir well and cook on sauté mode until cheese is melted.
8. Serve and enjoy.

Nutritional Value (Amount per Serving):
Calories 297; Fat 11.3 g; Carbohydrates 11.1 g; Sugar 6.2 g; Protein 37.1 g; Cholesterol 103 mg

Greek Chuck Roast

Preparation Time: 10 minutes; Cooking Time: 35 minutes; Serve: 6
Ingredients:
- 3 lbs beef chuck roast, boneless and cut into chunks
- 1/2 tsp dried basil
- 1 tsp oregano, chopped
- 1 small onion, chopped
- 1 cup tomatoes, diced
- 2 cups chicken broth
- 1 tbsp olive oil
- 1 tbsp garlic, minced
- Pepper
- Salt

Directions:
1. Add oil into the instant pot and set the pot on sauté mode.
2. Add onion and garlic and sauté for 3-5 minutes.
3. Add meat and sauté for 5 minutes.
4. Add remaining ingredients and stir well.
5. Seal pot with lid and cook on high for 25 minutes.
6. Once done, allow to release pressure naturally. Remove lid.
7. Serve and enjoy.

Nutritional Value (Amount per Serving):
Calories 869; Fat 66 g; Carbohydrates 3.2 g; Sugar 1.5 g; Protein 61.5 g; Cholesterol 234 mg

Beanless Beef Chili

Preparation Time: 10 minutes; Cooking Time: 20 minutes; Serve: 4

Ingredients:
- 1 lb ground beef
- 1/2 tsp dried rosemary
- 1/2 tsp paprika
- 1 tsp garlic powder
- 1/2 tsp chili powder
- 1/2 cup chicken broth
- 1 cup heavy cream
- 1 tbsp olive oil
- 1 tsp garlic, minced
- 1 small onion, chopped
- 1 bell pepper, chopped
- 2 cups tomatoes, diced
- Pepper
- Salt

Directions:
1. Add oil into the instant pot and set the pot on sauté mode.
2. Add meat, bell pepper, and onion and sauté for 5 minutes.
3. Add remaining ingredients except for heavy cream and stir well.
4. Seal pot with lid and cook on high for 5 minutes.
5. Once done, release pressure using quick release. Remove lid.
6. Add heavy cream and stir well and cook on sauté mode for 10 minutes.
7. Serve and enjoy.

Nutritional Value (Amount per Serving):
Calories 387; Fat 22.2 g; Carbohydrates 9.5 g; Sugar 5 g; Protein 37.2 g; Cholesterol 142 mg

Sage Tomato Beef

Preparation Time: 10 minutes; Cooking Time: 40 minutes; Serve: 4

Ingredients:
- 2 lbs beef stew meat, cubed
- 1/4 cup tomato paste
- 1 tsp garlic, minced
- 2 cups chicken stock
- 1 onion, chopped
- 2 tbsp olive oil
- 1 tbsp sage, chopped
- Pepper
- Salt

Directions:
1. Add oil into the instant pot and set the pot on sauté mode.
2. Add garlic and onion and sauté for 5 minutes.
3. Add meat and sauté for 5 minutes.
4. Add remaining ingredients and stir well.
5. Seal pot with lid and cook on high for 30 minutes.
6. Once done, allow to release pressure naturally. Remove lid.
7. Serve and enjoy.

Nutritional Value (Amount per Serving):
Calories 515; Fat 21.5 g; Carbohydrates 7 g; Sugar 3.6 g; Protein 70 g; Cholesterol 203 mg

Rosemary Beef Eggplant

Preparation Time: 10 minutes; Cooking Time: 30 minutes; Serve: 4

Ingredients:
- 1 lb beef stew meat, cubed
- 2 tbsp green onion, chopped
- 1/4 tsp red pepper flakes
- 1/2 tsp dried rosemary
- 1/2 tsp paprika
- 1 cup chicken stock
- 1 onion, chopped
- 1 eggplant, cubed

- 2 tbsp olive oil
- Pepper
- Salt

Directions:
1. Add oil into the instant pot and set the pot on sauté mode.
2. Add meat and onion and sauté for 5 minutes.
3. Add remaining ingredients and stir well.
4. Seal pot with lid and cook on high for 25 minutes.
5. Once done, allow to release pressure naturally. Remove lid.
6. Serve and enjoy.

Nutritional Value (Amount per Serving):
Calories 315; Fat 14.5 g; Carbohydrates 10 g; Sugar 4.9 g; Protein 36.1 g; Cholesterol 101 mg

Lemon Basil Beef

Preparation Time: 10 minutes; Cooking Time: 35 minutes; Serve: 4
Ingredients:
- 1 1/2 lb beef stew meat, cut into cubes
- 1/2 cup fresh basil, chopped
- 1/2 tsp dried thyme
- 2 cups chicken stock
- 1 tsp garlic, minced
- 2 tbsp lemon juice
- 1 onion, chopped
- 2 tbsp olive oil
- Pepper
- Salt

Directions:
1. Add oil into the instant pot and set the pot on sauté mode.
2. Add meat, garlic, and onion and sauté for 5 minutes.
3. Add remaining ingredients and stir well.
4. Seal pot with lid and cook on high for 30 minutes.
5. Once done, allow to release pressure naturally. Remove lid.
6. Serve and enjoy.

Nutritional Value (Amount per Serving):
Calories 396; Fat 18 g; Carbohydrates 3.5 g; Sugar 1.7 g; Protein 52.4 g; Cholesterol 152 mg

Thyme Ginger Garlic Beef

Preparation Time: 10 minutes; Cooking Time: 45 minutes; Serve: 2
Ingredients:
- 1 lb beef roast
- 2 whole cloves
- 1/2 tsp ginger, grated
- 1/2 cup beef stock
- 1/2 tsp garlic powder
- 1/2 tsp thyme
- 1/4 tsp pepper
- 1/4 tsp salt

Directions:
1. Mix together ginger, cloves, thyme, garlic powder, pepper, and salt and rub over beef.
2. Place meat into the instant pot. Pour stock around the meat.
3. Seal pot with lid and cook on high for 45 minutes.
4. Once done, release pressure using quick release. Remove lid.
5. Shred meat using a fork and serve.

Nutritional Value (Amount per Serving):
Calories 452; Fat 15.7 g; Carbohydrates 5.2 g; Sugar 0.4 g; Protein 70.1 g; Cholesterol 203 mg

Beef Shawarma

Preparation Time: 10 minutes; Cooking Time: 10 minutes; Serve: 2
Ingredients:
- 1/2 lb ground beef
- 1/4 tsp cinnamon

- 1/2 tsp dried oregano
- 1 cup cabbage, cut into strips
- 1/2 cup bell pepper, sliced
- 1/4 tsp ground coriander
- 1/4 tsp cumin
- 1/4 tsp cayenne pepper
- 1/4 tsp ground allspice
- 1/2 cup onion, chopped
- 1/2 tsp salt

Directions:
1. Set instant pot on sauté mode.
2. Add meat to the pot and sauté until brown.
3. Add remaining ingredients and stir well.
4. Seal pot with lid and cook on high for 5 minutes.
5. Once done, release pressure using quick release. Remove lid.
6. Stir and serve.

Nutritional Value (Amount per Serving):
Calories 245; Fat 7.4 g; Carbohydrates 7.9 g; Sugar 3.9 g; Protein 35.6 g; Cholesterol 101 mg

Beef Curry

Preparation Time: 10 minutes; Cooking Time: 30 minutes; Serve: 2

Ingredients:
- 1/2 lb beef stew meat, cubed
- 1 bell peppers, sliced
- 1 cup beef stock
- 1 tbsp fresh ginger, grated
- 1/2 tsp ground cumin
- 1 tsp ground coriander
- 1/2 tsp cayenne pepper
- 1/2 cup sun-roasted tomatoes, diced
- 2 tbsp olive oil
- 1 tsp garlic, crushed
- 1 green chili peppers, chopped

Directions:
1. Add all ingredients into the instant pot and stir well.
2. Seal pot with lid and cook on high for 30 minutes.
3. Once done, allow to release pressure naturally. Remove lid.
4. Serve and enjoy.

Nutritional Value (Amount per Serving):
Calories 391; Fat 21.9 g; Carbohydrates 11.6 g; Sugar 5.8 g; Protein 37.4 g; Cholesterol 101 mg

Chapter 10: Pork

Pork with Vegetables

Preparation Time: 10 minutes; Cooking Time: 22 minutes; Serve: 4
Ingredients:
- 1 lb pork, cut into chunks
- 2 potatoes, quarters
- 1 lb green beans
- 3 tomatoes, chopped
- 2 celery sticks, sliced
- 2 carrots, sliced
- 1/2 cup olive oil
- 1 onion, chopped
- Pepper
- Salt

Directions:
1. Add oil into the inner pot of instant pot and set the pot on sauté mode.
2. Add meat and cook for 5 minutes.
3. Add remaining ingredients and stir everything well.
4. Seal pot with lid and cook on high for 17 minutes.
5. Once done, release pressure using quick release. Remove lid.
6. Stir well and serve.

Nutritional Value (Amount per Serving):
Calories 527; Fat 29.6 g; Carbohydrates 34.1 g; Sugar 7.9 g; Protein 34.9 g; Cholesterol 83 mg

Garlic Parsley Pork Chops

Preparation Time: 10 minutes; Cooking Time: 25 minutes; Serve: 4
Ingredients:
- 4 pork chops, boneless
- 1 tbsp garlic, minced
- 1/2 cup tomato puree
- 1 cup chicken stock
- 1 onion, chopped
- 1 tbsp fresh parsley, chopped
- 1 tbsp olive oil
- Pepper
- Salt

Directions:
1. Add oil into the inner pot of instant pot and set the pot on sauté mode.
2. Add garlic and onion and sauté for 2 minutes.
3. Add pork chops and sauté for 3 minutes.
4. Add remaining ingredients and stir well.
5. Seal pot with lid and cook on high for 20 minutes.
6. Once done, allow to release pressure naturally for 10 minutes then release remaining using quick release. Remove lid.
7. Stir and serve.

Nutritional Value (Amount per Serving):
Calories 315; Fat 23.6 g; Carbohydrates 6.3 g; Sugar 2.9 g; Protein 19.1 g; Cholesterol 69 mg

Creamy Leek Pork Chops

Preparation Time: 10 minutes; Cooking Time: 35 minutes; Serve: 4
Ingredients:
- 4 pork chops
- 1/2 cup chicken stock
- 1 cup heavy cream
- 2 leek, sliced
- 2 tbsp olive oil
- 1 shallot, chopped
- 1 tbsp garlic, minced
- pepper
- salt

Directions:
1. Add oil into the inner pot of instant pot and set the pot on sauté mode.

2. Add garlic and shallot and sauté for 2 minutes.
3. Add pork chops and cook for 3 minutes.
4. Add remaining ingredients except for heavy cream and stir well.
5. Seal pot with lid and cook on high for 30 minutes.
6. Once done, release pressure using quick release. Remove lid.
7. Stir in heavy cream and serve.

Nutritional Value (Amount per Serving):
Calories 453; Fat 38.2 g; Carbohydrates 8.4 g; Sugar 1.9 g; Protein 19.6 g; Cholesterol 110 mg

Walnut Pork Chops

Preparation Time: 10 minutes; Cooking Time: 30 minutes; Serve: 4
Ingredients:
- 4 pork chops
- 1 cup chicken stock
- 2 red chili, chopped
- 2 tbsp walnuts, chopped
- 1 tbsp garlic, minced
- 1 small onion, chopped
- 1 tbsp olive oil
- Pepper
- Salt

Directions:
1. Add oil into the inner pot of instant pot and set the pot on sauté mode.
2. Add garlic and onion and sauté for 5 minutes.
3. Add pork chops and cook for 5 minutes.
4. Add remaining ingredients and stir well.
5. Seal pot with lid and cook on high for 20 minutes.
6. Once done, allow to release pressure naturally for 10 minutes then release remaining using quick release. Remove lid.
7. Serve and enjoy.

Nutritional Value (Amount per Serving):
Calories 324; Fat 25.9 g; Carbohydrates 3.1 g; Sugar 1.1 g; Protein 19.4 g; Cholesterol 69 mg

Balsamic Pork Chops

Preparation Time: 10 minutes; Cooking Time: 30 minutes; Serve: 4
Ingredients:
- 4 pork chops
- 1 1/2 cups onion, sliced
- 1 cup chicken stock
- 1 tbsp fresh parsley, chopped
- 1 tbsp paprika
- 1 tbsp olive oil
- 2 tbsp balsamic vinegar
- Pepper
- Salt

Directions:
1. Add oil into the inner pot of instant pot and set the pot on sauté mode.
2. Add onion and sauté for 5 minutes.
3. Add pork chops and cook for 5 minutes.
4. Add remaining ingredients and stir well.
5. Seal pot with lid and cook on high for 20 minutes.
6. Once done, allow to release pressure naturally for 10 minutes then release remaining using quick release. Remove lid.
7. Serve and enjoy.

Nutritional Value (Amount per Serving):
Calories 313; Fat 23.8 g; Carbohydrates 5.3 g; Sugar 2.2 g; Protein 18.9 g; Cholesterol 69 mg

Pork & Mushrooms

Preparation Time: 10 minutes; Cooking Time: 30 minutes; Serve: 4
Ingredients:
- 2 lbs pork stew meat, cut into cubes
- 1 tsp paprika
- 2 tbsp olive oil
- 1 onion, chopped
- 1 1/2 cups mushrooms, sliced
- 1 tbsp sage, chopped
- Pepper
- Salt

Directions:
1. Add oil into the inner pot of instant pot and set the pot on sauté mode.
2. Add meat and onion and sauté for 5 minutes.
3. Add remaining ingredients and stir well.
4. Seal pot with lid and cook on high for 25 minutes.
5. Once done, allow to release pressure naturally. Remove lid.
6. Serve and enjoy.

Nutritional Value (Amount per Serving):
Calories 561; Fat 29.2 g; Carbohydrates 4.1 g; Sugar 1.7 g; Protein 67.6 g; Cholesterol 195 mg

Pork Rice

Preparation Time: 10 minutes; Cooking Time: 40 minutes; Serve: 4
Ingredients:
- 2 lbs pork stew meat, cut into cubes
- 1 tbsp rosemary, chopped
- 1 tbsp garlic, minced
- 1/2 cup basil, chopped
- 2 cups wild rice
- 1 onion, chopped
- 4 cups chicken stock
- 1 tbsp olive oil
- Pepper
- Salt

Directions:
1. Add oil into the inner pot of instant pot and set the pot on sauté mode.
2. Add garlic and onion and sauté for 5 minutes.
3. Add meat and sauté for 5 minutes.
4. Add remaining ingredients and stir well.
5. Seal pot with lid and cook on high for 30 minutes.
6. Once done, allow to release pressure naturally. Remove lid.
7. Serve and enjoy.

Nutritional Value (Amount per Serving):
Calories 824; Fat 27 g; Carbohydrates 64.5 g; Sugar 3.9 g; Protein 79.4 g; Cholesterol 195 mg

Delicious Pork Roast

Preparation Time: 10 minutes; Cooking Time: 35 minutes; Serve: 4
Ingredients:
- 1 1/2 lbs pork roast
- 1 cup chicken stock
- 1 tbsp balsamic vinegar
- 1 tbsp olive oil
- 1 tsp dried oregano
- 2 tbsp chili powder
- 1 tbsp garlic, minced
- 14 oz can tomatoes, crushed
- 1 onion, chopped
- Pepper
- Salt

Directions:
1. Add oil into the inner pot of instant pot and set the pot on sauté mode.
2. Add garlic and onion and sauté for 5 minutes.
3. Add remaining ingredients and stir well.
4. Seal pot with lid and cook on high for 30 minutes.

5. Once done, allow to release pressure naturally. Remove lid.
6. Serve and enjoy.

Nutritional Value (Amount per Serving):
Calories 436; Fat 20.7 g; Carbohydrates 10.7 g; Sugar 5.2 g; Protein 50.4 g; Cholesterol 146 mg

Meatloaf

Preparation Time: 10 minutes; Cooking Time: 25 minutes; Serve: 4

Ingredients:
- 2 eggs
- 1 cup spinach, chopped
- 1 1/2 tsp dried basil
- 1 tsp garlic, minced
- 1 onion, chopped
- 1 1/2 lbs ground pork meat
- Pepper
- Salt

Directions:
1. Pour 1 1/2 cups of water into the instant pot then place the trivet in the pot.
2. Spray loaf pan with cooking spray.
3. Add all ingredients into the mixing bowl and mix until well combined.
4. Transfer meat mixture into the prepared loaf pan and place loaf pan on top of the trivet in the pot.
5. Seal pot with lid and cook on high for 25 minutes.
6. Once done, allow to release pressure naturally for 10 minutes then release remaining using quick release. Remove lid.
7. Serve and enjoy.

Nutritional Value (Amount per Serving):
Calories 497; Fat 38.4 g; Carbohydrates 3.3 g; Sugar 1.4 g; Protein 31.9 g; Cholesterol 202 mg

Pork Roast with Potatoes

Preparation Time: 10 minutes; Cooking Time: 30 minutes; Serve: 4

Ingredients:
- 2 lbs pork roast, sliced
- 1 tbsp fresh parsley, chopped
- 1 cup chicken stock
- 1 tbsp olive oil
- 1/2 tsp rosemary, chopped
- 1 tsp chili powder
- 1 cup heavy cream
- 1 onion, chopped
- 2 sweet potatoes, peeled and cubed
- Pepper
- Salt

Directions:
1. Add oil into the inner pot of instant pot and set the pot on sauté mode.
2. Add onion and meat and sauté for 5 minutes.
3. Add remaining ingredients except for heavy cream and stir well.
4. Seal pot with lid and cook on high for 25 minutes.
5. Once done, allow to release pressure naturally for 10 minutes then release remaining using quick release. Remove lid.
6. Stir in heavy cream and serve.

Nutritional Value (Amount per Serving):
Calories 664; Fat 36.4 g; Carbohydrates 14.6 g; Sugar 1.6 g; Protein 66.4 g; Cholesterol 236 mg

Herb Pork

Preparation Time: 10 minutes; Cooking Time: 30 minutes; Serve: 4

Ingredients:
- 1 lb pork stew meat, cut into cubes
- 1 cup can tomato, crushed
- 1 tbsp olive oil
- 1/2 tsp dried oregano

- 1 tbsp tarragon, chopped
- 1 onion, chopped
- Pepper
- Salt

Directions:
1. Add oil into the inner pot of instant pot and set the pot on sauté mode.
2. Add onion and meat and sauté for 5 minutes.
3. Add remaining ingredients and stir well.
4. Seal pot with lid and cook on high for 25 minutes.
5. Once done, allow to release pressure naturally. Remove lid.
6. Serve and enjoy.

Nutritional Value (Amount per Serving):
Calories 291; Fat 14.6 g; Carbohydrates 4.8 g; Sugar 1.2 g; Protein 34 g; Cholesterol 98 mg

Basil Pork Broccoli

Preparation Time: 10 minutes; Cooking Time: 30 minutes; Serve: 4

Ingredients:
- 1 1/2 lbs pork stew meat, cut into cubes
- 1 tbsp basil, chopped
- 1 1/2 cup chicken stock
- 1/4 cup can tomato, crushed
- 1 cup parmesan cheese, grated
- 2 cups broccoli florets
- 1 tbsp olive oil
- Pepper
- Salt

Directions:
1. Add oil into the inner pot of instant pot and set the pot on sauté mode.
2. Add meat and sauté for 5 minutes.
3. Add remaining ingredients except for cheese and stir well.
4. Seal pot with lid and cook on high for 25 minutes.
5. Once done, release pressure using quick release. Remove lid.
6. Sprinkle with cheese and serve.

Nutritional Value (Amount per Serving):
Calories 484; Fat 25.1 g; Carbohydrates 4.6 g; Sugar 1 g; Protein 58.7 g; Cholesterol 162 mg

Spinach Pork

Preparation Time: 10 minutes; Cooking Time: 25 minutes; Serve: 4

Ingredients:
- 1 lb pork stew meat, cut into chunks
- 1 tbsp dill, chopped
- 1 1/2 cups chicken stock
- 2 tomatoes, chopped
- 2 cups spinach, chopped
- 1/2 onion, chopped
- 2 tbsp olive oil
- Pepper
- Salt

Directions:
1. Add oil into the inner pot of instant pot and set the pot on sauté mode.
2. Add meat and sauté for 5 minutes.
3. Add remaining ingredients except for cheese and stir well.
4. Seal pot with lid and cook on high for 20 minutes.
5. Once done, allow to release pressure naturally. Remove lid.
6. Serve and enjoy.

Nutritional Value (Amount per Serving):
Calories 326; Fat 18.4 g; Carbohydrates 4.9 g; Sugar 2.5 g; Protein 34.7 g; Cholesterol 98 mg

Pork Chops with Sprouts

Preparation Time: 10 minutes; Cooking Time: 30 minutes; Serve: 4

Ingredients:
- 4 pork chops
- 1 tbsp parsley, chopped
- 1 cup chicken stock
- 1 tbsp Italian seasoning
- 1 lb Brussels sprouts
- Pepper
- Salt

Directions:
1. Add all ingredients into the inner pot of instant pot and stir well.
2. Seal pot with lid and cook on high for 30 minutes.
3. Once done, allow to release pressure naturally. Remove lid.
4. Serve and enjoy.

Nutritional Value (Amount per Serving):
Calories 319; Fat 21.5 g; Carbohydrates 11 g; Sugar 3 g; Protein 22.1 g; Cholesterol 71 mg

Pork with Beans

Preparation Time: 10 minutes; Cooking Time: 35 minutes; Serve: 4

Ingredients:
- 2 lbs pork shoulder, boneless and cut into chunks
- 1 tsp ground cumin
- 1 cup chicken stock
- 1 cup green beans, cut into pieces
- 1/2 cup corn
- 1 tsp garlic, minced
- Pepper
- Salt

Directions:
1. Add all ingredients into the inner pot of instant pot and stir well.
2. Seal pot with lid and cook on high for 35 minutes.
3. Once done, allow to release pressure naturally. Remove lid.
4. Serve and enjoy.

Nutritional Value (Amount per Serving):
Calories 693; Fat 49 g; Carbohydrates 6.3 g; Sugar 1.2 g; Protein 54.2 g; Cholesterol 204 mg

Bell Pepper Pork Chops

Preparation Time: 10 minutes; Cooking Time: 35 minutes; Serve: 4

Ingredients:
- 1 lb pork chops
- 1 tbsp parsley, chopped
- 2 cups chicken stock
- 1 onion, chopped
- 1 tsp garlic, minced
- 2 bell peppers, chopped
- 2 tbsp olive oil
- Pepper
- Salt

Directions:
1. Add oil into the inner pot of instant pot and set the pot on sauté mode.
2. Add pork chops and sauté for 2 minutes.
3. Add onion and garlic and sauté for 3 minutes.
4. Add remaining ingredients stir well.
5. Seal pot with lid and cook on high for 30 minutes.
6. Once done, allow to release pressure naturally for 10 minutes then release remaining using quick release. Remove lid.
7. Serve and enjoy.

Nutritional Value (Amount per Serving):
Calories 459; Fat 35.7 g; Carbohydrates 7.8 g; Sugar 4.5 g; Protein 26.8 g; Cholesterol 98 mg

Capers Pork Chops

Preparation Time: 10 minutes; Cooking Time: 25 minutes; Serve: 4

Ingredients:
- 4 pork chops
- 2 tbsp parsley, chopped
- 1/2 cup tomatoes, chopped
- 1 tsp paprika
- 1/2 tsp chili powder
- 1/2 tsp ground coriander
- 1 tbsp capers, chopped
- 1 tsp ground cumin
- 1 tbsp olive oil
- Pepper
- Salt

Directions:
1. Add oil into the inner pot of instant pot and set the pot on sauté mode.
2. Add pork chops and sauté for 5 minutes.
3. Add remaining ingredients stir well.
4. Seal pot with lid and cook on high for 20 minutes.
5. Once done, allow to release pressure naturally. Remove lid.
6. Serve and enjoy.

Nutritional Value (Amount per Serving):
Calories 269; Fat 23.7 g; Carbohydrates 1.8 g; Sugar 0.7 g; Protein 18.5 g; Cholesterol 69 mg

Balsamic Pork with Kale

Preparation Time: 10 minutes; Cooking Time: 30 minutes; Serve: 4

Ingredients:
- 2 lbs pork shoulder, cut into chunks
- 1/2 cup chicken stock
- 1 tbsp chives, chopped
- 2 tbsp balsamic vinegar
- 1 cup kale, torn
- 1 onion, sliced
- 2 tbsp olive oil
- Pepper
- Salt

Directions:
1. Add oil into the inner pot of instant pot and set the pot on sauté mode.
2. Add pork chops and onion and sauté for 5 minutes.
3. Add remaining ingredients stir well.
4. Seal pot with lid and cook on high for 25 minutes.
5. Once done, allow to release pressure naturally. Remove lid.
6. Serve and enjoy.

Nutritional Value (Amount per Serving):
Calories 745; Fat 55.6 g; Carbohydrates 4.5 g; Sugar 1.3 g; Protein 53.7 g; Cholesterol 204 mg

Simple Paprika Pork Chops

Preparation Time: 10 minutes; Cooking Time: 25 minutes; Serve: 4

Ingredients:
- 4 pork chops
- 1 tbsp paprika
- 1/4 cup can tomato, crushed
- 2 tbsp olive oil
- 1/2 tsp chili powder
- 1 onion, chopped
- 1 cup chicken stock
- Pepper
- Salt

Directions:
1. Add oil into the inner pot of instant pot and set the pot on sauté mode.
2. Add pork chops sauté for 5 minutes.
3. Add remaining ingredients stir well.
4. Seal pot with lid and cook on high for 20 minutes.

5. Once done, allow to release pressure naturally for 10 minutes then release remaining using quick release. Remove lid.
6. Serve and enjoy.

Nutritional Value (Amount per Serving):
Calories 338; Fat 27.4 g; Carbohydrates 4.4 g; Sugar 1.6 g; Protein 18.9 g; Cholesterol 69 mg

Delicious Pork Carnitas

Preparation Time: 10 minutes; Cooking Time: 40 minutes; Serve: 4
Ingredients:
- 2 lbs pork shoulder
- 1 jalapeno, chopped
- 1 tbsp olive oil
- 2 tsp garlic, minced
- 1 tsp cumin
- 1 tsp oregano
- 2 1/2 cups chicken broth
- 2 lime juice
- 1 onion, chopped

Directions:
1. Add oil into the inner pot of instant pot and set the pot on sauté mode.
2. Add the meat into the pot and sear until browned.
3. Add remaining ingredients stir well.
4. Seal pot with lid and cook on high for 30 minutes.
5. Once done, allow to release pressure naturally for 10 minutes then release remaining using quick release. Remove lid.
6. Shred the meat using a fork and serve.

Nutritional Value (Amount per Serving):
Calories 739; Fat 53.1 g; Carbohydrates 6.1 g; Sugar 2.1 g; Protein 56.5 g; Cholesterol 204 mg

Creamy Pork Chops

Preparation Time: 10 minutes; Cooking Time: 17 minutes; Serve: 4
Ingredients:
- 1 lb pork chops, boneless
- 1/2 cup sour cream
- 10 oz beef broth
- 10 oz onion soup
- Pepper
- Salt

Directions:
1. Add pork chops and broth into the instant pot.
2. Seal pot with lid and cook on high for 12 minutes.
3. Once done, allow to release pressure naturally. Open the lid.
4. Add remaining ingredients and stir well and cook on sauté mode for 5 minutes.
5. Serve and enjoy.

Nutritional Value (Amount per Serving):
Calories 468; Fat 35.6 g; Carbohydrates 6.3 g; Sugar 2.2 g; Protein 30 g; Cholesterol 110 mg

Pulled Pork Butt

Preparation Time: 10 minutes; Cooking Time: 60 minutes; Serve: 6
Ingredients:
- 4 lbs pork butt
- 1 1/2 cups beef broth
- 1 tbsp olive oil
- 1 tsp dried thyme
- 1 tsp dried oregano
- 1 tsp cayenne
- 1 1/2 tsp ground cumin
- 1 1/2 tsp chili powder
- 2 tsp paprika
- Pepper
- Salt

Directions:

1. In a small bowl, mix together paprika, chili powder, cumin, cayenne, oregano, thyme, pepper, and salt.
2. Coat meat with oil and rub with spice mixture.
3. Pour broth into the instant pot then place meat into the pot.
4. Seal pot with lid and cook on high for 60 minutes.
5. Once done, allow to release pressure naturally. Open the lid.
6. Remove meat from pot and shred using a fork.
7. Serve and enjoy.

Nutritional Value (Amount per Serving):
Calories 622; Fat 23.3 g; Carbohydrates 1.7 g; Sugar 0.3 g; Protein 95.7 g; Cholesterol 278 mg

Salsa Pork

Preparation Time: 10 minutes; Cooking Time: 45 minutes; Serve: 4
Ingredients:
- 2 lbs pork sirloin, sliced
- 2 tsp ground cumin
- 15 oz salsa
- 2 tsp garlic powder
- 1 tbsp olive oil
- Pepper
- Salt

Directions:
1. Add oil into the inner pot of instant pot and set the pot on sauté mode.
2. Add the meat into the pot and sear until browned.
3. Add remaining ingredients stir well.
4. Seal pot with lid and cook on high for 45 minutes.
5. Once done, release pressure using quick release. Remove lid.
6. Serve and enjoy.

Nutritional Value (Amount per Serving):
Calories 472; Fat 26.2 g; Carbohydrates 8.2 g; Sugar 3.6 g; Protein 48.7 g; Cholesterol 142 mg

Lime Salsa Pork Chops

Preparation Time: 10 minutes; Cooking Time: 25 minutes; Serve: 4
Ingredients:
- 1 1/2 lbs pork chops
- 1/2 tsp garlic powder
- 1/2 tsp ground cumin
- 2 tbsp lime juice
- 1/2 cup salsa
- 1 tbsp olive oil
- Pepper
- Salt

Directions:
1. Add oil into the inner pot of instant pot and set the pot on sauté mode.
2. Add pork chops and sauté until brown.
3. Add remaining ingredients and stir well.
4. Seal pot with lid and cook on high for 15 minutes.
5. Once done, release pressure using quick release. Remove lid.
6. Serve and enjoy.

Nutritional Value (Amount per Serving):
Calories 591; Fat 45.9 g; Carbohydrates 4.3 g; Sugar 1.5 g; Protein 38.9 g; Cholesterol 146 mg

Pork with Carrots Potatoes

Preparation Time: 10 minutes; Cooking Time: 15 minutes; Serve: 2
Ingredients:
- 2 pork chops, boneless
- 1/4 cup balsamic vinegar
- 2 tbsp honey
- 1 1/2 tsp ground ginger
- 1 tsp curry powder
- 1/2 cup chicken stock

- 1 tbsp olive oil
- 3 carrots, chopped
- 3 small potatoes, cubed
- 2 garlic cloves, chopped
- Pepper
- Salt

Directions:
1. Add oil into the instant pot and set the pot on sauté mode.
2. Add pork chops into the pot and brown them from both the sides.
3. Add remaining ingredients to the pot and stir well.
4. Seal pot with lid and cook on high for 10 minutes.
5. Once done, allow to release pressure naturally. Open the lid.
6. Serve and enjoy.

Nutritional Value (Amount per Serving):
Calories 615; Fat 27.5 g; Carbohydrates 69.4 g; Sugar 25.1 g; Protein 23.7 g; Cholesterol 69 mg

Simple Shredded Pork

Preparation Time: 10 minutes; Cooking Time: 35 minutes; Serve: 2
Ingredients:
- 1/2 lb pork belly, cut into cubes
- 1 tsp thyme
- 1/2 cup onion, chopped
- 1/2 cup chicken stock
- 1 1/2 tsp pepper
- 1/4 tsp salt

Directions:
1. Add all ingredients to the instant pot and stir well.
2. Seal pot with lid and cook on high for 35 minutes.
3. Once done, release pressure using quick release. Remove lid.
4. Remove meat from pot and shred using a fork.
5. Serve and enjoy.

Nutritional Value (Amount per Serving):
Calories 543; Fat 30.8 g; Carbohydrates 4.2 g; Sugar 1.4 g; Protein 53.1 g; Cholesterol 131 mg

Cheese Pork Chops

Preparation Time: 10 minutes; Cooking Time: 15 minutes; Serve: 2
Ingredients:
- 2 pork chops, boneless
- 1/2 tbsp olive oil
- 1/2 tbsp Italian seasoning
- 3 oz feta cheese, crumbled
- 3/4 cup chicken stock
- 1/2 tsp garlic powder
- Pepper
- Salt

Directions:
1. Season pork chops with Italian seasoning, garlic powder, pepper, and salt and set aside.
2. Add oil into the instant pot and set the pot on sauté mode.
3. Add pork chops and cook until brown. Pour stock over pork chops.
4. Seal pot with lid and cook on high for 10 minutes.
5. Once done, allow to release pressure naturally for 10 minutes then release remaining using quick release. Remove lid.
6. Top with cheese and serve.

Nutritional Value (Amount per Serving):
Calories 415; Fat 33.7 g; Carbohydrates 2.9 g; Sugar 2.5 g; Protein 24.4 g; Cholesterol 109 mg

Tasty Pork Carnitas

Preparation Time: 10 minutes; Cooking Time: 35 minutes; Serve: 4
Ingredients:
- 1 lb pork shoulder
- 1/4 cup of water
- 1 cup chicken broth
- 1/2 tbsp olive oil

- 1 tsp garlic, minced
- 1/2 tsp cumin
- 1/2 tsp oregano
- 1/2 onion, chopped
- 1 lime juice
- Pepper
- Salt

Directions:
1. Add oil into the instant pot and set the pot on sauté mode.
2. Add meat to the pot and sauté until browned.
3. Add remaining ingredients and stir well.
4. Seal pot with lid and cook on high for 30 minutes.
5. Once done, allow to release pressure naturally. Open the lid.
6. Remove meat from pot and shred using a fork and serve.

Nutritional Value (Amount per Serving):
Calories 367; Fat 26.5 g; Carbohydrates 2.9 g; Sugar 1 g; Protein 27.9 g; Cholesterol 102 mg

Pork Rice

Preparation Time: 10 minutes; Cooking Time: 30 minutes; Serve: 2

Ingredients:
- 1 lb pork tenderloin, cut into 1-inch pieces
- 1/2 cup rice
- 7 oz can black beans, rinsed and drained
- 1 tsp garlic, chopped
- 1/4 cup orange juice
- 1 tbsp fresh cilantro, chopped
- 1/2 tbsp fresh lime juice
- 1 cup chicken broth
- 1 tbsp olive oil
- 1/2 tsp ground cumin
- Salt

Directions:
1. Add oil into the instant pot and set the pot on sauté mode.
2. Add meat to the pot and sauté for 5 minutes.
3. Stir in orange juice, cumin, garlic, broth, rice, and beans.
4. Seal pot with lid and cook on high for 12 minutes.
5. Once done, release pressure using quick release. Remove lid.
6. Stir in lime juice and garnish with cilantro.
7. Serve and enjoy.

Nutritional Value (Amount per Serving):
Calories 685; Fat 16.5 g; Carbohydrates 59.8 g; Sugar 4 g; Protein 70.9 g; Cholesterol 166 mg

Simple Lemon Pepper Pork Chops

Preparation Time: 10 minutes; Cooking Time: 15 minutes; Serve: 2

Ingredients:
- 1/2 lb pork chops
- 1 1/2 tbsp lemon pepper seasoning
- 1/4 cup chicken stock
- Salt

Directions:
1. Season pork chops with lemon pepper seasoning and salt.
2. Set pot on sauté mode.
3. Add pork chops and sauté until brown. Pour stock over pork chops.
4. Seal pot with lid and cook on high for 10 minutes.
5. Once done, release pressure using quick release. Remove lid.
6. Serve and enjoy.

Nutritional Value (Amount per Serving):
Calories 376; Fat 28.4 g; Carbohydrates 3.2 g; Sugar 0.1 g; Protein 26.1 g; Cholesterol 98 mg

Chapter 11: Lamb

Lamb Stew

Preparation Time: 10 minutes; Cooking Time: 30 minutes; Serve: 4
Ingredients:
- 2 lbs lamb shoulder, cut into cubes
- 1 tsp dried basil
- 1 tsp dried oregano
- 1 tbsp olive oil
- 2 onion, chopped
- 14 oz can tomatoes, chopped
- 1 tbsp garlic, minced
- Pepper
- Salt

Directions:
1. Add oil into the inner pot of instant pot and set the pot on sauté mode.
2. Add meat, onion, and garlic and sauté for 5 minutes.
3. Add remaining ingredients and stir well.
4. Seal pot with lid and cook on high for 25 minutes.
5. Once done, allow to release pressure naturally for 10 minutes then release remaining using quick release. Remove lid.
6. Stir well and serve.

Nutritional Value (Amount per Serving):
Calories 499; Fat 20.2 g; Carbohydrates 11.2 g; Sugar 5.7 g; Protein 65.4 g; Cholesterol 204 mg

Carrot Bean Lamb Stew

Preparation Time: 10 minutes; Cooking Time: 20 minutes; Serve: 4
Ingredients:
- 1 lb lamb shoulder, cut into chunks
- 1/4 cup fresh parsley, chopped
- 2 carrots, chopped
- 2 cups beef stock
- 1/2 lb green beans, trimmed and halved
- 1 onion, chopped
- Pepper
- Salt

Directions:
1. Add all ingredients into the inner pot of instant pot and stir well.
2. Seal pot with lid and cook on high for 20 minutes.
3. Once done, allow to release pressure naturally. Remove lid.
4. Stir well and serve.

Nutritional Value (Amount per Serving):
Calories 262; Fat 8.7 g; Carbohydrates 9.9 g; Sugar 3.5 g; Protein 34.9 g; Cholesterol 102 mg

Delicious Salsa Lamb

Preparation Time: 10 minutes; Cooking Time: 35 minutes; Serve: 4
Ingredients:
- 1 lb lamb shoulder, cut into chunks
- 1/4 cup fresh cilantro, chopped
- 2 tbsp olive oil
- 1 onion, chopped
- 1 tsp garlic, minced
- 1 1/2 cups salsa
- Pepper
- Salt

Directions:
1. Add oil into the inner pot of instant pot and set the pot on sauté mode.
2. Add garlic and onion and sauté for 5 minutes.
3. Add remaining ingredients and stir well.
4. Seal pot with lid and cook on high for 30 minutes.
5. Once done, allow to release pressure naturally. Remove lid.

6. Stir well and serve.

Nutritional Value (Amount per Serving):
Calories 310; Fat 15.5 g; Carbohydrates 9 g; Sugar 4.2 g; Protein 33.7 g; Cholesterol 102 mg

Tomato Lamb Chops

Preparation Time: 10 minutes; Cooking Time: 30 minutes; Serve: 4

Ingredients:
- 4 lamb chopped
- 1 cup chicken stock
- 1 tsp herb de province
- 1 tsp garlic, minced
- 2 cups can tomatoes, chopped
- Pepper
- Salt

Directions:
1. Add all ingredients into the inner pot of instant pot and stir well.
2. Seal pot with lid and cook on high for 30 minutes.
3. Once done, allow to release pressure naturally. Remove lid.
4. Stir well and serve.

Nutritional Value (Amount per Serving):
Calories 375; Fat 17.1 g; Carbohydrates 6.4 g; Sugar 4.2 g; Protein 23 g; Cholesterol 82 mg

Healthy Quinoa Lamb

Preparation Time: 10 minutes; Cooking Time: 25 minutes; Serve: 4

Ingredients:
- 1 lb lamb shoulder, cut into chunks
- 1 tbsp chives, chopped
- 1/4 cup can tomatoes, crushed
- 2 cups beef stock
- 1 onion, chopped
- 1 1/2 cups quinoa, rinsed and drained
- Pepper
- Salt

Directions:
1. Add all ingredients into the inner pot of instant pot and stir well.
2. Seal pot with lid and cook on high for 25 minutes.
3. Once done, allow to release pressure naturally for 10 minutes then release remaining using quick release. Remove lid.
4. Stir well and serve.

Nutritional Value (Amount per Serving):
Calories 469; Fat 12.5 g; Carbohydrates 44.3 g; Sugar 1.7 g; Protein 42.7 g; Cholesterol 102 mg

Sweet Potato lamb

Preparation Time: 10 minutes; Cooking Time: 35 minutes; Serve: 4

Ingredients:
- 1 lb lamb shoulder, cut into chunks
- 2 tbsp olive oil
- 1 cup beef stock
- 2 sweet potatoes, cubed
- 1 tsp garlic, minced
- 1 onion, chopped
- 1 carrot, chopped
- Pepper
- Salt

Directions:
1. Add oil into the inner pot of instant pot and set the pot on sauté mode.
2. Add garlic and onion and sauté for 2 minutes.
3. Add meat and sauté for 3 minutes.
4. Add remaining ingredients and stir well.
5. Seal pot with lid and cook on high for 30 minutes.
6. Once done, allow to release pressure naturally. Remove lid.

7. Stir well and serve.

Nutritional Value (Amount per Serving):
Calories 338; Fat 15.5 g; Carbohydrates 14.8 g; Sugar 2.1 g; Protein 33.6 g; Cholesterol 102 mg

Lamb & Kale

Preparation Time: 10 minutes; Cooking Time: 35 minutes; Serve: 4

Ingredients:
- 1 1/2 lbs lamb, cut into chunks
- 1 tbsp olive oil
- 2 tbsp tomato paste
- 1 tsp garlic, minced
- 1 onion, chopped
- 4 tomatoes, chopped
- 1 cup kale, chopped
- Pepper
- Salt

Directions:
1. Add oil into the inner pot of instant pot and set the pot on sauté mode.
2. Add meat and sauté for 2 minutes.
3. Add garlic and onion and sauté for 3 minutes.
4. Add remaining ingredients and stir well.
5. Seal pot with lid and cook on high for 30 minutes.
6. Once done, allow to release pressure naturally. Remove lid.
7. Stir well and serve.

Nutritional Value (Amount per Serving):
Calories 395; Fat 16.3 g; Carbohydrates 10.9 g; Sugar 5.4 g; Protein 50 g; Cholesterol 153 mg

Tomato Pea Lamb Chops

Preparation Time: 10 minutes; Cooking Time: 40 minutes; Serve: 4

Ingredients:
- 4 lamb chops
- 2 tbsp fresh parsley, chopped
- 12 oz can tomatoes, chopped
- 1 cup green peas
- 1 tsp garlic, minced
- 1 onion, chopped
- 2 tbsp olive oil
- Pepper
- Salt

Directions:
1. Add oil into the inner pot of instant pot and set the pot on sauté mode.
2. Add meat and sauté for 2 minutes.
3. Add garlic and onion and sauté for 3 minutes.
4. Add remaining ingredients and stir well.
5. Seal pot with lid and cook on high for 30 minutes.
6. Once done, allow to release pressure naturally. Remove lid.
7. Stir well and serve.

Nutritional Value (Amount per Serving):
Calories 278; Fat 13.4 g; Carbohydrates 12.5 g; Sugar 6.2 g; Protein 27 g; Cholesterol 77 mg

Delicious Lamb Curry

Preparation Time: 10 minutes; Cooking Time: 30 minutes; Serve: 4

Ingredients:
- 2 lbs lamb, cut into chunks
- 1 tbsp parsley, chopped
- 1 onion, chopped
- 2 tbsp olive oil
- 1 tsp curry powder
- 1/2 cup heavy cream
- 1 cup of coconut milk
- Pepper
- Salt

Directions:
1. Add oil into the inner pot of instant pot and set the pot on sauté mode.
2. Add onion and sauté for 5 minutes.
3. Add meat and sauté for 5 minutes.
4. Add remaining ingredients except for heavy cream and stir well.
5. Seal pot with lid and cook on high for 20 minutes.
6. Once done, release pressure using quick release. Remove lid.
7. Stir in heavy cream and serve.

Nutritional Value (Amount per Serving):
Calories 685; Fat 43.6 g; Carbohydrates 6.7 g; Sugar 3.2 g; Protein 65.8 g; Cholesterol 225 mg

Flavors Lamb Ribs

Preparation Time: 10 minutes; Cooking Time: 25 minutes; Serve: 4
Ingredients:
- 4 lamb ribs
- 2 tomatoes, chopped
- 2 tbsp olive oil
- 1 1/2 cups chicken stock
- 1 tbsp sage, chopped
- 1 tbsp garlic, minced
- Pepper
- Salt

Directions:
1. Add oil into the inner pot of instant pot and set the pot on sauté mode.
2. Add lamb ribs and sear for 5 minutes.
3. Add remaining ingredients except for heavy cream and stir well.
4. Seal pot with lid and cook on high for 20 minutes.
5. Once done, allow to release pressure naturally for 10 minutes then release remaining using quick release. Remove lid.
6. Serve and enjoy.

Nutritional Value (Amount per Serving):
Calories 539; Fat 46.1 g; Carbohydrates 10.9 g; Sugar 7.2 g; Protein 22.6 g; Cholesterol 0 mg

Meatballs in Sauce

Preparation Time: 10 minutes; Cooking Time: 11 minutes; Serve: 6
Ingredients:
- 1 egg
- 1 1/2 lbs ground lamb
- 2 tbsp fresh parsley, chopped
- 28 oz can tomatoes, chopped
- 1/2 cup almond flour
- 1 tsp oregano
- 1 tbsp water
- 1 tbsp mint, chopped
- 1/2 cup feta cheese, crumbled
- 1 onion, chopped
- 1 bell pepper, chopped
- 1 tsp garlic, minced
- 2 tbsp olive oil
- Pepper
- Salt

Directions:
1. In a bowl, mix together egg, meat, feta, parsley, mint, water, almond flour, garlic, pepper, and salt.
2. Make small balls from meat mixture.
3. Add oil into the inner pot of instant pot and set the pot on sauté mode.
4. Add bell pepper and onion and sauté for 3 minutes.
5. Add remaining ingredients and stir well.
6. Add meatballs. Seal pot with lid and cook on high for 8 minutes.
7. Once done, release pressure using quick release. Remove lid.
8. Serve and enjoy.

Nutritional Value (Amount per Serving):
Calories 392; Fat 20.9 g; Carbohydrates 12.4 g; Sugar 6.3 g; Protein 38.2 g; Cholesterol 140 mg

Lamb Basil Salad

Preparation Time: 10 minutes; Cooking Time: 40 minutes; Serve: 4

Ingredients:
- 1 1/2 lbs lamb, boneless and cut into chunks
- 1 1/2 tbsp fresh lemon juice
- 2 cups spinach
- 4 oz feta cheese, crumbled
- 1 cup basil, chopped
- 1/4 cup pecans, chopped
- 2 cups beef stock
- 1/4 tsp dried thyme
- 1 tsp cumin
- 5 tbsp olive oil
- Pepper
- Salt

Directions:
1. Add meat, thyme, 1 tbsp olive oil, garlic, pepper, stock, and salt into the instant pot and stir well.
2. Seal pot with lid and cook on high for 40 minutes.
3. Once done, release pressure using quick release. Remove lid.
4. Transfer meat to the large mixing bowl.
5. Add remaining ingredients into the bowl and mix well.
6. Serve and enjoy.

Nutritional Value (Amount per Serving):
Calories 564; Fat 37.2 g; Carbohydrates 2.5 g; Sugar 1.4 g; Protein 54 g; Cholesterol 178 mg

Lamb Shanks

Preparation Time: 10 minutes; Cooking Time: 25 minutes; Serve: 4

Ingredients:
- 4 lamb shanks
- 1 tomato, chopped
- 1/4 cup leeks, chopped
- 2 celery stalks, chopped
- 1 tsp garlic, minced
- 1 onion, chopped
- 1/4 cup balsamic vinegar
- 3 tbsp olive oil
- 3 cups beef broth
- 8 oz mushrooms, sliced
- 1 tsp dried rosemary
- Pepper
- Salt

Directions:
1. Add all ingredients into the inner pot of instant pot and stir well.
2. Seal pot with lid and cook on high for 25 minutes.
3. Once done, allow to release pressure naturally. Remove lid.
4. Stir well and serve.

Nutritional Value (Amount per Serving):
Calories 763; Fat 35.8 g; Carbohydrates 7.3 g; Sugar 3.5 g; Protein 97.9 g; Cholesterol 83 mg

Vegetable Lamb Chops

Preparation Time: 10 minutes; Cooking Time: 15 minutes; Serve: 4

Ingredients:
- 4 lamb chops
- 1 bay leaf
- 1 cup beef stock
- 1 bell pepper, chopped
- 1 cup cauliflower florets
- 1 cup onion, sliced
- 2 tbsp olive oil
- Pepper
- Salt

Directions:
1. Add all ingredients into the inner pot of instant pot and stir well.
2. Seal pot with lid and cook on high for 15 minutes.
3. Once done, allow to release pressure naturally. Remove lid.
4. Stir well and serve.

Nutritional Value (Amount per Serving):
Calories 701; Fat 31.3 g; Carbohydrates 6.7 g; Sugar 3.3 g; Protein 93.7 g; Cholesterol 294 mg

Italian Lamb Tomatoes

Preparation Time: 10 minutes; Cooking Time: 10 minutes; Serve: 4

Ingredients:
- 1 lb lamb loin, cut into chunks
- 1/4 tsp garlic powder
- 1 tsp cumin powder
- 1/2 tsp dried rosemary
- 1 tbsp olive oil
- 1 cup beef broth
- 1/2 cup fresh parsley, chopped
- 1 cup grape tomatoes
- 1 onion, chopped
- Pepper
- Salt

Directions:
1. Add oil into the inner pot of instant pot and set the pot on sauté mode.
2. Add lamb ribs and sear for 3 minutes.
3. Add remaining ingredients and stir well.
4. Seal pot with lid and cook on high for 7 minutes.
5. Once done, release pressure using quick release. Remove lid.
6. Serve and enjoy.

Nutritional Value (Amount per Serving):
Calories 386; Fat 30.3 g; Carbohydrates 5.5 g; Sugar 2.6 g; Protein 21.3 g; Cholesterol 80 mg

Lamb with Sprouts

Preparation Time: 10 minutes; Cooking Time: 15 minutes; Serve: 4

Ingredients:
- 1 lb lamb, cut into chunks
- 1 tsp rosemary
- 1/2 tsp dried sage
- 1/2 tsp chili powder
- 1 cup sour cream
- 3 cups beef stock
- 2 tbsp olive oil
- 2 celery stalks, chopped
- 1/2 cup mushrooms, sliced
- 1 cup grape tomatoes
- 1 cup Brussels sprouts
- Pepper
- Salt

Directions:
1. Add all ingredients except sour cream into the inner pot of instant pot and stir well.
2. Seal pot with lid and cook on high for 15 minutes.
3. Once done, release pressure using quick release. Remove lid.
4. Stir in cream and serve.

Nutritional Value (Amount per Serving):
Calories 430; Fat 28.1 g; Carbohydrates 7.3 g; Sugar 2 g; Protein 37.3 g; Cholesterol 127 mg

Garlic Mushrooms Lamb Chops

Preparation Time: 10 minutes; Cooking Time: 15 minutes; Serve: 4

Ingredients:
- 1 lb lamb chops
- 2 cups beef stock
- 1 cup mushrooms, sliced
- 2 tbsp olive oil

- 1 tsp garlic, minced
- Pepper
- Salt

Directions:
1. Add all ingredients into the inner pot of instant pot and stir well.
2. Seal pot with lid and cook on high for 15 minutes.
3. Once done, release pressure using quick release. Remove lid.
4. Stir and serve.

Nutritional Value (Amount per Serving):
Calories 284; Fat 15.6 g; Carbohydrates 0.9 g; Sugar 0.3 g; Protein 33.8 g; Cholesterol 102 mg

Eggplant & Lamb

Preparation Time: 10 minutes; Cooking Time: 35 minutes; Serve: 4

Ingredients:
- 2 lamb shanks
- 1 bay leaf
- 2 tbsp cumin seeds
- 1 tbsp oregano
- 1/2 eggplant, cubed
- 1/4 cup yogurt
- 4 cups beef broth
- 2 tbsp olive oil
- 1 tbsp garlic, minced
- 2 green chili, chopped
- Pepper
- Salt

Directions:
1. Add oil into the inner pot of instant pot and set the pot on sauté mode.
2. Add cumin, oregano, garlic, pepper, and salt and sauté for 2 minutes.
3. Add meat and sauté for 3 minutes.
4. Add eggplant and cook for 5 minutes.
5. Add remaining ingredients and stir well.
6. Seal pot with lid and cook on high for 30 minutes.
7. Once done, release pressure using quick release. Remove lid.
8. Stir and serve.

Nutritional Value (Amount per Serving):
Calories 452; Fat 21.5 g; Carbohydrates 9.5 g; Sugar 4.1 g; Protein 53 g; Cholesterol 148 mg

Lemon Garlic Lamb Riblets

Preparation Time: 10 minutes; Cooking Time: 40 minutes; Serve: 4

Ingredients:
- 2 lbs lamb riblets
- 2 tsp chili powder
- 1/4 cup fresh coriander, chopped
- 1 tsp garlic, minced
- 2 tbsp olive oil
- 1 tbsp lemon juice
- 5 cups beef broth
- Pepper
- Salt

Directions:
1. Add all ingredients into the inner pot of instant pot and stir well.
2. Seal pot with lid and cook on high for 40 minutes.
3. Once done, allow to release pressure naturally. Remove lid.
4. Serve and enjoy.

Nutritional Value (Amount per Serving):
Calories 496; Fat 29 g; Carbohydrates 2.2 g; Sugar 1.1 g; Protein 52.5 g; Cholesterol 151 mg

Mediterranean Lamb

Preparation Time: 10 minutes; Cooking Time: 35 minutes; Serve: 4
Ingredients:

- 2 1/2 lbs lamb shoulder, cut into chunks
- 1 bay leaf
- 1 cup vegetable stock
- 10 oz prunes, soaked
- 1 tsp garlic, minced
- 2 tbsp honey
- 2 onions, sliced
- 1 tsp ground cumin
- 1 tsp ground ginger
- 1 tsp ground turmeric
- 1/4 tsp cinnamon
- 3 oz almonds sliced
- Pepper
- Salt

Directions:
1. Add all ingredients into the inner pot of instant pot and stir well.
2. Seal pot with lid and cook on high for 35 minutes.
3. Once done, allow to release pressure naturally. Remove lid.
4. Serve and enjoy.

Nutritional Value (Amount per Serving):
Calories 886; Fat 32 g; Carbohydrates 65.3 g; Sugar 38.8 g; Protein 86.5 g; Cholesterol 255 mg

Tasty Lamb Leg

Preparation Time: 10 minutes; Cooking Time: 20 minutes; Serve: 4
Ingredients:
- 2 lbs leg of lamb, boneless and cut into chunks
- 1 tbsp olive oil
- 1 tbsp garlic, sliced
- 1 cup red wine
- 1 cup onion, chopped
- 2 carrots, chopped
- 1 tsp rosemary, chopped
- 2 tsp thyme, chopped
- 1 tsp oregano, chopped
- 1/2 cup beef stock
- 2 tbsp tomato paste
- Pepper
- Salt

Directions:
1. Add oil into the inner pot of instant pot and set the pot on sauté mode.
2. Add meat and sauté until browned.
3. Add remaining ingredients and stir well.
4. Seal pot with lid and cook on high for 15 minutes.
5. Once done, allow to release pressure naturally. Remove lid.
6. Stir well and serve.

Nutritional Value (Amount per Serving):
Calories 540; Fat 20.4 g; Carbohydrates 10.3 g; Sugar 4.2 g; Protein 65.2 g; Cholesterol 204 mg

Kale Sprouts & Lamb

Preparation Time: 10 minutes; Cooking Time: 30 minutes; Serve: 4
Ingredients:
- 2 lbs lamb, cut into chunks
- 1 tbsp parsley, chopped
- 2 tbsp olive oil
- 1 cup kale, chopped
- 1 cup Brussels sprouts, halved
- 1 cup beef stock
- Pepper
- Salt

Directions:
1. Add all ingredients into the inner pot of instant pot and stir well.
2. Seal pot with lid and cook on high for 30 minutes.
3. Once done, allow to release pressure naturally. Remove lid.
4. Serve and enjoy.

Nutritional Value (Amount per Serving):
Calories 504; Fat 23.8 g; Carbohydrates 3.9 g; Sugar 0.5 g; Protein 65.7 g; Cholesterol 204 mg

Herb Veggie Lamb

Preparation Time: 10 minutes; Cooking Time: 30 minutes; Serve: 4
Ingredients:
- 1 1/2 lbs lamb stew meat, cubed
- 1 tbsp cilantro, chopped
- 1 cup tomato puree
- 1 eggplant, chopped
- 1 tomato, chopped
- 1 carrot, chopped
- 1 zucchini, chopped
- 1 cup beef stock
- 1 tbsp tarragon, chopped
- 1 onion, chopped
- Pepper
- Salt

Directions:
1. Add oil into the inner pot of instant pot and set the pot on sauté mode.
2. Add meat and onion and sauté for 5 minutes.
3. Add remaining ingredients and stir well.
4. Seal pot with lid and cook on high for 25 minutes.
5. Once done, allow to release pressure naturally. Remove lid.
6. Serve and enjoy.

Nutritional Value (Amount per Serving):
Calories 405; Fat 13.2 g; Carbohydrates 19.5 g; Sugar 10 g; Protein 52 g; Cholesterol 153 mg

Italian Lamb Stew

Preparation Time: 10 minutes; Cooking Time: 30 minutes; Serve: 4
Ingredients:
- 2 lbs lamb, cut into chunks
- 1/2 cup cilantro, chopped
- 1 tsp dried oregano
- 1 tbsp olive oil
- 1 cup tomatoes, chopped
- 1 cup olives, pitted and sliced
- 1 onion, chopped
- 1 tbsp garlic, minced
- Pepper
- Salt

Directions:
1. Add oil into the inner pot of instant pot and set the pot on sauté mode.
2. Add oregano, garlic, and onion and sauté for 5 minutes.
3. Add meat and sauté for 5 minutes.
4. Add the rest of the ingredients and stir well.
5. Seal pot with lid and cook on high for 20 minutes.
6. Once done, allow to release pressure naturally. Remove lid.
7. Serve and enjoy.

Nutritional Value (Amount per Serving):
Calories 514; Fat 23.9 g; Carbohydrates 7.4 g; Sugar 2.4 g; Protein 64.9 g; Cholesterol 204 mg

Curried Lamb Stew

Preparation Time: 10 minutes; Cooking Time: 20 minutes; Serve: 4
Ingredients:
- 1 lb lamb shoulder, cut into cubes
- 1/4 cup heavy cream
- 2 cups beef stock
- 1 tbsp basil, chopped
- 1 tsp chili powder
- 1/2 tbsp curry powder
- 1 onion, chopped
- 1 tbsp olive oil
- Pepper
- Salt

Directions:
1. Add oil into the inner pot of instant pot and set the pot on sauté mode.
2. Add onion and sauté for 5 minutes.
3. Add meat and sauté for 5 minutes.

4. Add the rest of ingredients except cream and stir well.
5. Seal pot with lid and cook on high for 10 minutes.
6. Once done, release pressure using quick release. Remove lid.
7. Stir in cream and serve.

Nutritional Value (Amount per Serving):
Calories 291; Fat 15.1 g; Carbohydrates 3.7 g; Sugar 1.3 g; Protein 33.9 g; Cholesterol 112 mg

Artichoke Lamb Curry

Preparation Time: 10 minutes; Cooking Time: 35 minutes; Serve: 4

Ingredients:
- 2 lb lamb meat, cut into chunks
- 1 tbsp dill, chopped
- 1/2 cup heavy cream
- 1 cup of coconut milk
- 1 onion, chopped
- 2 tbsp olive oil
- 1 tbsp curry powder
- 1 cup jar artichoke hearts, chopped
- Pepper
- Salt

Directions:
1. Add oil into the inner pot of instant pot and set the pot on sauté mode.
2. Add artichokes and onion and sauté for 5 minutes.
3. Add meat and sauté for 5 minutes.
4. Add the rest of the ingredients and stir well.
5. Seal pot with lid and cook on high for 25 minutes.
6. Once done, allow to release pressure naturally. Remove lid.
7. Serve and enjoy.

Nutritional Value (Amount per Serving):
Calories 738; Fat 57.2 g; Carbohydrates 9.2 g; Sugar 3.5 g; Protein 45 g; Cholesterol 181 mg

Lamb with Beans

Preparation Time: 10 minutes; Cooking Time: 35 minutes; Serve: 4

Ingredients:
- 2 lbs lamb meat, cut into chunks
- 1/4 cup cilantro, chopped
- 1 tbsp garlic, minced
- 1/4 cup can tomato, crushed
- 1 cup beef stock
- 2 cups can red beans, rinsed and drained
- 1 onion, chopped
- 2 tbsp olive oil
- Pepper
- Salt

Directions:
1. Add oil into the inner pot of instant pot and set the pot on sauté mode.
2. Add garlic, onion, and meat and sauté for 5 minutes.
3. Add the rest of the ingredients and stir well.
4. Seal pot with lid and cook on high for 30 minutes.
5. Once done, allow to release pressure naturally. Remove lid.
6. Serve and enjoy.

Nutritional Value (Amount per Serving):
Calories 650; Fat 37.8 g; Carbohydrates 23.7 g; Sugar 3.6 g; Protein 50.1 g; Cholesterol 161 mg

Garlic Coriander Lamb Chops

Preparation Time: 10 minutes; Cooking Time: 30 minutes; Serve: 4

Ingredients:
- 4 lamb chops
- 1 tbsp cilantro, chopped
- 1 cup beef stock
- 1/2 tsp ground coriander

- 1 tsp chili powder
- 1 tsp turmeric powder
- 1 tbsp garlic, minced
- 2 tbsp olive oil
- Pepper
- Salt

Directions:
1. Add oil into the inner pot of instant pot and set the pot on sauté mode.
2. Add garlic, lamb chops, chili powder, and turmeric and sauté for 5 minutes.
3. Add the rest of the ingredients and stir well.
4. Seal pot with lid and cook on high for 25 minutes.
5. Once done, allow to release pressure naturally. Remove lid.
6. Serve and enjoy.

Nutritional Value (Amount per Serving):
Calories 680; Fat 31.3 g; Carbohydrates 1.6 g; Sugar 0.1 g; Protein 92.8 g; Cholesterol 294 mg

Healthy Lamb & Couscous

Preparation Time: 10 minutes; Cooking Time: 43 minutes; Serve: 4
Ingredients:
- 4 lamb chops
- 2 celery stalks, chopped
- 1 tbsp olive oil
- 1 tbsp basil, chopped
- 1 tbsp oregano, chopped
- 1 tbsp almonds, chopped
- 3 cups beef stock
- 1 1/2 cusp couscous
- Pepper
- Salt

Directions:
1. Add oil into the inner pot of instant pot and set the pot on sauté mode.
2. Add the meat into the pot and sauté for 3 minutes.
3. Add the rest of the ingredients and stir well.
4. Seal pot with lid and cook on low pressure for 40 minutes.
5. Once done, allow to release pressure naturally. Remove lid.
6. Serve and enjoy.

Nutritional Value (Amount per Serving):
Calories 908; Fat 29.2 g; Carbohydrates 51.7 g; Sugar 0.2 g; Protein 102.7 g; Cholesterol 294 mg

Tomato Oregano Lamb Stew

Preparation Time: 10 minutes; Cooking Time: 40 minutes; Serve: 4
Ingredients:
- 4 lamb shanks
- 2 cups beef stock
- 1 tbsp oregano, chopped
- 1 1/2 cups tomatoes, chopped
- 1 tsp garlic, minced
- 1 onion, chopped
- 2 tbsp olive oil
- Pepper
- Salt

Directions:
1. Add oil into the inner pot of instant pot and set the pot on sauté mode.
2. Add lamb and sear for 5 minutes.
3. Add the rest of the ingredients and stir well.
4. Seal pot with lid and cook on low pressure for 35 minutes.
5. Once done, allow to release pressure naturally. Remove lid.
6. Serve and enjoy.

Nutritional Value (Amount per Serving):
Calories 704; Fat 31.5 g; Carbohydrates 6.2 g; Sugar 3 g; Protein 94.2 g; Cholesterol 294 mg

Chapter 12: Seafood & Fish

Delicious Lemon Butter Cod

Preparation Time: 10 minutes; Cooking Time: 8 minutes; Serve: 6
Ingredients:
- 1 1/2 lbs fresh cod fillets
- 28 oz can tomatoes, diced
- 1 tsp oregano
- 1 onion, sliced
- 1 lemon juice
- 3 tbsp butter
- Pepper
- Salt

Directions:
1. Add butter into the instant pot and set the pot on sauté mode.
2. Add onion and sauté for 5 minutes.
3. Add remaining ingredients and stir everything well.
4. Seal pot with lid and cook on high for 3 minutes.
5. Once done, release pressure using quick release. Remove lid.
6. Stir well and serve.

Nutritional Value (Amount per Serving):
Calories 231; Fat 6.9 g; Carbohydrates 29 g; Sugar 7.5 g; Protein 14.7 g; Cholesterol 51 mg

Italian White Fish Fillets

Preparation Time: 10 minutes; Cooking Time: 4 minutes; Serve: 4
Ingredients:
- 4 white fish fillets, frozen
- 2 tbsp olive oil
- 1/3 cup roasted red peppers, sliced
- 2 tbsp capers
- 3/4 cup olives
- 3/4 cup cherry tomatoes
- 1/4 cup water
- 1/2 tsp salt

Directions:
1. Add water into the inner pot of instant pot then place fish fillets in the pot.
2. Pour remaining ingredients over fish fillets.
3. Seal pot with lid and cook on high for 4 minutes.
4. Once done, allow to release pressure naturally for 5 minutes then release remaining using quick release. Remove lid.
5. Serve and enjoy.

Nutritional Value (Amount per Serving):
Calories 365; Fat 21.4 g; Carbohydrates 4 g; Sugar 1.6 g; Protein 38.4 g; Cholesterol 119 mg

Rosemary Salmon

Preparation Time: 10 minutes; Cooking Time: 3 minutes; Serve: 3
Ingredients:
- 1 lb salmon
- 1 tbsp fresh lemon juice
- 1 tbsp olive oil
- 1/2 cup cherry tomatoes, halved
- 1 fresh rosemary sprig
- 10 oz fresh asparagus, trimmed
- Pepper
- Salt

Directions:
1. Pour 1 cup of water into the instant pot then place steamer rack into the pot.
2. Place salmon on steamer rack then arrange asparagus and rosemary on top of salmon.
3. Seal pot with lid and cook on high for 3 minutes.
4. Once done, release pressure using quick release. Remove lid.
5. Transfer salmon and asparagus on a plate.
6. Add cherry tomatoes on top of salmon. Season with pepper and salt.

7. Drizzle oil and lemon juice over salmon.
8. Serve and enjoy.

Nutritional Value (Amount per Serving):
Calories 269; Fat 14.4 g; Carbohydrates 5.7 g; Sugar 2.7 g; Protein 31.8 g; Cholesterol 67 mg

Shrimp Salad

Preparation Time: 10 minutes; Cooking Time: 7 minutes; Serve: 4

Ingredients:
- 1 1/2 lbs shrimp, peeled and deveined
- 1 1/2 tbsp fresh basil, chopped
- 1 tbsp olive oil
- 1/2 cup vinegar
- 1/2 tsp hot sauce
- 1 onion, chopped
- 1/4 cup fresh lemon juice
- Pepper
- Salt

Directions:
1. Add oil into the inner pot of instant pot and set the pot on sauté mode.
2. Add onion and sauté for 2-3 minutes.
3. Add remaining ingredients and stir everything well.
4. Seal pot with lid and cook on high for 4 minutes.
5. Once done, allow to release pressure naturally for 5 minutes then release remaining using quick release. Remove lid.
6. Stir well and serve.

Nutritional Value (Amount per Serving):
Calories 253; Fat 6.5 g; Carbohydrates 5.8 g; Sugar 1.6 g; Protein 39.2 g; Cholesterol 358 mg

Chili Lime Salmon

Preparation Time: 10 minutes; Cooking Time: 12 minutes; Serve: 4

Ingredients:
- 1 lb salmon, skinless, boneless, and cubed
- 1 cup fish stock
- 1 tbsp olive oil
- 1/2 tsp ground coriander
- 1/2 tbsp fresh lime juice
- 1 small onion, chopped
- 2 green chilies, chopped
- 1 tsp garlic, minced
- Pepper
- Salt

Directions:
1. Add oil into the inner pot of instant pot and set the pot on sauté mode.
2. Add garlic, onion, green chilies, and ground coriander and cook for 2 minutes.
3. Add remaining ingredients and stir well.
4. Seal pot with lid and cook on high for 10 minutes.
5. Once done, release pressure using quick release. Remove lid.
6. Stir well and serve.

Nutritional Value (Amount per Serving):
Calories 200; Fat 11 g; Carbohydrates 2.5 g; Sugar 0.9 g; Protein 23.6 g; Cholesterol 51 mg

Steamed Salmon

Preparation Time: 10 minutes; Cooking Time: 5 minutes; Serve: 4

Ingredients:
- 4 salmon fillets, frozen
- 1/4 cup fresh lemon juice
- 3/4 cup water
- 1 tbsp dill, chopped
- 1 tbsp olive oil
- Pepper
- Salt

Directions:
1. Pour lemon juice and water into the instant pot.
2. Place a steamer basket in the pot. Place salmon fillets in the basket and season with pepper and salt.
3. Seal pot with a lid and select manual and cook on low for 5 minutes.
4. Once done, release pressure using quick release. Remove lid.
5. Transfer salmon fillets on a plate. Sprinkle dill over salmon.
6. Drizzle olive oil over salmon fillets and serve.

Nutritional Value (Amount per Serving):
Calories 271; Fat 14.6 g; Carbohydrates 0.8 g; Sugar 0.3 g; Protein 34.8 g; Cholesterol 78 mg

Rosemary Mussels

Preparation Time: 10 minutes; Cooking Time: 9 minutes; Serve: 4
Ingredients:
- 1 lb mussels, cleaned
- 1/2 cup sour cream
- 1/2 tsp garlic, minced
- 1/2 onion, chopped
- 1 tbsp olive oil
- 2 tbsp fresh lemon juice
- 1/2 cup fish stock
- 1/2 tsp dried rosemary
- Pepper
- Salt

Directions:
1. Add oil into the inner pot of instant pot and set the pot on sauté mode.
2. Add onion and sauté for 3 minutes.
3. Add rosemary and garlic and sauté for a minute.
4. Add remaining ingredients and stir well.
5. Seal pot with lid and cook on high for 5 minutes.
6. Once done, release pressure using quick release. Remove lid.
7. Serve and enjoy.

Nutritional Value (Amount per Serving):
Calories 202; Fat 12.4 g; Carbohydrates 7.1 g; Sugar 0.8 g; Protein 15.3 g; Cholesterol 45 mg

Basil Fish Curry

Preparation Time: 10 minutes; Cooking Time: 8 minutes; Serve: 4
Ingredients:
- 10 oz tilapia fillets, chopped
- 1/2 tsp turmeric
- 1 tsp ground cumin
- 1 1/2 tsp chili powder
- 1 tsp ground coriander
- 1/2 cup fresh basil, chopped
- 1 tsp fresh lemon juice
- 3 tbsp olive oil
- 1 chili pepper, chopped
- 1/2 cup grape tomatoes, chopped
- 2 cups of coconut milk
- 1 tsp garlic, minced
- 1 small onion, chopped
- Salt

Directions:
1. Add oil into the inner pot of instant pot and set the pot on sauté mode.
2. Add garlic, onion, salt, and all spices and cook for 2-4 minutes.
3. Add coconut milk and stir well.
4. Add chili pepper, fish, and grape tomatoes and stir well.
5. Seal pot with lid and cook on high for 4 minutes.
6. Once done, release pressure using quick release. Remove lid.
7. Stir in basil and serve.

Nutritional Value (Amount per Serving):
Calories 444; Fat 40.2 g; Carbohydrates 10.5 g; Sugar 5.5 g; Protein 16.7 g; Cholesterol 35 mg

Italian Fish Stew

Preparation Time: 10 minutes; Cooking Time: 7 minutes; Serve: 2

Ingredients:
- 10 oz catfish fillets, cut into chunks
- 1 tsp dried dill
- 1 tsp garlic powder
- 1/4 tsp red pepper flakes
- 1 tsp Italian seasoning
- 3 tbsp olive oil
- 2 cups spinach, chopped
- 2 cups grape tomatoes, chopped
- 2 cups fish stock
- 1/2 tsp salt

Directions:
1. Add all ingredients except spinach into the instant pot and stir well.
2. Seal pot with lid and cook on high for 7 minutes.
3. Once done, allow to release pressure naturally for 5 minutes then release remaining using quick release. Remove lid.
4. Add spinach and stir until spinach is wilted.
5. Serve and enjoy.

Nutritional Value (Amount per Serving):
Calories 464; Fat 34.9 g; Carbohydrates 9.8 g; Sugar 5.4 g; Protein 30.1 g; Cholesterol 71 mg

Thyme Mussels

Preparation Time: 10 minutes; Cooking Time: 5 minutes; Serve: 4

Ingredients:
- 1 lb mussels, cleaned
- 2 tbsp fresh parsley, chopped
- 1/2 tsp red pepper flakes
- 1 tsp dried thyme
- 2 tbsp olive oil
- 2 tbsp fresh lemon juice
- 1 tbsp garlic, minced
- 2 cups fish stock

Directions:
1. Add all ingredients except mussels into the instant pot and stir well.
2. Add mussels and stir well.
3. Seal pot with lid and cook on high for 5 minutes.
4. Once done, release pressure using quick release. Remove lid.
5. Serve and enjoy.

Nutritional Value (Amount per Serving):
Calories 184; Fat 10.6 g; Carbohydrates 5.4 g; Sugar 0.2 g; Protein 16.4 g; Cholesterol 33 mg

Mediterranean Fish Fillets

Preparation Time: 10 minutes; Cooking Time: 3 minutes; Serve: 4

Ingredients:
- 4 cod fillets
- 1 lb grape tomatoes, halved
- 1 cup olives, pitted and sliced
- 2 tbsp capers
- 1 tsp dried thyme
- 2 tbsp olive oil
- 1 tsp garlic, minced
- Pepper
- Salt

Directions:
1. Pour 1 cup water into the instant pot then place steamer rack in the pot.
2. Spray heat-safe baking dish with cooking spray.
3. Add half grape tomatoes into the dish and season with pepper and salt.
4. Arrange fish fillets on top of cherry tomatoes. Drizzle with oil and season with garlic, thyme, capers, pepper, and salt.
5. Spread olives and remaining grape tomatoes on top of fish fillets.
6. Place dish on top of steamer rack in the pot.

7. Seal pot with a lid and select manual and cook on high for 3 minutes.
8. Once done, release pressure using quick release. Remove lid.
9. Serve and enjoy.

Nutritional Value (Amount per Serving):
Calories 212; Fat 11.9 g; Carbohydrates 7.1 g; Sugar 3 g; Protein 21.4 g; Cholesterol 55 mg

Flavors Cioppino

Preparation Time: 10 minutes; Cooking Time: 5 minutes; Serve: 6
Ingredients:
- 1 lb codfish, cut into chunks
- 1 1/2 lbs shrimp
- 28 oz can tomatoes, diced
- 1 cup dry white wine
- 1 bay leaf
- 1 tsp cayenne
- 1 tsp oregano
- 1 shallot, chopped
- 1 tsp garlic, minced
- 1 tbsp olive oil
- 1/2 tsp salt

Directions:
1. Add oil into the inner pot of instant pot and set the pot on sauté mode.
2. Add shallot and garlic and sauté for 2 minutes.
3. Add wine, bay leaf, cayenne, oregano, and salt and cook for 3 minutes.
4. Add remaining ingredients and stir well.
5. Seal pot with a lid and select manual and cook on low for 0 minutes.
6. Once done, release pressure using quick release. Remove lid.
7. Serve and enjoy.

Nutritional Value (Amount per Serving):
Calories 281; Fat 5 g; Carbohydrates 10.5 g; Sugar 4.9 g; Protein 40.7 g; Cholesterol 266 mg

Delicious Shrimp Alfredo

Preparation Time: 10 minutes; Cooking Time: 3 minutes; Serve: 4
Ingredients:
- 12 shrimp, remove shells
- 1 tbsp garlic, minced
- 1/4 cup parmesan cheese
- 2 cups whole wheat rotini noodles
- 1 cup fish broth
- 15 oz alfredo sauce
- 1 onion, chopped
- Salt

Directions:
1. Add all ingredients except parmesan cheese into the instant pot and stir well.
2. Seal pot with lid and cook on high for 3 minutes.
3. Once done, release pressure using quick release. Remove lid.
4. Stir in cheese and serve.

Nutritional Value (Amount per Serving):
Calories 669; Fat 23.1 g; Carbohydrates 76 g; Sugar 2.4 g; Protein 37.8 g; Cholesterol 190 mg

Tomato Olive Fish Fillets

Preparation Time: 10 minutes; Cooking Time: 8 minutes; Serve: 4
Ingredients:
- 2 lbs halibut fish fillets
- 2 oregano sprigs
- 2 rosemary sprigs
- 2 tbsp fresh lime juice
- 1 cup olives, pitted
- 28 oz can tomatoes, diced
- 1 tbsp garlic, minced
- 1 onion, chopped
- 2 tbsp olive oil

Directions:

1. Add oil into the inner pot of instant pot and set the pot on sauté mode.
2. Add onion and sauté for 3 minutes.
3. Add garlic and sauté for a minute.
4. Add lime juice, olives, herb sprigs, and tomatoes and stir well.
5. Seal pot with lid and cook on high for 3 minutes.
6. Once done, release pressure using quick release. Remove lid.
7. Add fish fillets and seal pot again with lid and cook on high for 2 minutes.
8. Once done, release pressure using quick release. Remove lid.
9. Serve and enjoy.

Nutritional Value (Amount per Serving):
Calories 333; Fat 19.1 g; Carbohydrates 31.8 g; Sugar 8.4 g; Protein 13.4 g; Cholesterol 5 mg

Shrimp Scampi

Preparation Time: 10 minutes; Cooking Time: 8 minutes; Serve: 6
Ingredients:
- 1 lb whole wheat penne pasta
- 1 lb frozen shrimp
- 2 tbsp garlic, minced
- 1/4 tsp cayenne
- 1/2 tbsp Italian seasoning
- 1/4 cup olive oil
- 3 1/2 cups fish stock
- Pepper
- Salt

Directions:
1. Add all ingredients into the inner pot of instant pot and stir well.
2. Seal pot with lid and cook on high for 6 minutes.
3. Once done, release pressure using quick release. Remove lid.
4. Stir well and serve.

Nutritional Value (Amount per Serving):
Calories 435; Fat 12.6 g; Carbohydrates 54.9 g; Sugar 0.1 g; Protein 30.6 g; Cholesterol 116 mg

Easy Salmon Stew

Preparation Time: 10 minutes; Cooking Time: 8 minutes; Serve: 6
Ingredients:
- 2 lbs salmon fillet, cubed
- 1 onion, chopped
- 2 cups fish broth
- 1 tbsp olive oil
- Pepper
- salt

Directions:
1. Add oil into the inner pot of instant pot and set the pot on sauté mode.
2. Add onion and sauté for 2 minutes.
3. Add remaining ingredients and stir well.
4. Seal pot with lid and cook on high for 6 minutes.
5. Once done, release pressure using quick release. Remove lid.
6. Stir and serve.

Nutritional Value (Amount per Serving):
Calories 243; Fat 12.6 g; Carbohydrates 0.8 g; Sugar 0.3 g; Protein 31 g; Cholesterol 78 mg

Italian Tuna Pasta

Preparation Time: 10 minutes; Cooking Time: 5 minutes; Serve: 6
Ingredients:
- 15 oz whole wheat pasta
- 2 tbsp capers
- 3 oz tuna
- 2 cups can tomatoes, crushed
- 2 anchovies
- 1 tsp garlic, minced

- 1 tbsp olive oil
- Salt

Directions:
1. Add oil into the inner pot of instant pot and set the pot on sauté mode.
2. Add anchovies and garlic and sauté for 1 minute.
3. Add remaining ingredients and stir well. Pour enough water into the pot to cover the pasta.
4. Seal pot with a lid and select manual and cook on low for 4 minutes.
5. Once done, release pressure using quick release. Remove lid.
6. Stir and serve.

Nutritional Value (Amount per Serving):
Calories 339; Fat 6 g; Carbohydrates 56.5 g; Sugar 5.2 g; Protein 15.2 g; Cholesterol 10 mg

Garlicky Clams

Preparation Time: 10 minutes; Cooking Time: 5 minutes; Serve: 4

Ingredients:
- 3 lbs clams, clean
- 4 garlic cloves
- 1/4 cup olive oil
- 1/2 cup fresh lemon juice
- 1 cup white wine
- Pepper
- Salt

Directions:
1. Add oil into the inner pot of instant pot and set the pot on sauté mode.
2. Add garlic and sauté for 1 minute.
3. Add wine and cook for 2 minutes.
4. Add remaining ingredients and stir well.
5. Seal pot with lid and cook on high for 2 minutes.
6. Once done, allow to release pressure naturally. Remove lid.
7. Serve and enjoy.

Nutritional Value (Amount per Serving):
Calories 332; Fat 13.5 g; Carbohydrates 40.5 g; Sugar 12.4 g; Protein 2.5 g; Cholesterol 0 mg

Delicious Fish Tacos

Preparation Time: 10 minutes; Cooking Time: 8 minutes; Serve: 8

Ingredients:
- 4 tilapia fillets
- 1/4 cup fresh cilantro, chopped
- 1/4 cup fresh lime juice
- 2 tbsp paprika
- 1 tbsp olive oil
- Pepper
- Salt

Directions:
1. Pour 2 cups of water into the instant pot then place steamer rack in the pot.
2. Place fish fillets on parchment paper.
3. Season fish fillets with paprika, pepper, and salt and drizzle with oil and lime juice.
4. Fold parchment paper around the fish fillets and place them on a steamer rack in the pot.
5. Seal pot with lid and cook on high for 8 minutes.
6. Once done, release pressure using quick release. Remove lid.
7. Remove fish packet from pot and open it.
8. Shred the fish with a fork and serve.

Nutritional Value (Amount per Serving):
Calories 67; Fat 2.5 g; Carbohydrates 1.1 g; Sugar 0.2 g; Protein 10.8 g; Cholesterol 28 mg

Pesto Fish Fillet

Preparation Time: 10 minutes; Cooking Time: 8 minutes; Serve: 4

Ingredients:
- 4 halibut fillets
- 1/2 cup water
- 1 tbsp lemon zest, grated
- 1 tbsp capers
- 1/2 cup basil, chopped
- 1 tbsp garlic, chopped
- 1 avocado, peeled and chopped
- Pepper
- Salt

Directions:
1. Add lemon zest, capers, basil, garlic, avocado, pepper, and salt into the blender blend until smooth.
2. Place fish fillets on aluminum foil and spread a blended mixture on fish fillets.
3. Fold foil around the fish fillets.
4. Pour water into the instant pot and place trivet in the pot.
5. Place foil fish packet on the trivet.
6. Seal pot with lid and cook on high for 8 minutes.
7. Once done, allow to release pressure naturally. Remove lid.
8. Serve and enjoy.

Nutritional Value (Amount per Serving):
Calories 426; Fat 16.6 g; Carbohydrates 5.5 g; Sugar 0.4 g; Protein 61.8 g; Cholesterol 93 mg

Tuna Risotto

Preparation Time: 10 minutes; Cooking Time: 23 minutes; Serve: 6

Ingredients:
- 1 cup of rice
- 1/3 cup parmesan cheese, grated
- 1 1/2 cups fish broth
- 1 lemon juice
- 1 tbsp garlic, minced
- 1 onion, chopped
- 2 tbsp olive oil
- 2 cups can tuna, cut into chunks
- Pepper
- Salt

Directions:
1. Add oil into the inner pot of instant pot and set the pot on sauté mode.
2. Add garlic, onion, and tuna and cook for 3 minutes.
3. Add remaining ingredients except for parmesan cheese and stir well.
4. Seal pot with lid and cook on high for 20 minutes.
5. Once done, release pressure using quick release. Remove lid.
6. Stir in parmesan cheese and serve.

Nutritional Value (Amount per Serving):
Calories 228; Fat 7 g; Carbohydrates 27.7 g; Sugar 1.2 g; Protein 12.6 g; Cholesterol 21 mg

Salsa Fish Fillets

Preparation Time: 10 minutes; Cooking Time: 2 minutes; Serve: 4

Ingredients:
- 1 lb tilapia fillets
- 1/2 cup salsa
- 1 cup of water
- Pepper
- Salt

Directions:
1. Place fish fillets on aluminum foil and top with salsa and season with pepper and salt.
2. Fold foil around the fish fillets.
3. Pour water into the instant pot and place trivet in the pot.
4. Place foil fish packet on the trivet.

5. Seal pot with lid and cook on high for 2 minutes.
6. Once done, release pressure using quick release. Remove lid.
7. Serve and enjoy.

Nutritional Value (Amount per Serving):
Calories 342; Fat 10.5 g; Carbohydrates 41.5 g; Sugar 1.9 g; Protein 18.9 g; Cholesterol 31 mg

Coconut Clam Chowder

Preparation Time: 10 minutes; Cooking Time: 7 minutes; Serve: 6

Ingredients:
- 6 oz clams, chopped
- 1 cup heavy cream
- 1/4 onion, sliced
- 1 cup celery, chopped
- 1 lb cauliflower, chopped
- 1 cup fish broth
- 1 bay leaf
- 2 cups of coconut milk
- Salt

Directions:
1. Add all ingredients except clams and heavy cream and stir well.
2. Seal pot with lid and cook on high for 5 minutes.
3. Once done, release pressure using quick release. Remove lid.
4. Add heavy cream and clams and stir well and cook on sauté mode for 2 minutes.
5. Stir well and serve.

Nutritional Value (Amount per Serving):
Calories 301; Fat 27.2 g; Carbohydrates 13.6 g; Sugar 6 g; Protein 4.9 g; Cholesterol 33 mg

Feta Tomato Sea Bass

Preparation Time: 10 minutes; Cooking Time: 8 minutes; Serve: 4

Ingredients:
- 4 sea bass fillets
- 1 1/2 cups water
- 1 tbsp olive oil
- 1 tsp garlic, minced
- 1 tsp basil, chopped
- 1 tsp parsley, chopped
- 1/2 cup feta cheese, crumbled
- 1 cup can tomatoes, diced
- Pepper
- Salt

Directions:
1. Season fish fillets with pepper and salt.
2. Pour 2 cups of water into the instant pot then place steamer rack in the pot.
3. Place fish fillets on steamer rack in the pot.
4. Seal pot with lid and cook on high for 5 minutes.
5. Once done, release pressure using quick release. Remove lid.
6. Remove fish fillets from the pot and clean the pot.
7. Add oil into the inner pot of instant pot and set the pot on sauté mode.
8. Add garlic and sauté for 1 minute.
9. Add tomatoes, parsley, and basil and stir well and cook for 1 minute.
10. Add fish fillets and top with crumbled cheese and cook for a minute.
11. Serve and enjoy.

Nutritional Value (Amount per Serving):
Calories 219; Fat 10.1 g; Carbohydrates 4 g; Sugar 2.8 g; Protein 27.1 g; Cholesterol 70 mg

Stewed Mussels & Scallops

Preparation Time: 10 minutes; Cooking Time: 11 minutes; Serve: 4

Ingredients:
- 2 cups mussels
- 1 cup scallops

- 2 cups fish stock
- 2 bell peppers, diced
- 2 cups cauliflower rice
- 1 onion, chopped
- 1 tbsp olive oil
- Pepper
- Salt

Directions:
1. Add oil into the inner pot of instant pot and set the pot on sauté mode.
2. Add onion and peppers and sauté for 3 minutes.
3. Add scallops and cook for 2 minutes.
4. Add remaining ingredients and stir well.
5. Seal pot with lid and cook on high for 6 minutes.
6. Once done, allow to release pressure naturally. Remove lid.
7. Stir and serve.

Nutritional Value (Amount per Serving):
Calories 191; Fat 7.4 g; Carbohydrates 13.7 g; Sugar 6.2 g; Protein 18 g; Cholesterol 29 mg

Healthy Halibut Soup

Preparation Time: 10 minutes; Cooking Time: 13 minutes; Serve: 4
Ingredients:
- 1 lb halibut, skinless, boneless, & cut into chunks
- 2 tbsp ginger, minced
- 2 celery stalks, chopped
- 1 carrot, sliced
- 1 onion, chopped
- 1 cup of water
- 2 cups fish stock
- 1 tbsp olive oil
- Pepper
- Salt

Directions:
1. Add oil into the inner pot of instant pot and set the pot on sauté mode.
2. Add onion and sauté for 3-4 minutes.
3. Add water, celery, carrot, ginger, and stock and stir well.
4. Seal pot with lid and cook on high for 5 minutes.
5. Once done, release pressure using quick release. Remove lid.
6. Add fish and stir well. Seal pot again and cook on high for 4 minutes.
7. Once done, release pressure using quick release. Remove lid.
8. Stir and serve.

Nutritional Value (Amount per Serving):
Calories 4586; Fat 99.6 g; Carbohydrates 6.3 g; Sugar 2.1 g; Protein 861 g; Cholesterol 1319 mg

Creamy Fish Stew

Preparation Time: 10 minutes; Cooking Time: 8 minutes; Serve: 6
Ingredients:
- 1 lb white fish fillets, cut into chunks
- 2 tbsp olive oil
- 1 cup kale, chopped
- 1 cup cauliflower, chopped
- 1 cup broccoli, chopped
- 3 cups fish broth
- 1 cup heavy cream
- 2 celery stalks, diced
- 1 carrot, sliced
- 1 onion, diced
- Pepper
- Salt

Directions:
1. Add oil into the inner pot of instant pot and set the pot on sauté mode.
2. Add onion and sauté for 3 minutes.
3. Add remaining ingredients except for heavy cream and stir well.
4. Seal pot with lid and cook on high for 5 minutes.

5. Once done, allow to release pressure naturally. Remove lid.
6. Stir in heavy cream and serve.

Nutritional Value (Amount per Serving):
Calories 296; Fat 19.3 g; Carbohydrates 7.5 g; Sugar 2.6 g; Protein 22.8 g; Cholesterol 103 mg

Nutritious Broccoli Salmon

Preparation Time: 10 minutes; Cooking Time: 4 minutes; Serve: 4
Ingredients:
- 4 salmon fillets
- 10 oz broccoli florets
- 1 1/2 cups water
- 1 tbsp olive oil
- Pepper
- Salt

Directions:
1. Pour water into the instant pot then place steamer basket in the pot.
2. Place salmon in the steamer basket and season with pepper and salt and drizzle with oil.
3. Add broccoli on top of salmon in the steamer basket.
4. Seal pot with lid and cook on high for 4 minutes.
5. Once done, release pressure using quick release. Remove lid.
6. Serve and enjoy.

Nutritional Value (Amount per Serving):
Calories 290; Fat 14.7 g; Carbohydrates 4.7 g; Sugar 1.2 g; Protein 36.5 g; Cholesterol 78 mg

Shrimp Zoodles

Preparation Time: 10 minutes; Cooking Time: 5 minutes; Serve: 4
Ingredients:
- 2 zucchini, spiralized
- 1 lb shrimp, peeled and deveined
- 1/2 tsp paprika
- 1 tbsp basil, chopped
- 1/2 lemon juice
- 1 tsp garlic, minced
- 2 tbsp olive oil
- 1 cup vegetable stock
- Pepper
- Salt

Directions:
1. Add oil into the inner pot of instant pot and set the pot on sauté mode.
2. Add garlic and sauté for a minute.
3. Add shrimp and lemon juice and stir well and cook for 1 minute.
4. Add remaining ingredients and stir well.
5. Seal pot with lid and cook on high for 3 minutes.
6. Once done, release pressure using quick release. Remove lid.
7. Serve and enjoy.

Nutritional Value (Amount per Serving):
Calories 215; Fat 9.2 g; Carbohydrates 5.8 g; Sugar 2 g; Protein 27.3 g; Cholesterol 239 mg

Healthy Carrot & Shrimp

Preparation Time: 10 minutes; Cooking Time: 6 minutes; Serve: 4
Ingredients:
- 1 lb shrimp, peeled and deveined
- 1 tbsp chives, chopped
- 1 onion, chopped
- 1 tbsp olive oil
- 1 cup fish stock
- 1 cup carrots, sliced
- Pepper
- Salt

Directions:
1. Add oil into the inner pot of instant pot and set the pot on sauté mode.
2. Add onion and sauté for 2 minutes.

3. Add shrimp and stir well.
4. Add remaining ingredients and stir well.
5. Seal pot with lid and cook on high for 4 minutes.
6. Once done, release pressure using quick release. Remove lid.
7. Serve and enjoy.

Nutritional Value (Amount per Serving):
Calories 197; Fat 5.9 g; Carbohydrates 7 g; Sugar 2.5 g; Protein 27.7 g; Cholesterol 239 mg

Salmon with Potatoes

Preparation Time: 10 minutes; Cooking Time: 15 minutes; Serve: 4
Ingredients:
- 1 1/2 lbs Salmon fillets, boneless and cubed
- 2 tbsp olive oil
- 1 cup fish stock
- 2 tbsp parsley, chopped
- 1 tsp garlic, minced
- 1 lb baby potatoes, halved
- Pepper
- Salt

Directions:
1. Add oil into the inner pot of instant pot and set the pot on sauté mode.
2. Add garlic and sauté for 2 minutes.
3. Add remaining ingredients and stir well.
4. Seal pot with lid and cook on high for 13 minutes.
5. Once done, release pressure using quick release. Remove lid.
6. Serve and enjoy.

Nutritional Value (Amount per Serving):
Calories 362; Fat 18.1 g; Carbohydrates 14.5 g; Sugar 0 g; Protein 37.3 g; Cholesterol 76 mg

Honey Garlic Shrimp

Preparation Time: 10 minutes; Cooking Time: 5 minutes; Serve: 4
Ingredients:
- 1 lb shrimp, peeled and deveined
- 1/4 cup honey
- 1 tbsp garlic, minced
- 1 tbsp ginger, minced
- 1 tbsp olive oil
- 1/4 cup fish stock
- Pepper
- Salt

Directions:
1. Add shrimp into the large bowl. Add remaining ingredients over shrimp and toss well.
2. Transfer shrimp into the instant pot and stir well.
3. Seal pot with lid and cook on high for 5 minutes.
4. Once done, release pressure using quick release. Remove lid.
5. Serve and enjoy.

Nutritional Value (Amount per Serving):
Calories 240; Fat 5.6 g; Carbohydrates 20.9 g; Sugar 17.5 g; Protein 26.5 g; Cholesterol 239 mg

Simple Lemon Clams

Preparation Time: 10 minutes; Cooking Time: 10 minutes; Serve: 4
Ingredients:
- 1 lb clams, clean
- 1 tbsp fresh lemon juice
- 1 lemon zest, grated
- 1 onion, chopped
- 1/2 cup fish stock
- Pepper
- Salt

Directions:

1. Add all ingredients into the inner pot of instant pot and stir well.
2. Seal pot with lid and cook on high for 10 minutes.
3. Once done, release pressure using quick release. Remove lid.
4. Serve and enjoy.

Nutritional Value (Amount per Serving):
Calories 76; Fat 0.6 g; Carbohydrates 16.4 g; Sugar 5.4 g; Protein 1.8 g; Cholesterol 0 mg

Crab Stew

Preparation Time: 10 minutes; Cooking Time: 13 minutes; Serve: 2
Ingredients:
- 1/2 lb lump crab meat
- 2 tbsp heavy cream
- 1 tbsp olive oil
- 2 cups fish stock
- 1/2 lb shrimp, shelled and chopped
- 1 celery stalk, chopped
- 1/2 tsp garlic, chopped
- 1/4 onion, chopped
- Pepper
- Salt

Directions:
1. Add oil into the inner pot of instant pot and set the pot on sauté mode.
2. Add onion and sauté for 3 minutes.
3. Add garlic and sauté for 30 seconds.
4. Add remaining ingredients except for heavy cream and stir well.
5. Seal pot with lid and cook on high for 10 minutes.
6. Once done, release pressure using quick release. Remove lid.
7. Stir in heavy cream and serve.

Nutritional Value (Amount per Serving):
Calories 376; Fat 25.5 g; Carbohydrates 5.8 g; Sugar 0.7 g; Protein 48.1 g; Cholesterol 326 mg

Honey Balsamic Salmon

Preparation Time: 10 minutes; Cooking Time: 3 minutes; Serve: 2
Ingredients:
- 2 salmon fillets
- 1/4 tsp red pepper flakes
- 2 tbsp honey
- 2 tbsp balsamic vinegar
- 1 cup of water
- Pepper
- Salt

Directions:
1. Pour water into the instant pot and place trivet in the pot.
2. In a small bowl, mix together honey, red pepper flakes, and vinegar.
3. Brush fish fillets with honey mixture and place on top of the trivet.
4. Seal pot with lid and cook on high for 3 minutes.
5. Once done, release pressure using quick release. Remove lid.
6. Serve and enjoy.

Nutritional Value (Amount per Serving):
Calories 303; Fat 11 g; Carbohydrates 17.6 g; Sugar 17.3 g; Protein 34.6 g; Cholesterol 78 mg

Spicy Tomato Crab Mix

Preparation Time: 10 minutes; Cooking Time: 12 minutes; Serve: 4
Ingredients:
- 1 lb crab meat
- 1 tsp paprika
- 1 cup grape tomatoes, cut into half
- 2 tbsp green onion, chopped
- 1 tbsp olive oil
- Pepper
- Salt

Directions:
1. Add oil into the inner pot of instant pot and set the pot on sauté mode.
2. Add paprika and onion and sauté for 2 minutes.
3. Add the rest of the ingredients and stir well.
4. Seal pot with lid and cook on high for 10 minutes.
5. Once done, release pressure using quick release. Remove lid.
6. Serve and enjoy.

Nutritional Value (Amount per Serving):
Calories 142; Fat 5.7 g; Carbohydrates 4.3 g; Sugar 1.3 g; Protein 14.7 g; Cholesterol 61 mg

Dijon Fish Fillets

Preparation Time: 10 minutes; Cooking Time: 3 minutes; Serve: 2
Ingredients:
- 2 white fish fillets
- 1 tbsp Dijon mustard
- 1 cup of water
- Pepper
- Salt

Directions:
1. Pour water into the instant pot and place trivet in the pot.
2. Brush fish fillets with mustard and season with pepper and salt and place on top of the trivet.
3. Seal pot with lid and cook on high for 3 minutes.
4. Once done, release pressure using quick release. Remove lid.
5. Serve and enjoy.

Nutritional Value (Amount per Serving):
Calories 270; Fat 11.9 g; Carbohydrates 0.5 g; Sugar 0.1 g; Protein 38 g; Cholesterol 119 mg

Lemoney Prawns

Preparation Time: 10 minutes; Cooking Time: 3 minutes; Serve: 2
Ingredients:
- 1/2 lb prawns
- 1/2 cup fish stock
- 1 tbsp fresh lemon juice
- 1 tbsp lemon zest, grated
- 1 tbsp olive oil
- 1 tbsp garlic, minced
- Pepper
- Salt

Directions:
1. Add all ingredients into the inner pot of instant pot and stir well.
2. Seal pot with lid and cook on high for 3 minutes.
3. Once done, release pressure using quick release. Remove lid.
4. Drain prawns and serve.

Nutritional Value (Amount per Serving):
Calories 215; Fat 9.5 g; Carbohydrates 3.9 g; Sugar 0.4 g; Protein 27.6 g; Cholesterol 239 mg

Lemon Cod Peas

Preparation Time: 10 minutes; Cooking Time: 10 minutes; Serve: 4
Ingredients:
- 1 lb cod fillets, skinless, boneless and cut into chunks
- 1 cup fish stock
- 1 tbsp fresh parsley, chopped
- 1/2 tbsp lemon juice
- 1 green chili, chopped
- 3/4 cup fresh peas
- 2 tbsp onion, chopped
- Pepper
- Salt

Directions:

1. Add all ingredients into the inner pot of instant pot and stir well.
2. Seal pot with lid and cook on high for 10 minutes.
3. Once done, release pressure using quick release. Remove lid.
4. Stir and serve.

Nutritional Value (Amount per Serving):
Calories 128; Fat 1.6 g; Carbohydrates 5 g; Sugar 2.1 g; Protein 23.2 g; Cholesterol 41 mg

Quick & Easy Shrimp

Preparation Time: 10 minutes; Cooking Time: 1 minute; Serve: 6
Directions:
- 1 3/4 lbs shrimp, frozen and deveined
- 1/2 cup fish stock
- 1/2 cup apple cider vinegar
- Pepper
- Salt

Directions:
1. Add all ingredients into the inner pot of instant pot and stir well.
2. Seal pot with lid and cook on high for 1 minute.
3. Once done, release pressure using quick release. Remove lid.
4. Stir and serve.

Nutritional Value (Amount per Serving):
Calories 165; Fat 2.4 g; Carbohydrates 2.2 g; Sugar 0.1 g; Protein 30.6 g; Cholesterol 279 mg

Chapter 13: Desserts

Chocolate Nut Spread

Preparation Time: 10 minutes; Cooking Time: 10 minutes; Serve: 4
Ingredients:
- 1/4 cup unsweetened cocoa powder
- 1/4 tsp nutmeg
- 1 tsp vanilla
- 1/4 cup coconut oil
- 1 tsp liquid stevia
- 1/4 cup coconut cream
- 3 tbsp walnuts
- 1 cup almonds

Directions:
1. Add walnut and almonds into the food processor and process until smooth.
2. Add oil and process for 1 minute. Transfer to the bowl and stir in vanilla, nutmeg, and liquid stevia.
3. Add coconut cream into the instant pot and set the pot on sauté mode.
4. Add almond mixture and cocoa powder and stir well and cook for 5 minutes.
5. Pour into the container and store it in the refrigerator for 30 minutes.
6. Serve and enjoy.

Nutritional Value (Amount per Serving):
Calories 342; Fat 33.3 g; Carbohydrates 9.6 g; Sugar 1.8 g; Protein 7.8 g; Cholesterol 0 mg

Fruit Nut Bowl

Preparation Time: 10 minutes; Cooking Time: 10 minutes; Serve: 2
Ingredients:
- 1/4 cup pecans, chopped
- 1/4 cup shredded coconut
- 1 cup of water
- 3 tbsp coconut oil
- 1/2 tsp cinnamon
- 1 pear, chopped
- 1 plum, chopped
- 2 tbsp Swerve
- 1 apple, chopped

Directions:
1. In a heat-safe dish add coconut, coconut oil, pear, apple, plum, and swerve and mix well.
2. Pour water into the instant pot then place the trivet in the pot.
3. Place dish on top of the trivet.
4. Seal pot with lid and cook on high for 10 minutes.
5. Once done, release pressure using quick release. Remove lid.
6. Remove dish from pot carefully. Top with pecans and serve.

Nutritional Value (Amount per Serving):
Calories 338; Fat 25.4 g; Carbohydrates 47.2 g; Sugar 37.6 g; Protein 1.4 g; Cholesterol 0 mg

Applesauce

Preparation Time: 10 minutes; Cooking Time: 1 minute; Serve: 12
Ingredients:
- 3 lbs apples, peeled, cored, and diced
- 1/3 cup apple juice
- 1/2 tsp ground cinnamon

Directions:
1. Add all ingredients into the instant pot and stir well.
2. Seal pot with lid and cook on high for 1 minute.
3. Once done, allow to release pressure naturally. Remove lid.
4. Blend apple mixture using an immersion blender until smooth.
5. Serve and enjoy.

Nutritional Value (Amount per Serving):

Calories 32; Fat 0.1 g; Carbohydrates 8.6 g; Sugar 6.5 g; Protein 0.2 g; Cholesterol 0 mg

Sweet Coconut Raspberries

Preparation Time: 10 minutes; Cooking Time: 2 minutes; Serve: 12
Ingredients:
- 1/2 cup dried raspberries
- 3 tbsp swerve
- 1/2 cup shredded coconut
- 1/2 cup coconut oil
- 1/2 cup coconut butter

Directions:
1. Set instant pot on sauté mode.
2. Add coconut butter into the pot and let it melt.
3. Add raspberries, coconut, oil, and swerve and stir well.
4. Seal pot with lid and cook on high for 2 minutes.
5. Once done, release pressure using quick release. Remove lid.
6. Spread berry mixture on a parchment-lined baking tray and place in the refrigerator for 3-4 hours.
7. Slice and serve.

Nutritional Value (Amount per Serving):
Calories 101; Fat 10.6 g; Carbohydrates 6.2 g; Sugar 5.1 g; Protein 0.3 g; Cholesterol 0 mg

Creamy Fruit Bowls

Preparation Time: 10 minutes; Cooking Time: 1 minute; Serve: 4
Ingredients:
- 1 cup heavy cream
- 1 cup grapes, halved
- 1 avocado, peeled and cubed
- 3 cups pineapple, peeled and cubed
- 1 cup mango, peeled and cubed
- 1/2 tsp vanilla

Directions:
1. Add mango, pineapple, avocado, and grapes into the instant pot and stir well.
2. Seal pot with lid and cook on high for 1 minute.
3. Once done, release pressure using quick release. Remove lid.
4. Stir in vanilla and heavy cream.
5. Serve and enjoy.

Nutritional Value (Amount per Serving):
Calories 309; Fat 21.3 g; Carbohydrates 31.6 g; Sugar 21.9 g; Protein 2.7 g; Cholesterol 41 mg

Delicious Berry Crunch

Preparation Time: 10 minutes; Cooking Time: 4 minutes; Serve: 2
Ingredients:
- 2 tbsp almond flour
- 1 tsp cinnamon
- 1/2 cup pecans, chopped
- 2 tbsp coconut oil
- 1/4 tsp Xanthan gum
- 1/4 cup Erythritol
- 1 tsp vanilla
- 20 blackberries

Directions:
1. Add blackberries, vanilla, erythritol, and xanthan gum into the heat-safe dish. Stir well.
2. Mix together almond flour, cinnamon, pecans, and coconut oil and sprinkle over blackberry mixture. Cover dish with foil.
3. Pour 1 cup of water into the instant pot then place the trivet in the pot.
4. Place dish on top of the trivet.
5. Seal pot with lid and cook on high for 4 minutes.
6. Once done, release pressure using quick release. Remove lid.

7. Serve and enjoy.

Nutritional Value (Amount per Serving):
Calories 224; Fat 19.8 g; Carbohydrates 40.3 g; Sugar 33.9 g; Protein 2.9 g; Cholesterol 0 mg

Cinnamon Apple

Preparation Time: 10 minutes; Cooking Time: 20 minutes; Serve: 4

Ingredients:
- 4 apples, cored and cut into chunks
- 1/2 cup apple juice
- 1 tsp liquid stevia
- 2 tsp cinnamon

Directions:
1. Add all ingredients into the instant pot and stir well.
2. Seal pot with lid and cook on low pressure for 20 minutes.
3. Once done, release pressure using quick release. Remove lid.
4. Serve and enjoy.

Nutritional Value (Amount per Serving):
Calories 133; Fat 0.5 g; Carbohydrates 35.2 g; Sugar 26.2 g; Protein 0.7 g; Cholesterol 0 mg

Sweet Vanilla Pears

Preparation Time: 10 minutes; Cooking Time: 15 minutes; Serve: 4

Ingredients:
- 4 pears, cored & cut into wedges
- 1 tsp vanilla
- 2 tbsp maple syrup
- 1/4 cup raisins
- 1 cup apple juice

Directions:
1. Add all ingredients into the instant pot and stir well.
2. Seal pot with lid and cook on high for 15 minutes.
3. Once done, release pressure using quick release. Remove lid.
4. Serve and enjoy.

Nutritional Value (Amount per Serving):
Calories 205; Fat 0.4 g; Carbohydrates 52.8 g; Sugar 37.8 g; Protein 1.1 g; Cholesterol 0 mg

Tapioca Pudding

Preparation Time: 10 minutes; Cooking Time: 10 minutes; Serve: 4

Ingredients:
- 2 1/2 cups almond milk
- 1 tsp cinnamon
- 1 tsp liquid stevia
- 1/2 cup quinoa
- 1/3 cup tapioca pearls, rinsed
- Pinch of salt

Directions:
1. Spray instant pot from inside with cooking spray.
2. Add all ingredients into the inner pot of instant pot and stir well.
3. Seal pot with lid and cook on high for 10 minutes.
4. Once done, allow to release pressure naturally for 10 minutes then release remaining using quick release. Remove lid.
5. Stir well and serve.

Nutritional Value (Amount per Serving):
Calories 470; Fat 37.1 g; Carbohydrates 33.7 g; Sugar 5.4 g; Protein 6.5 g; Cholesterol 0 mg

Apple Orange Stew

Preparation Time: 10 minutes; Cooking Time: 10 minutes; Serve: 4

Ingredients:

- 4 apples, cored and cut into wedges
- 1 tsp liquid stevia
- 1/2 cup orange juice
- 1 cup apple juice
- 1 tsp vanilla

Directions:
1. Add all ingredients into the inner pot of instant pot and stir well.
2. Seal pot with lid and cook on high for 10 minutes.
3. Once done, allow to release pressure naturally for 10 minutes then release remaining using quick release. Remove lid.
4. Stir well and serve.

Nutritional Value (Amount per Serving):
Calories 161; Fat 0.5 g; Carbohydrates 41.2 g; Sugar 31.9 g; Protein 0.9 g; Cholesterol 0 mg

Lime Pears

Preparation Time: 10 minutes; Cooking Time: 10 minutes; Serve: 4
Ingredients:
- 4 pears, cored & cut into wedges
- 1/2 tsp vanilla
- 1 cup apple juice
- 1 tsp lime zest, grated
- 1 lime juice

Directions:
1. Add all ingredients into the inner pot of instant pot and stir well.
2. Seal pot with lid and cook on high for 10 minutes.
3. Once done, allow to release pressure naturally for 10 minutes then release remaining using quick release. Remove lid.
4. Stir and serve.

Nutritional Value (Amount per Serving):
Calories 151; Fat 0.4 g; Carbohydrates 39.9 g; Sugar 26.7 g; Protein 0.9 g; Cholesterol 0 mg

Cauliflower Rice Pudding

Preparation Time: 10 minutes; Cooking Time: 15 minutes; Serve: 4
Ingredients:
- 2 cups cauliflower rice
- 1 tsp cinnamon
- 1 tsp vanilla
- 1 tsp liquid stevia
- 3 cups almond milk
- 1 cup apples, cored and cubed
- Pinch of salt

Directions:
1. Add all ingredients into the inner pot of instant pot and stir well.
2. Seal pot with lid and cook on high for 15 minutes.
3. Once done, allow to release pressure naturally for 10 minutes then release remaining using quick release. Remove lid.
4. Stir and serve.

Nutritional Value (Amount per Serving):
Calories 475; Fat 43.9 g; Carbohydrates 21.6 g; Sugar 14 g; Protein 6.2 g; Cholesterol 0 mg

Lime Orange Jam

Preparation Time: 10 minutes; Cooking Time: 40 minutes; Serve: 6
Ingredients:
- 1 lb oranges, peeled, and cut into segments
- 1 3/4 cups coconut sugar
- 1 tsp lime zest, grated
- 2 lime juice
- 3 cups of water

Directions:

1. Add all ingredients into the inner pot of instant pot and stir well.
2. Seal pot with lid and cook on low pressure for 40 minutes.
3. Once done, allow to release pressure naturally for 10 minutes then release remaining using quick release. Remove lid.
4. Blend the orange mixture using an immersion blender.
5. Serve and enjoy.

Nutritional Value (Amount per Serving):
Calories 67; Fat 0.1 g; Carbohydrates 15.7 g; Sugar 7.3 g; Protein 1.1 g; Cholesterol 0 mg

Sweet Pear Stew

Preparation Time: 10 minutes; Cooking Time: 15 minutes; Serve: 4
Ingredients:
- 4 pears, cored and cut into wedges
- 1 tsp vanilla
- 1/4 cup apple juice
- 2 cups grapes, halved

Directions:
1. Add all ingredients into the inner pot of instant pot and stir well.
2. Seal pot with lid and cook on high for 15 minutes.
3. Once done, allow to release pressure naturally for 10 minutes then release remaining using quick release. Remove lid.
4. Stir and serve.

Nutritional Value (Amount per Serving):
Calories 162; Fat 0.5 g; Carbohydrates 41.6 g; Sugar 29.5 g; Protein 1.1 g; Cholesterol 0 mg

Vanilla Apple Compote

Preparation Time: 10 minutes; Cooking Time: 15 minutes; Serve: 6
Ingredients:
- 3 cups apples, cored and cubed
- 1 tsp vanilla
- 3/4 cup coconut sugar
- 1 cup of water
- 2 tbsp fresh lime juice

Directions:
1. Add all ingredients into the inner pot of instant pot and stir well.
2. Seal pot with lid and cook on high for 15 minutes.
3. Once done, allow to release pressure naturally for 10 minutes then release remaining using quick release. Remove lid.
4. Stir and serve.

Nutritional Value (Amount per Serving):
Calories 76; Fat 0.2 g; Carbohydrates 19.1 g; Sugar 11.9 g; Protein 0.5 g; Cholesterol 0 mg

Apple Dates Mix

Preparation Time: 10 minutes; Cooking Time: 15 minutes; Serve: 4
Ingredients:
- 4 apples, cored and cut into chunks
- 1 tsp vanilla
- 1 tsp cinnamon
- 1/2 cup dates, pitted
- 1 1/2 cups apple juice

Directions:
1. Add all ingredients into the inner pot of instant pot and stir well.
2. Seal pot with lid and cook on high for 15 minutes.
3. Once done, allow to release pressure naturally for 10 minutes then release remaining using quick release. Remove lid.
4. Stir and serve.

Nutritional Value (Amount per Serving):
Calories 226; Fat 0.6 g; Carbohydrates 58.6 g; Sugar 46.4 g; Protein 1.3 g; Cholesterol 0 mg

Choco Rice Pudding

Preparation Time: 10 minutes; Cooking Time: 20 minutes; Serve: 4
Ingredients:
- 1 1/4 cup rice
- 1/4 cup dark chocolate, chopped
- 1 tsp vanilla
- 1/3 cup coconut butter
- 1 tsp liquid stevia
- 2 1/2 cups almond milk

Directions:
1. Add all ingredients into the inner pot of instant pot and stir well.
2. Seal pot with lid and cook on high for 20 minutes.
3. Once done, allow to release pressure naturally. Remove lid.
4. Stir well and serve.

Nutritional Value (Amount per Serving):
Calories 632; Fat 39.9 g; Carbohydrates 63.5 g; Sugar 12.5 g; Protein 8.6 g; Cholesterol 2 mg

Grapes Stew

Preparation Time: 10 minutes; Cooking Time: 15 minutes; Serve: 4
Ingredients:
- 1 cup grapes, halved
- 1 tsp vanilla
- 1 tbsp fresh lemon juice
- 1 tbsp honey
- 2 cups rhubarb, chopped
- 2 cups of water

Directions:
1. Add all ingredients into the inner pot of instant pot and stir well.
2. Seal pot with lid and cook on high for 15 minutes.
3. Once done, allow to release pressure naturally for 10 minutes then release remaining using quick release. Remove lid.
4. Stir and serve.

Nutritional Value (Amount per Serving):
Calories 48; Fat 0.2 g; Carbohydrates 11.3 g; Sugar 8.9 g; Protein 0.7 g; Cholesterol 0 mg

Chocolate Rice

Preparation Time: 10 minutes; Cooking Time: 20 minutes; Serve: 4
Ingredients:
- 1 cup of rice
- 1 tbsp cocoa powder
- 2 tbsp maple syrup
- 2 cups almond milk

Directions:
1. Add all ingredients into the inner pot of instant pot and stir well.
2. Seal pot with lid and cook on high for 20 minutes.
3. Once done, allow to release pressure naturally for 10 minutes then release remaining using quick release. Remove lid.
4. Stir and serve.

Nutritional Value (Amount per Serving):
Calories 474; Fat 29.1 g; Carbohydrates 51.1 g; Sugar 10 g; Protein 6.3 g; Cholesterol 0 mg

Raisins Cinnamon Peaches

Preparation Time: 10 minutes; Cooking Time: 15 minutes; Serve: 4
Ingredients:
- 4 peaches, cored and cut into chunks
- 1 tsp vanilla

- 1 tsp cinnamon
- 1/2 cup raisins
- 1 cup of water

Directions:
1. Add all ingredients into the inner pot of instant pot and stir well.
2. Seal pot with lid and cook on high for 15 minutes.
3. Once done, allow to release pressure naturally for 10 minutes then release remaining using quick release. Remove lid.
4. Stir and serve.

Nutritional Value (Amount per Serving):
Calories 118; Fat 0.5 g; Carbohydrates 29 g; Sugar 24.9 g; Protein 2 g; Cholesterol 0 mg

Lemon Pear Compote

Preparation Time: 10 minutes; Cooking Time: 15 minutes; Serve: 6
Ingredients:
- 3 cups pears, cored and cut into chunks
- 1 tsp vanilla
- 1 tsp liquid stevia
- 1 tbsp lemon zest, grated
- 2 tbsp lemon juice

Directions:
1. Add all ingredients into the inner pot of instant pot and stir well.
2. Seal pot with lid and cook on high for 15 minutes.
3. Once done, allow to release pressure naturally for 10 minutes then release remaining using quick release. Remove lid.
4. Stir and serve.

Nutritional Value (Amount per Serving):
Calories 50; Fat 0.2 g; Carbohydrates 12.7 g; Sugar 8.1 g; Protein 0.4 g; Cholesterol 0 mg

Strawberry Stew

Preparation Time: 10 minutes; Cooking Time: 15 minutes; Serve: 4
Ingredients:
- 12 oz fresh strawberries, sliced
- 1 tsp vanilla
- 1 1/2 cups water
- 1 tsp liquid stevia
- 2 tbsp lime juice

Directions:
1. Add all ingredients into the inner pot of instant pot and stir well.
2. Seal pot with lid and cook on high for 15 minutes.
3. Once done, allow to release pressure naturally for 10 minutes then release remaining using quick release. Remove lid.
4. Stir and serve.

Nutritional Value (Amount per Serving):
Calories 36; Fat 0.3 g; Carbohydrates 8.5 g; Sugar 4.7 g; Protein 0.7 g; Cholesterol 0 mg

Walnut Apple Pear Mix

Preparation Time: 10 minutes; Cooking Time: 10 minutes; Serve: 4
Ingredients:
- 2 apples, cored and cut into wedges
- 1/2 tsp vanilla
- 1 cup apple juice
- 2 tbsp walnuts, chopped
- 2 apples, cored and cut into wedges

Directions:
1. Add all ingredients into the inner pot of instant pot and stir well.
2. Seal pot with lid and cook on high for 10 minutes.

3. Once done, allow to release pressure naturally for 10 minutes then release remaining using quick release. Remove lid.
4. Serve and enjoy.

Nutritional Value (Amount per Serving):
Calories 132; Fat 2.6 g; Carbohydrates 28.3 g; Sugar 21.9 g; Protein 1.3 g; Cholesterol 0 mg

Cinnamon Pear Jam

Preparation Time: 10 minutes; Cooking Time: 4 minutes; Serve: 12
Ingredients:
- 8 pears, cored and cut into quarters
- 1 tsp cinnamon
- 1/4 cup apple juice
- 2 apples, peeled, cored and diced

Directions:
1. Add all ingredients into the inner pot of instant pot and stir well.
2. Seal pot with lid and cook on high for 4 minutes.
3. Once done, allow to release pressure naturally. Remove lid.
4. Blend pear apple mixture using an immersion blender until smooth.
5. Serve and enjoy.

Nutritional Value (Amount per Serving):
Calories 103; Fat 0.3 g; Carbohydrates 27.1 g; Sugar 18 g; Protein 0.6 g; Cholesterol 0 mg

Delicious Apple Pear Cobbler

Preparation Time: 10 minutes; Cooking Time: 12 minutes; Serve: 4
Ingredients:
- 3 apples, cored and cut into chunks
- 1 cup steel-cut oats
- 2 pears, cored and cut into chunks
- 1/4 cup maple syrup
- 1 1/2 cups water
- 1 tsp cinnamon

Directions:
1. Spray instant pot from inside with cooking spray.
2. Add all ingredients into the inner pot of instant pot and stir well.
3. Seal pot with lid and cook on high for 12 minutes.
4. Once done, release pressure using quick release. Remove lid.
5. Sere and enjoy.

Nutritional Value (Amount per Serving):
Calories 278; Fat 1.8 g; Carbohydrates 66.5 g; Sugar 39.5 g; Protein 3.5 g; Cholesterol 0 mg

Coconut Rice Pudding

Preparation Time: 10 minutes; Cooking Time: 3 minutes; Serve: 4
Ingredients:
- 1/2 cup rice
- 1/4 cup shredded coconut
- 3 tbsp swerve
- 1 1/2 cups water
- 14 oz can coconut milk
- Pinch of salt

Directions:
1. Spray instant pot from inside with cooking spray.
2. Add all ingredients into the inner pot of instant pot and stir well.
3. Seal pot with lid and cook on high for 3 minutes.
4. Once done, allow to release pressure naturally for 10 minutes then release remaining using quick release. Remove lid.
5. Serve and enjoy.

Nutritional Value (Amount per Serving):
Calories 298; Fat 23 g; Carbohydrates 33.3 g; Sugar 11.6 g; Protein 3.8 g; Cholesterol 0 mg

Pear Sauce

Preparation Time: 10 minutes; Cooking Time: 15 minutes; Serve: 6
Ingredients:
- 10 pears, sliced
- 1 cup apple juice
- 1 1/2 tsp cinnamon
- 1/4 tsp nutmeg

Directions:
1. Add all ingredients into the instant pot and stir well.
2. Seal pot with lid and cook on high for 15 minutes.
3. Once done, allow to release pressure naturally for 10 minutes then release remaining using quick release. Remove lid.
4. Blend the pear mixture using an immersion blender until smooth.
5. Serve and enjoy.

Nutritional Value (Amount per Serving):
Calories 222; Fat 0.6 g; Carbohydrates 58.2 g; Sugar 38 g; Protein 1.3 g; Cholesterol 0 mg

Sweet Peach Jam

Preparation Time: 10 minutes; Cooking Time: 16 minutes; Serve: 20
Ingredients:
- 1 1/2 lb fresh peaches, pitted and chopped
- 1/2 tbsp vanilla
- 1/4 cup maple syrup

Directions:
1. Add all ingredients into the instant pot and stir well.
2. Seal pot with lid and cook on high for 1 minute.
3. Once done, allow to release pressure naturally. Remove lid.
4. Set pot on sauté mode and cook for 15 minutes or until jam thickened.
5. Pour into the container and store it in the fridge.

Nutritional Value (Amount per Serving):
Calories 16; Fat 0 g; Carbohydrates 3.7 g; Sugar 3.4 g; Protein 0.1 g; Cholesterol 0 mg

Warm Peach Compote

Preparation Time: 10 minutes; Cooking Time: 1 minute; Serve: 4
Ingredients:
- 4 peaches, peeled and chopped
- 1 tbsp water
- 1/2 tbsp cornstarch
- 1 tsp vanilla

Directions:
1. Add water, vanilla, and peaches into the instant pot.
2. Seal pot with lid and cook on high for 1 minute.
3. Once done, allow to release pressure naturally. Remove lid.
4. In a small bowl, whisk together 1 tablespoon of water and cornstarch and pour into the pot and stir well.
5. Serve and enjoy.

Nutritional Value (Amount per Serving):
Calories 66; Fat 0.4 g; Carbohydrates 15 g; Sugar 14.1 g; Protein 1.4 g; Cholesterol 0 mg

Spiced Pear Sauce

Preparation Time: 10 minutes; Cooking Time: 6 hours; Serve: 12
Ingredients:
- 8 pears, cored and diced
- 1/2 tsp ground cinnamon
- 1/4 tsp ground nutmeg
- 1/4 tsp ground cardamom
- 1 cup of water

Directions:
1. Add all ingredients into the instant pot and stir well.
2. Seal the pot with a lid and select slow cook mode and cook on low for 6 hours.
3. Mash the sauce using potato masher.
4. Pour into the container and store it in the fridge.

Nutritional Value (Amount per Serving):
Calories 81; Fat 0.2 g; Carbohydrates 21.4 g; Sugar 13.6 g; Protein 0.5 g; Cholesterol 0 mg

Honey Fruit Compote

Preparation Time: 10 minutes; Cooking Time: 3 minutes; Serve: 4

Ingredients:
- 1/3 cup honey
- 1 1/2 cups blueberries
- 1 1/2 cups raspberries

Directions:
1. Add all ingredients into the instant pot and stir well.
2. Seal pot with lid and cook on high for 3 minutes.
3. Once done, allow to release pressure naturally. Remove lid.
4. Serve and enjoy.

Nutritional Value (Amount per Serving):
Calories 141; Fat 0.5 g; Carbohydrates 36.7 g; Sugar 30.6 g; Protein 1 g; Cholesterol 0 mg

Creamy Brown Rice Pudding

Preparation Time: 10 minutes; Cooking Time: 20 minutes; Serve: 8

Ingredients:
- 1 cup of rice
- 1 cup of brown rice
- 1 cup of water
- 1 cup half and half
- 1/2 cup pecans, chopped
- 2 tsp vanilla
- 1 tbsp coconut butter
- 1/2 cup heavy cream
- Pinch of salt

Directions:
1. Add coconut butter into the instant pot and set the pot on sauté mode.
2. Add pecans into the pot and stir until toasted.
3. Add remaining ingredients except for heavy cream and vanilla. Stir well.
4. Seal pot with lid and cook on high for 20 minutes.
5. Once done, allow to release pressure naturally for 10 minutes then release remaining using quick release. Remove lid.
6. Add vanilla and heavy cream. Stir well and serve.

Nutritional Value (Amount per Serving):
Calories 276; Fat 10.9 g; Carbohydrates 39.2 g; Sugar 0.5 g; Protein 5 g; Cholesterol 21 mg

Lemon Cranberry Sauce

Preparation Time: 10 minutes; Cooking Time: 14 minutes; Serve: 8

Ingredients:
- 10 oz fresh cranberries
- 3/4 cup Swerve
- 1/4 cup water
- 1 tsp lemon zest
- 1 tsp vanilla extract

Directions:
1. Add cranberries and water into the instant pot.
2. Seal pot with lid and cook on high for 1 minute.

3. Once done, allow to release pressure naturally for 10 minutes then release remaining using quick release. Remove lid.
4. Set pot on sauté mode.
5. Add remaining ingredients and cook for 2-3 minutes.
6. Pour in container and store in fridge.

Nutritional Value (Amount per Serving):
Calories 21; Fat 0 g; Carbohydrates 25.8 g; Sugar 23.9 g; Protein 0 g; Cholesterol 0 mg

Blackberry Jam

Preparation Time: 10 minutes; Cooking Time: 6 hours; Serve: 6
Ingredients:
- 3 cups fresh blackberries
- 1/4 cup chia seeds
- 4 tbsp Swerve
- 1/4 cup fresh lemon juice
- 1/4 cup coconut butter

Directions:
1. Add all ingredients into the instant pot and stir well.
2. Seal the pot with a lid and select slow cook mode and cook on low for 6 hours.
3. Pour in container and store in fridge.

Nutritional Value (Amount per Serving):
Calories 101; Fat 6.8 g; Carbohydrates 20 g; Sugar 14.4 g; Protein 2 g; Cholesterol 0 mg

Chunky Apple Sauce

Preparation Time: 10 minutes; Cooking Time: 12 minutes; Serve: 16
Ingredients:
- 4 apples, peeled, cored and diced
- 1 tsp vanilla
- 4 pears, diced
- 2 tbsp cinnamon
- 1/4 cup maple syrup
- 3/4 cup water

Directions:
1. Add all ingredients into the instant pot and stir well.
2. Seal pot with lid and cook on high for 12 minutes.
3. Once done, allow to release pressure naturally for 10 minutes then release remaining using quick release. Remove lid.
4. Serve and enjoy.

Nutritional Value (Amount per Serving):
Calories 75; Fat 0.2 g; Carbohydrates 19.7 g; Sugar 13.9 g; Protein 0.4 g; Cholesterol 0 mg

Maple Syrup Cranberry Sauce

Preparation Time: 10 minutes; Cooking Time: 5 minutes; Serve: 8
Ingredients:
- 12 oz fresh cranberries, rinsed
- 1 apple, peeled, cored, and chopped
- 1/2 cup maple syrup
- 1/2 cup apple cider
- 1 tsp orange zest, grated
- 1 orange juice

Directions:
1. Add all ingredients into the instant pot and stir well.
2. Seal pot with lid and cook on high for 5 minutes.
3. Once done, allow to release pressure naturally for 10 minutes then release remaining using quick release. Remove lid.
4. Pour in container and store in fridge.

Nutritional Value (Amount per Serving):
Calories 101; Fat 0.1 g; Carbohydrates 23.9 g; Sugar 18.8 g; Protein 0.2 g; Cholesterol 0 mg

Raisin Pecan Baked Apples

Preparation Time: 10 minutes; Cooking Time: 4 minutes; Serve: 6
Ingredients:
- 6 apples, cored and cut into wedges
- 1 cup red wine
- 1/4 cup pecans, chopped
- 1/4 cup raisins
- 1/4 tsp nutmeg
- 1 tsp cinnamon
- 1/3 cup honey

Directions:
1. Add all ingredients into the instant pot and stir well.
2. Seal pot with lid and cook on high for 4 minutes.
3. Once done, allow to release pressure naturally for 10 minutes then release remaining using quick release. Remove lid.
4. Stir well and serve.

Nutritional Value (Amount per Serving):
Calories 229; Fat 0.9 g; Carbohydrates 52.6 g; Sugar 42.6 g; Protein 1 g; Cholesterol 0 mg

Healthy Zucchini Pudding

Preparation Time: 10 minutes; Cooking Time: 10 minutes; Serve: 4
Ingredients:
- 2 cups zucchini, shredded
- 1/4 tsp cardamom powder
- 5 oz half and half
- 5 oz almond milk
- 1/4 cup Swerve

Directions:
1. Add all ingredients except cardamom into the instant pot and stir well.
2. Seal pot with lid and cook on high for 10 minutes.
3. Once done, allow to release pressure naturally for 10 minutes then release remaining using quick release. Remove lid.
4. Stir in cardamom and serve.

Nutritional Value (Amount per Serving):
Calories 137; Fat 12.6 g; Carbohydrates 20.5 g; Sugar 17.2 g; Protein 2.6 g; Cholesterol 13 mg

Cinnamon Apple Rice Pudding

Preparation Time: 10 minutes; Cooking Time: 15 minutes; Serve: 8
Ingredients:
- 1 cup of rice
- 1 tsp vanilla
- 1/4 apple, peeled and chopped
- 1/2 cup water
- 1 1/2 cup almond milk
- 1 tsp cinnamon
- 1 cinnamon stick

Directions:
1. Add all ingredients into the instant pot and stir well.
2. Seal pot with lid and cook on high for 15 minutes.
3. Once done, release pressure using quick release. Remove lid.
4. Stir and serve.

Nutritional Value (Amount per Serving):
Calories 206; Fat 11.5 g; Carbohydrates 23.7 g; Sugar 2.7 g; Protein 3 g; Cholesterol 0 mg

Coconut Risotto Pudding

Preparation Time: 10 minutes; Cooking Time: 20 minutes; Serve: 6
Ingredients:
- 3/4 cup rice
- 1/2 cup shredded coconut

- 1 tsp lemon juice
- 1/2 tsp vanilla
- 14.5 oz can coconut milk
- 1/4 cup maple syrup
- 1 1/2 cups water

Directions:
1. Add all ingredients into the instant pot and stir well.
2. Seal pot with lid and cook on high for 20 minutes.
3. Once done, allow to release pressure naturally for 10 minutes then release remaining using quick release. Remove lid.
4. Blend pudding mixture using an immersion blender until smooth.
5. Serve and enjoy.

Nutritional Value (Amount per Serving):
Calories 205; Fat 8.6 g; Carbohydrates 29.1 g; Sugar 9 g; Protein 2.6 g; Cholesterol 0 mg

Chapter 14: 30-Day Meal Plan

Day 1

Breakfast-Vegetable Quinoa

Lunch-Nutritious Kidney Bean Soup

Dinner-Delicious Lemon Butter Cod

Day 2

Breakfast-Quinoa Breakfast Bowls

Lunch-Mixed Lentil Stew

Dinner-Italian White Fish Fillets

Day 3

Breakfast-Delicious Breakfast Potato Mix

Lunch-Spinach Chicken Stew

Dinner-Rosemary Salmon

Day 4

Breakfast-Perfect Breakfast Oatmeal

Lunch-Delicious Okra Chicken Stew

Dinner-Shrimp Salad

Day 5

Breakfast-Mix Berry Oatmeal

Lunch-Lamb Stew

Dinner-Chili Lime Salmon

Day 6

Breakfast-Warm Pumpkin Oats

Lunch-Easy & Delicious Beef Stew

Dinner-Steamed Salmon

Day 7

Breakfast-Blueberry Breakfast Oatmeal

Lunch-Tomato Chickpeas Stew

Dinner-Basil Fish Curry

Day 8

Breakfast-Pear Oatmeal

Lunch-Healthy Vegetable Soup

Dinner-Italian Fish Stew

Day 9
Breakfast-Sprout Potato Salad
Lunch-Hearty Pork Stew
Dinner-Mediterranean Fish Fillets

Day 10
Breakfast-Peach Blueberry Oatmeal
Lunch-Flavorful Mac & Cheese
Dinner-Tomato Olive Fish Fillets

Day 11
Breakfast-Breakfast Jalapeno Egg Cups
Lunch-Cucumber Olive Rice
Dinner-Easy Salmon Stew

Day 12
Breakfast-Almond Peach Oatmeal
Lunch-Flavors Herb Risotto
Dinner-Pesto Fish Fillet

Day 13
Breakfast-Breakfast Cobbler
Lunch-Potato Salad
Dinner-Tuna Risotto

Day 14
Breakfast-Breakfast Cauliflower Rice Bowl
Lunch-Chicken Lentil Stew
Dinner-Salsa Fish Fillets

Day 15
Breakfast-Healthy Zucchini Kale Tomato Salad
Lunch-Delicious Chicken Pasta
Dinner-Coconut Clam Chowder

Day 16
Breakfast-Walnut Banana Oatmeal
Lunch-Flavors Taco Rice Bowl
Dinner-Feta Tomato Sea Bass

Day 17
Breakfast-Breakfast Rice Bowls

Lunch-Healthy Garlic Eggplant

Dinner-Creamy Fish Stew

Day 18

Breakfast-Healthy Dry Fruit Porridge

Lunch-Carrot Potato Medley

Dinner-Nutritious Broccoli Salmon

Day 19

Breakfast-Rosemary Broccoli Cauliflower Mash

Lunch-Lemon Herb Potatoes

Dinner-Shrimp Zoodles

Day 20

Breakfast-Zucchini Pudding

Lunch-Flavors Basil Lemon Ratatouille

Dinner-Healthy Carrot & Shrimp

Day 21

Breakfast-Mushroom Tomato Egg Cups

Lunch-Garlic Basil Zucchini

Dinner-Delicious Lemon Butter Cod

Day 22

Breakfast-Feta Spinach Egg Cups

Lunch-Feta Green Beans

Dinner-Italian White Fish Fillets

Day 23

Breakfast-Breakfast Carrot Oatmeal

Lunch-Greek Green Beans

Dinner-Rosemary Salmon

Day 24

Breakfast-Potato Breakfast Hash

Lunch-Healthy Vegetable Medley

Dinner-Shrimp Salad

Day 25

Breakfast-Cranberry Oatmeal

Lunch-Spicy Zucchini

Dinner-Chili Lime Salmon

Day 26
Breakfast-Healthy Buckwheat Porridge
Lunch-Flavorful Mediterranean Chicken
Dinner-Steamed Salmon

Day 27
Breakfast-Apricot Oats
Lunch-Artichoke Olive Chicken
Dinner-Basil Fish Curry

Day 28
Breakfast-Simple Breakfast Quinoa
Lunch-Easy Chicken Piccata
Dinner-Italian Fish Stew

Day 29
Breakfast-Irish Oatmeal
Lunch-Garlic Thyme Chicken Drumsticks
Dinner-Mediterranean Fish Fillets

Day 30
Breakfast-Coconut Strawberry Oatmeal
Lunch-Tender Chicken & Mushrooms
Dinner-Tomato Olive Fish Fillets

Conclusion

The Mediterranean diet is one of the most studied diets worldwide. It is the oldest diet plan that comes from Mediterranean regions situated on the coast of the Mediterranean Sea. In this book, you have found all about the Mediterranean diet from its history to the health benefits of the Mediterranean diet and science behind the diet.

The books also introduce you with a healthy cooking appliance known as an instant pot with its benefits. There are different types of Mediterranean recipes found in this book. The recipes written in this book are easy to understand and easy to prepare.